THE VIKING
DISCOVERY OF AMERICA:

The Excavation of a Norse Settlement
in L'Anse aux Meadows, Newfoundland

The Viking discovery of America : The excavation of a Norse settlement in
L'Anse aux Meadows, Newfoundland

Copyright © 2001 by Checkmark Books

Checkmark Books
An imprint of Facts On File, Inc.
132 W. 31st Street
New York, NY 10001

Library of Congress Cataloging-in-publication Data

Ingstad, Helge, 1899—2001

The Viking discovery of America : The excavation of a Norse settlement in
L'Anse aux Meadows, Newfoundland / Helge Ingstad & Anne Stine Ingstad.
    p. cm.
Includes bibliographical references (p.) and index.
ISBN 0-8160-4716-2 (hardcover : alk. paper)
1. America—Discovery and exploration—Norse. 2. Vikings—Newfoundland—
L'Anse aux Meadows—Antiquities.3. Vikings—Folklore. 4. Sagas. 5. Vikings—
Newfoundland—L'Anse aux Meadows—History. 6. Excavations (Archaeology)—
Newfoundland—L'Anse aux Meadows. 7. L'Anse aux Meadows (Nfld.)—Antiquities. I. Ingstad, Anne
Stine, 1918-

E105 .I54 2001
970.01'3—dc21   2001033051

Published in cooperation with
Breakwater Books Ltd.
100 Water Street
P.O. Box 2188
St. John's, NF
A1C 6E6

Printed and bound in Canada

TABLE OF CONTENTS

FOREWORD

This book provides the reader with a popular account of my archaeological expeditions to North America that led to the discovery of a group of house-sites of Norse origin in Newfoundland.

It was around the year 1000 that Leif Eiriksson according to the Icelandic sagas sailed south across the ocean with 35 Norsemen from Greenland. He discovered a new and promising land that he named Vinland. He settled here, built large houses and explored the surroundings before he returned to his home in Greenland. Inspired by this discovery, three expeditions followed from Greenland carrying men, women and domestic animals. This time, they were emigrating to the new country. However, these expeditions did not stay long in Vinland. Most probably, they feared the native populations that far outnumbered them.

The historical and geographical background for these voyages to Vinland is the Norse settlements in south-west Greenland, founded by Eirik the Red. Around the year A.D. 986, he discovered Greenland. This society would exist for about 500 years.

Where was Vinland? This question has occupied the thoughts of many outstanding scholars for about two hundred years. The sagas mention that the Norsemen found grapes in Vinland and it consequently became a common belief that Vinland must be located far to the south on the North American continent—in a region of wild grapes. Many examinations have been done, but no Norse sites had previously been discovered in America.

After my expedition in 1953 to the old Norse settlement in Greenland and the study of sources, I concluded that Vinland must be located further to the north and most probably in Newfoundland. In 1960, I undertook a systematic investigation of the north-east coast of Newfoundland, and after a long search and many disappointments, I succeeded.

At the northernmost tip of Newfoundland, at L' Anse aux Meadows, I came to a small fishing village where I met George Decker, who showed me traces of some very old overgrown house-sites that seemed to be very promising.

I subsequently organized seven archaeological expeditions (from 1961 to 1968) with international teams of scientists. My wife Dr. Anne Stine Ingstad was the leader of the archaeological work. Eight, perhaps nine, remains of house-sites made of turf were excavated. They were of a similar type as old house-types found in Iceland and Greenland. A few of the houses were rather large. Of great interest is the find of a ringheaded pin of bronze of the late Viking type commonly used as a clothfastening, and of a spindle whorl of soapstone indicating that women had been on the site as well. We also found a smithy dug into a terrace with a large stone as anvil. Here, iron had been produced from bog-iron in the same way as in Norway and Iceland.

Furthermore, we made a series of carbon-dates (C14) that place the sites of L' Anse aux Meadows to around year 1000 A.D. Interestingly, the sagas also indicate this as the time for Leif Eiriksson's voyage to Vinland, which is believed to be part of America.

iv

Based on the substantive arguments that are briefly described above, one can hardly arrive at any other conclusion than that Norsemen discovered America about 500 years before Columbus. UNESCO is among the institutions that recognize these findings as such.

My work dealing with the Vinland problem has carried on for many years. It has been very fascinating, sometimes exciting work. I wish to thank the many people and outstanding scientists who have contributed to the result, and the fisherman George Decker in Newfoundland. But the person to whom I owe the greatest thanks is my wife, Dr. Anne Stine Ingstad.

Helge Ingstad
Brattahlid, Oslo, August 15, 2000

vi

SHIPS AND NAVIGATION

The Viking Age developed with an almost explosive force in the Scandinavian countries somewhat before A.D. 800. Young men hoisted sail, and made for many countries in Europe, and also for lands further east. The Swedes tended to go east, to Russia and other regions, while the Danes made for the North Sea coast, for England, France and the south. Norwegian Vikings also went south, as far as the Mediterranean, but most of their voyages led across the North Sea, to the British Isles. One route, however, they plied almost alone, except for the Icelanders once Iceland had been discovered and settled: this was the route west, over the northern part of the Atlantic. This was entirely natural, seeing that the homelands of these Norsemen faced that ocean.

And thus, in the course of time, Norse seafarers gradually sailed further and further west. First they came to Shetland, Orkney, the Hebrides and the Faeroes, to Scotland, Ireland and the Isle of Man. Conflict and fighting were often involved, and many Norsemen settled in these lands. Towards the end of the ninth century, Iceland was discovered, an event which led to a veritable tide of emigration, especially from Norway, but also from the Norse settlements in the Western Isles. From Iceland, Eirik the Red discovered Greenland, and the west coast of Greenland was colonized. And finally, in about A.D. 1000, came the natural consequence of these events: Leif Eiriksson discovered North America. The westward main had been sailed to its very end.

There may have been many and diverse reasons for these Viking Age voyages. One of them may well be overpopulation, but no less important were a desire for profit and a craving for adventure. We know perfectly well that the people of the North could be ruthless, but this must not be permitted to eclipse the fact that they also engaged in trade, and that in their voyages of discovery for new lands hard work meant

Fig. 1. facing page. Carved head of a man, from the Oseberg find (c. A.D. 800-850). Photo courtesy of University Museum of Cultural Heritage, University of Oslo; Ove Holst, photographer.

Fig. 2. In a scene from the past, the Gaia, a replica Viking ship, enters Newfoundland's misty waters in 1991.

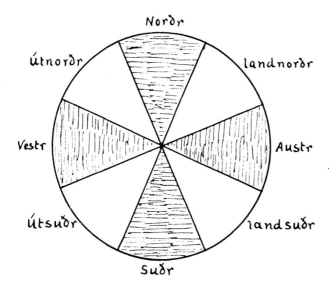

Fig. 3. The Norsemen sailed without a compass. They operated with eight cardinal points – ættir – and navigated by means of the sun and the stars.

more than the brandishing of swords.

For centuries the Norsemen crossed the enormous northern ocean from the west coast of Norway to North America; in their open ships with square sails they sailed here in all kinds of weather, often through masses of drift-ice. Such long and demanding, often perilous voyages could not have been carried out without a high standard of ship-building and brilliant seamanship.

In this field Norway had ancient traditions. There were various kinds of ships. The men-of-war, the so-called long-ships, were fairly narrow in the beam, their sides were low, and the deck covered the entire length of the ship. There were oar holes along the whole length of the ship. It seems likely that the normal number of oarsmen was forty, but there could be up to seventy. Then there were the merchant and cargo vessels, a separate category. They were considerably broader in the beam, and had two half-decks with room for only one pair of oars in the bow and one in the stem. The entire midship was an open hold for cargo. To this category belong the *knǫrr* and the *byrðingr*, and such ocean-going types as the *skúta* and the *karfi*. Significant in this connection is the fact that a Viking Age type of craft, the *fembøring*, was still in use as a fishing vessel in northern Norway at the beginning of the present century.

As an example of the superb art of the Norwegian ship-builder during the Viking Age, we can do no better than to point to the famous Gokstad ship, which dates from c. A. D. 850-900. This ocean-going vessel, which was found in a barrow in southern Norway, is clinker-built of oak. The ship is about 23 m long, and the maximum beam is 5.20 m. From the bottom of the keel to the gunwale amidships the height is 2.02 m. The eight first strakes are lashed to the ribs, a method which makes for a light, supple ship. The mast was set in a sturdy mast partner, which was made in such a way that the mast could easily be raised and lowered. The Gokstad ship had a side rudder and a square sail; there were sixteen oar-holes, so that thirty-two oars men were required. When she was fully loaded, the ship drew no more than about one metre of water, which is of great advantage when sailing in unknown, perilous seas.

This vessel, an exquisite piece of craftsmanship, must have been a chieftain's ship. Her excellent ocean-going qualities were clearly demonstrated when Magnus Andersen, a Norwegian mariner, sailed a replica of the Gokstad ship across the Atlantic in 1893. Her speed was surprisingly high, an average of about 4-5 knots with an occasional maximum speed of 11 knots. And she rode off the storms.

The sight of this splendid craft, tall, supple and elegant, calls to mind the chieftain who set out to sea, be it for battle or for trade, about eleven hundred years ago. We have reason to believe that this chieftain may have been King Olaf Geirstad-alv. The skeleton of the man who was buried in the ship provides important documentation in this respect: this is the skeleton of an elderly, sturdy and unusually tall man. He suffered not only from pronounced chronic arthritis, but also from advanced muscular rheumatism. This syndrome corresponds well with an ancient source which states that Olaf died of 'foot pains'. In Snorri's *Heimskringla* we read that in his youth he was a mighty chieftain and a great warrior, the most handsome, strongest and tallest of them all.

Materials for ship-building were an important matter for these people. While Norway had forests with oak as well as pine, Iceland and Greenland had only a scattered occurrence of wind-blown birches here and there, and there was much driftwood along the shore. These materials could at best be used for building small boats, but no more. All material for ship-building had to be imported from Norway; one might also purchase ships in that country. Ships were absolutely essential for the people of these two distant islands, Iceland and Greenland. True, they were farmers, but they could not live without fishing, hunting and catching, activities which often had to be carried out far from their homes. Below we shall see that once the Vinland voyages had led to the discovery of the great forests of Labrador and Newfoundland, the Greenlanders are likely to have obtained ship-building materials there.

The Norsemen's ability to find their way on the great oceans with the simple aids at their disposal is remarkable. We are reminded of the instinct for directions and distances which the Indians and the Eskimos possess. The firmament was divided into four cardinal points, *hǫvuðættir*, north, south, east and west, by axes perpendicular to each other. Four more points were inserted between the cardinals, so that there were eight in all.

They had no compasses, but possessed their own method of navigation by means of observations of the sun and the stars, the pole star being of particular importance in this connection. But during storms or long periods with fog, even the most accomplished of mariners might lose his bearings. Sometimes the sunstone, *sølarsteinn*, could be of help under such conditions. This may have been a piece of double-refractive feld spar able to catch polarizing light in overcast weather (*Kult. Leks.* XII: col. 261). The Norse seafarers must have possessed a highly developed sense of observation, which could be useful in various ways. They noted winds and waves and their direction, currents, the colour and temperature of the sea, the movement and form of the drifting ice, mirages, high and low tide, birds and whales.

It was of great advantage if the route was such that one could, by means of observations of the sun, one could stay on the same latitude all the time, for instance when sailing from Bergen to the southernmost part of Greenland. But when one sailed on the high sea in a southerly or northerly direction, it was very difficult to keep a steady course. The Norsemen had no facilities for using their observations of heavenly bodies to determine the longitude of their position. Sailing along the coasts would be given preference, unless the shorter route across the open sea was well known. The route of the Vinland voyagers included coasting as well as sailing with the current for almost the entire distance from Leif Eiriksson's home on the west coast of Greenland to Vinland in North America.

The Icelandic sources often give sailing times in terms of *dægr*; this applies also to the Vinland expeditions. There has been considerable disagreement about the meaning of this term as applied to sailing. It seems likely that *dægr* means twelve hours when applied to coastal sailing, and twenty-four hours when it refers to sailing on the high seas.

The ice conditions in the waters around Greenland and in the Davis Strait, the regions of the Vinland route, made sailing particularly difficult.

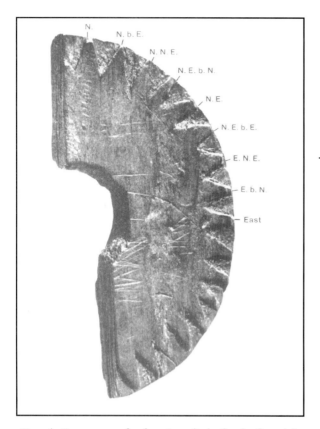

N.
N. b. E.
N. N. E.
N. E. b. N.
N. E.
N. E. b. E.
E. N. E.
E. b. N.
East

Fig. 4. Fragment of a bearing-dial of oak, found by C. L. Vebæk during the excavation of a convent in the Eastern Settlement of Greenland. Photo courtesy of The National Museum, Cpn.

One had to have a ship constructed in such a way as to make rowing really effective. In the drift-ice, fast rowing could be essential if one was to save one's life, but sometimes the only way out was to pull the ship up on to the ice.

The square sail was usually of wadmal. According to ancient Norwegian tradition, the sail was impregnated with an extract of boiled birch bark mixed with horse grease and a little red pigment. The grease was taken from under the mane of the horse, as it is particularly soft in this part of the body, and easily dissolved.

The Viking Age ships were quite swift. Some of them could attain a speed of about twelve knots. It is difficult to be certain about the average speed during long voyages, since so many factors

must be taken into consideration – fog, storms, headwind and ice. An average speed of three to four knots may be reasonable. The voyage of the Gokstad replica shows that even with a square sail one can tack against the wind to some extent.

An important question to consider is the following: what is the best time of the summer to start sailing to Greenland, and from Greenland to Vinland? The ice conditions were the decisive factor in this connection. Several sources state that the best time for setting out from Bergen to Greenland was the beginning of August, and the same must indubitably apply also to the voyage across the Davis Strait from Greenland to Vinland. How late in the year could one sail in these western waters? In the *King's Mirror* (1945: 6) from about 1250 we read that one should not sail on the ocean after the beginning of October, for then the storms grew stronger.

Some simple descriptions of sailing routes appear in the sources. In *Hauksbók* we read:

'Thus say knowledgeable men that from Stad in Norway it is seven *dægr's* sailing to Horn on the east coast of Iceland, but from Snæfellsnes it is four *dægr's* sailing to Hvarf in Greenland (near the southern point). From Bergen in Norway one must usually sail west to Hvarf in Greenland, and then one sails north of Hetland (Shetland) in such a way that one can just glimpse land when the weather is clear, but south of the Faeroes in such a way that one sees only half the height of the land, and so far south of Iceland that that country's seabirds and whales become visible...'

A remarkable combination of sterling shipbuilding and excellent seamanship enabled

Fig. 5, p. 5. Helge Ingstad and Anne Stine Ingstad on board the Halten, *the ship that took them on their expeditions.*

Fig. 6. King Olaf's ship 'Visund' is being built. Drawing by G. Munthe in 'Heimskringla'.

the Norse seafarers to sail the great oceans and master their open vessels in storm, fog and icy waters on their expeditions to unknown and dangerous coasts, the White Sea, Greenland and North America. At times continuous bailing was a matter of life and death. One of the greatest hazards during voyages in the northern oceans was that of icing, which would add a crushing weight to both ship and rigging. Theirs was a life which demanded not only knowledge, skill and the ability to attend to sail and oars without delay, but also a will of iron and a character able to endure privation and pain without a murmur. Not infrequently there were women on board, they must have been cast in the same mould.

Nor did superstition make the times of peril any easier to bear. The Norsemen firmly believed in terrible sea trolls; the *King's Mirror* calls them *hafstrambar* and *margýgjar*. Then there were the fearful *hafgerðingar*, thought to hold all storms and all waves gathered into three mountainous swells that would crush any ship. And those who sailed far out on the high seas might be confronted with the greatest danger of all: they risked sailing over the edge of the world, only to plunge into the great abyss, *Ginnungagap (cf p.* 114).

The sources have sporadic accounts of ship-wrecks, but they can no more than give us a slight idea of the actual number. We are only given a few glimpses of the sailors' tremendous hardships and their struggle for life. It is difficult to imagine the life of Viking Age seafarers sailing the northern oceans drenched to the skin in the biting cold, or when furious storms tore at the sail and the sea rushed into the ship. A small rune-stick from Greenland speaks for itself. It was found in a coffin when the Herjolfsnes cemetery in Greenland was excavated (Nørlund 1924: 62). A huge boulder, weighing about a ton and a half lay on the grave, perhaps as a protection against evil spirits. From the inscription on the rune-stick it appears that this is not a burial but a cenotaph: 'This woman, whose name was Gudveig, was buried at sea in the Greenland ocean.'

Fig. 7. Gudveig's rune-stick. Photo courtesy of The National Museum, Cpn.

THE NORSE COMMUNITY

in

Greenland

The people of the Norse community of Greenland form the background of the Vinland expeditions, and we must therefore view these voyages in the light of our knowledge of this society. Considering that we are here dealing with a community in existence for almost five hundred years, the sources are sparse indeed. Most of them are Icelandic, but these are primarily concerned with matters of interest to the Icelanders, and they tell us little about life in Greenland. Outstanding among the Norwegian sources is the *King's Mirror*; other occasional sources include documents such as papal letters. Not a single document from Greenland has come down to us. A great deal of our knowledge about life in Norse Greenland is due to the evidence resulting from excavations carried out there by Danish archaeologists.

The conditions for life afforded by an arctic island such as Greenland, the people's struggle for survival and their general outlook can give us a good idea of their yearning for distant shores. The hardships they had to endure and their distinctive culture provide a background for a better understanding of the kind of land the Greenlanders would choose for settling when they were sailing south along the coast of North America. Moreover, in the course of the centuries the social structure changed and resources diminished, and this must be considered in an appraisal of whether the Greenlanders could also have journeyed to North America *after* the Vinland voyages of which the sagas tell. And any assessment of the Norse settlement site discovered in Newfoundland and of the life of the people who lived there, must needs include a comparison with the conditions and cultural elements of the Norse society of Greenland.

The settlement of Iceland began at the end of the ninth century and according to Ari Thorgilsson the country was fully settled by about 930 (Benediktsson 1968: 9). The majority of the settlers, as we saw above, came from Norway,

Fig. 8. Thor's hammer, incised on soapstone, found at Brattahlið. Photo courtesy of The National Museum, Cpn.

while others came from the Norse colonies of the Atlantic islands. During the period of settlement, many ships must have sailed on the northern ocean, and it is not unlikely that some of them should have drifted so far west that those on board might catch a glimpse of the high mountains and glaciers of eastern Greenland. We know that Gunnbjorn Ulfsson drifted westwards beyond Iceland, and that he found some islands which were then called *Gunnbjarnarsker*. Were these, perhaps, the islands of Angmagssalik?

Eirik the Red was one of the late immigrants from Norway. In the *Book of the Settlements* we read:

'There was a man called Thorvald, son of Asvald, son of Ulf Oxen-Thorir's son. Thorvald and his son Eirik the Red went from the Jaeder (Jæren on the west coast of Norway) to Iceland because of a slaying, and took land at Homstrandir, and lived on the farm Drangar.'

Eirik must have been a strong personality, a leader type. First he settled in the north of Iceland, but later he moved south, married and had children. It seems that it was not easy for him to adapt himself to the society of Iceland, however. He came into conflict with powerful families and finally he was outlawed by the Thorsnes Thing in 982, and had to flee the country.

He sailed out to sea, to the west, in order to find the land Gunnbjorn was said to have sighted. He reached the west coast of Greenland, stayed in that country for three years, and explored it. He found it to be a good land, and called it Greenland, thinking that such a name would tempt people to settle there.

Then he returned to Iceland, and organized one of the most striking northern colonization expeditions known to us. The expedition comprised twenty-five ships, with perhaps as many as 300 people on board. They also took horses, cattle, sheep, goats, pigs and dogs with them, as well as various kinds of equipment. This fleet sailed for Greenland in 986, a dangerous voyage in ice filled waters.

They came to a land with wild mountains and many bluish-white glaciers running down from the inland ice. But along the fjords and in the valleys they found good pasture for their cattle, and knurled birches grew in sheltered places. But there was no forest to provide them with materials for ship-building. Considerable quantities of driftwood had in the course of time accumulated on the shores, carried there from Siberia on the arctic current. Game and marine fauna were abundant here.

The *Book of the Settlements* mentions a number of men who took land along the different fjords. of Greenland. Eirik the Red settled at Eiriksfjord, the modern Tunugdilarfik. He called his farm Brattahlið. This farm has been found in the upper part of the fjord, in the district now known as Kagssiarsuk, which is one of the most favour-able parts of Greenland. After Eirik's death, his son Leif took over Brattahlið. The farm has been excavated, and the archaeological results are highly interesting, but the complex of buildings uncovered seems largely to have been built above an earlier house. Turf walls, which presumably represent the earliest building here, have been found below the complex. Brattahlið was to become the point of departure for the Vinland expeditions.

The colonists founded two settlements, the Eastern Settlement in the south, and the Western Settlement considerably further north, in the fjord district where Godthib now lies, and where life was harder than in the Eastern Settlement. In both these places the people tended to settle some way up the fjords, where the climate was more favourable and the pasture better. But ruins of farms have also been found down by the coast and in inland areas, right up to the limit of the permanent ice. It is difficult to establish, however, when these latter farms were built. The earliest settlers presumably built their farms in

Fig. 9. Eiriksfjord. Eirik Rauðis farm, Brattahlið, lay at the head of the fjord. Photo by Chr. Keller.

the best districts. The Norsemen could live in Greenland only by exploiting every possible means of subsistence. Animal husbandry was of prime importance, but fishing, hunting caribou, polar bear, whale, seal, walrus, etc. were also vital. A comparison of the Greenlanders' life with that of the Eskimos reveals a difference in that the Norse Greenlanders could fall back on their cattle, if need be. Their methods of hunting and trapping, and the primitive equipment at their disposal – bow and arrow, spear and traps – did not, however, differ much from those of the Eskimos.

We know from the large number of excavations of farms and middens carried out by Danish archaeologists that the Greenlanders had cattle, sheep, horses, goats and pigs. Well-built cattle sheds with thick walls of turf show that for most of the winter, at least, the cattle were not out on the pasture. Sheep and horses probably grazed out in the open all winter, as they still do today.

9

Fig. 10. This rune stone was found in what was once a cairn, on the island of Kingigtorssuaq, off the west coast of Greenland (72° 57' N). The inscription reads: 'Erling Sigvatsson, Bjarne Tordsson and Eindride Oddsson erected these cairns on the Saturday before Rogation Day, and runed well'. Photo courtesy of The National Museum, Cpn.

Cod fishing in the fjords by which the settlements lay must have been of great importance. There is often a great deal of cod in many of these fjords, but the temperature of the water is very close to what this fish can stand, and when it drops slightly, the cod may make for the open sea. Char (*salmo alpinus*) fishing in rivers and lakes is also of consequence, especially for those living on the inland farms. Gathering plants and berries must also have been essential, as it was in Norway and Iceland.

When Eirik the Red and his company settled in Greenland, there must have been rich fauna in the districts around the settlements, for this was virgin country. Large herds of caribou roamed about the country, there were polar bears and a multitude of fowl, the sea held seal, walrus, Greenland whale and other game. But the increasing population hunted so intensely that the resources of the nearby districts must have been overtaxed. And so the Norsemen were gradually forced to make for more distant virgin regions, just as people dependent on hunting have always done. The sources (*Grønl. Hist. Mind.* III: 234 ff.) tell of hunting and trapping in the north, off the west coast of Greenland.

This is where the large schools of walrus were to be found, and these animals were of great value. Walrus tooth was the ivory of the Middle Ages, and walrus hide was used for hawsers which were in great demand on the European market. The collection of driftwood further north was also of importance.

The Greenlanders' customary hunting grounds were at *Norðrseta*, far north of the settlements, and probably between 69° and 71°N. We may assume that the Disko region was particularly favoured by hunters, for there has been a rich stand of walrus, Greenland whale, seal and polar bear here throughout the ages.

In the course of time, the Greenlanders penetrated further and further north along the west coast. We know this from an account of an expedition which took place in 1267, and which may have reached about 76° N (*Grønl. Hist. Mind* III: 238-43). Moreover, a rune stone has been found on the island Kingigtorssuaq, at about 73° N, and this is assumed to date from the beginning of the fourteenth century (*Norges innskrifter med de yngre runer* V: 223, 233). In a great many Eskimo settlements, as far north as Marshall Bay (79° N), objects of Norse origin have been found (Holtved 1945: 78-84), and recently some Norse objects were found in Eskimo settlements on Ellesmere Island, Devon Island and Baffin Island. The question is whether these objects were transported by Eskimos from the Greenland settlements to the places where they were found, or whether we here have evidence testifying to voyages undertaken by the Norse Greenlanders. This will be discussed in the Epilogue.

With regard to the east coast the sources give some information suggesting that the Norsemen were familiar with many districts far in the north, where they probably hunted and fished (Ingstad 1966: 87 ff.), and concerning the southern part of the east coast, Ivar Bardarson (F. Jónsson 1930a: 21, 22) mentions *Finnbuder* (Finnsbu) and *Kaarsøø* (Korsøy), two districts in

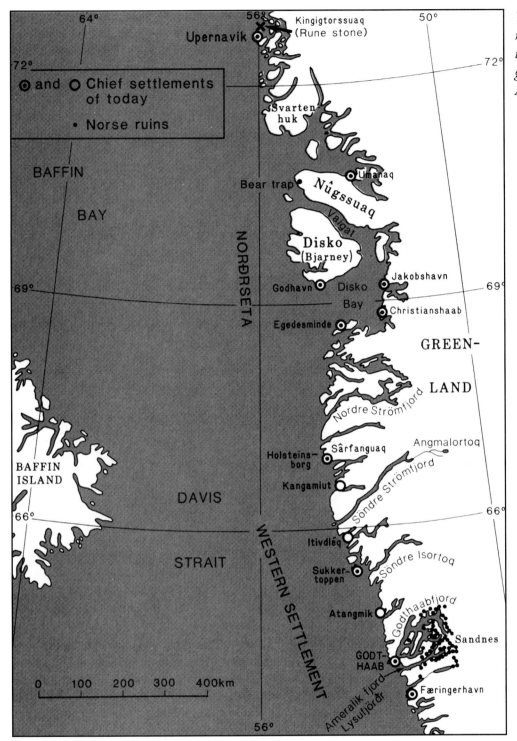

64°

56°

Kingigtorssuaq
(Rune stone)

Upernavik

50°

72°

72°

Svarten
huk

and Chief settlements
of today

Norse ruins

BAFFIN

BAY

Bear trap

Umanaq

Nûgssuaq

Vaigat

Disko
(Bjarney)

NORÐRSETA

Jakobshavn

69°

Godhavn

Disko
Bay

Christianshaab

69°

Egedesminde

GREEN-

LAND

Nordre Strömfjord

Angmalortoq

BAFFIN
ISLAND

Sârfanguaq

Holsteins—
borg

Sôndre Strömfjord

66°

Kangamiut

DAVIS

66°

Itivdléq

Sôndre Isortoq

STRAIT

Sukker-
toppen

WESTERN SETTLEMENT

Atangmik

Godthaabfjord

Sandnes

GODT-
HAAB

0   100   200   300   400km

Ameralik fjord

Lysufjörðr

56°

Færingerhavn

*The Western Settle-
ment and Norðrseta,
the northern hunting
grounds.
After E. Kopperud.*

11

Fig. 11. Ruins of the farm Sandnes in the Western Settlement, Greenland. Photo by Helge Ingstad.

the possession of the Church, where the polar bear was hunted. A ruin thought to be Norse has been found by the Lindenow fjord.

A sailing direction from Hauk's *Book of the Settlements* (Benediktsson 1968: 35) states: '... It is one day's and one night's sailing north to the uninhabited areas of Greenland from Kolbeinsey.' Kolbeinsey is also mentioned in *Svarfdæla Saga* (Kristjánsson 1956: 170), where it is said to be a small island north-west of Grimsey. There can hardly be any doubt that the reference is to eastern Greenland, even though the time of sailing is too short. In this connection we would also cite the information in the Icelandic annals for 1285 (Storm 1888b: 142, 196 and 337), concerning the discovery of Nýjaland (or Dúneyar), by two priests, Adalbrand and Thorvald (*Grønl. Hist. Mind.* 111: 12). This must be a district of eastern Greenland. A few years later the Norwegian king Eirik Magnusson sent Hrolf, known as Landa-Hrolf, to Iceland (Storm 1888b: 384), where he was to organize an expedition to the new land which must presumably have been so rich in game, not least in walrus, that there was a good chance of economic profit.

Further, there are in Björn Jónsson's version of the ancient Gripla (Halldórsson 1978:37, cf. 233) and in Arngrimur Jónssons *Gronlandia (Grønl. Hist. Mind.* 111: 24 ff. and note 460-1) some strange interpolations concerning a district of Greenland which can hardly lie anywhere except on the east coast. We are told that there are sheep, sauðum, of which there is testimony in Norway, for heads of these animals had been hung up in churches in Nidaros and in Bergen, and also in other public buildings. This cannot refer to anything as commonplace as ordinary sheep – the sources must mean the musk-ox (Ingstad 1966: 103 ff.). These animals, which are related to sheep, are somewhat reminiscent of their domesticated relatives. It was common practice in Norway to hang up or otherwise display in churches things considered worth seeing, such as the fur of polar bears, walrus ivory, etc. In fact, in Nidaros Cathedral a large and a small hide-boat had, according to Claudius Clavus (Storm 1889: 140), been hung up – probably a kayak and a woman's boat. Olaus Magnus (1909 B 1: 92) writes in 1555 of a hide-boat which had been hung up in the church of St. Hallvard in Oslo. Musk-ox heads were certainly something strange and new.

This opens a greater vista, for in eastern Greenland there is a definite southern limit for the musk-ox in the region by Scoresby Sound, at about 70° N. Mountains and glaciers prevent the animals from penetrating further south. In this connection we would mention an archaeological find from an Eskimo settlement at Dunholmen, a little way south of Scoresby Sound. Here a comb and a needle-case of bone with an incised cross were found (*Medd. om Grønl.* 28, VI, 1909: 472-6). The astonishing fact that heads were taken from Greenland to Norway and displayed in churches there can hardly be explained in any way except that the prey of the Norse hunters and trappers must have included the musk-ox. In any case, along the east coast of Greenland

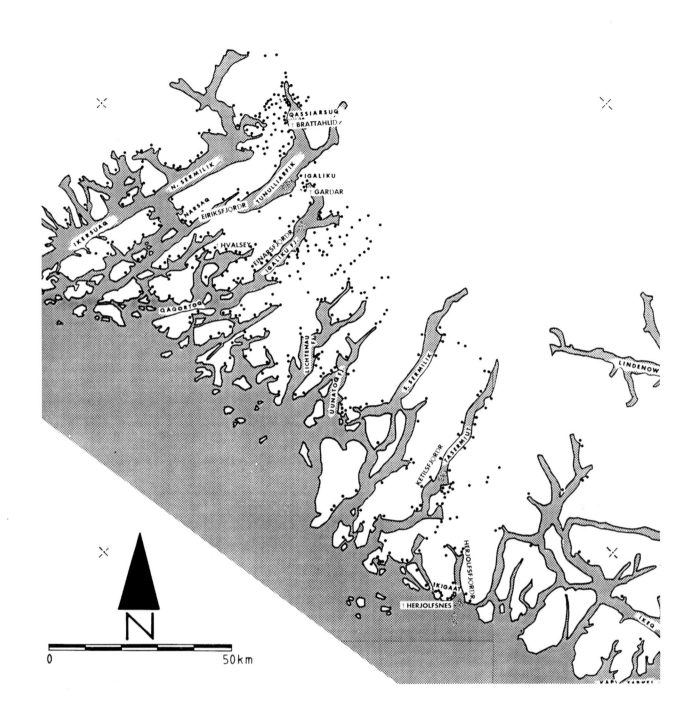

QASSIARSUQ
† BRATTAHLID

N. SERMILIK

NARSAQ

IGALIKU

TUNULLIARFIK
EIRIKSFJORDR
† GARDAR

IKERJUAG

EINARSFJORDR

HVALSEY

IGALIKU F.

QAQORTOQ

LICHTENAU
IGALIKU F.

UUNATOQ

S. SERMILIK

LINDENOW

KETILSFJORDR
TASERMIUT

HERJOLFSFJORDR

IKIGAAT

† HERJOLFSNES

IKEQ

VAP KARVEL

N

0   50km

Greenland, The Eastern Settlement. Medieval Norse groups of ruins. Christian Keller.

13

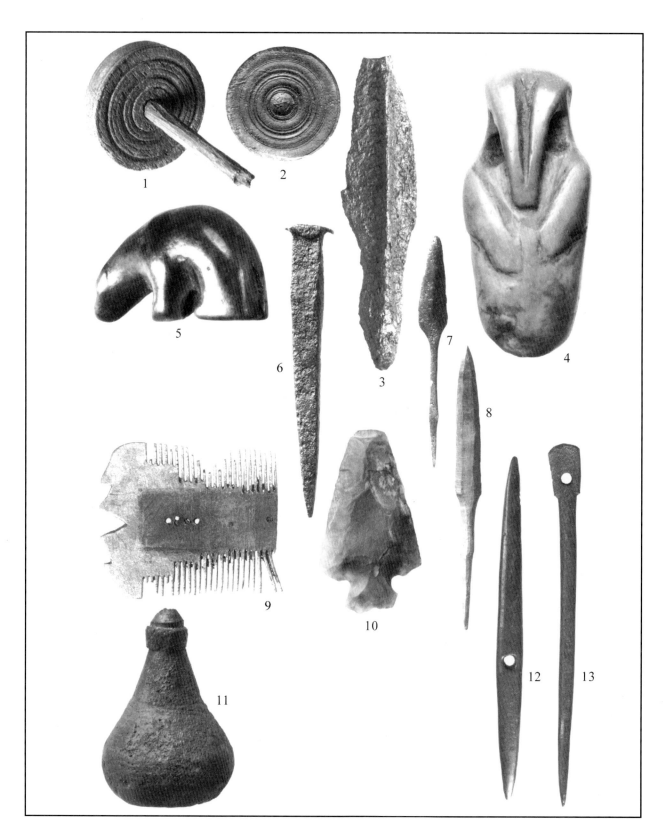

the Norsemen came as far north as Scoresby Sound, one of the districts of eastern Greenland richest in game. There is a plentiful stand of musk-ox there to this day.

Thus in the course of time the Greenlanders journeyed far north along the west coast of Greenland, and also along a part of the east coast. The sailing directions and information about Landa-Hrolf in the Icelandic annals may also be indicative of a direct voyage from Iceland to the northern parts of the east coast. This would imply an interesting extension of the geographic knowledge of the northern regions at the command of the Norsemen, a knowledge based on experience gained at sea, from the White Sea in the east to Greenland in the west.

Especially as concerns the Greenlanders' repeated expeditions to Norðrseta by the west coast far north of the settlements, to their established hunting and trapping grounds here, which must have covered the Disko fjord as well as other districts, it seems natural to assume that they must have gained new knowledge about the geography of the regions west of Greenland. This is of importance when we try to assess the possibility of any later voyages to North America which the Greenlanders may have undertaken. During their many expeditions to Norðrseta, they probably acquired some information about the narrowest part of the Davis Strait, which is no more than about 250 nautical miles wide. And it seems very unlikely that they should not have caught a glimpse of the high, snow-capped mountains of Baffin Island. Even the assumption that these expert sailors should have found the multitude of walrus there hardly seems too

Fig. 12.1, 2: draughtsmen, Innugsuk and Sandnes; 3, 9, 11: spearhead, bone comb and gaming piece, Brattahlið; 4, 6: walrus carving and iron wedge, Umiviarssuk; 5, 10: polar bear and Indian-type arrowhead, Sandnes; 7, 8: arrowheads; 12, 13: bone needles. Photo courtesy of National Museum, Cpn.

bold. The east coast of Baffin Island must have been the starting point for the Vinland route southwards along the coast of North America, and it seems unlikely that the traditional knowledge of this route should not have been remembered as long as there were Norsemen in Greenland.

When we consider the farms and the activities connected with them, we shall find elements of a Norse character more or less adapted to conditions in Greenland. The houses were built of turf and stone. The earliest type was the so called *long house*, a rectangular building, often with curved walls. Some had one room only, others had several, and rooms could also be added as, for instance, at the farm Sandnes in the Western Settlement (Roussell 1936: 12). A particularly interesting long house of the earliest type has been excavated at Narssaq in the Eastern Settlement (Vebæk 1964: 200-14); a runic inscription found there indicates that it may date back to the days of Eirik the Red. House-sites of a similar type have also been found at L'Anse aux Meadows.

Two other types of houses were evolved in Greenland as time went by; probably the increasing difficulties with regard to fuel were a contributory cause. One of them is the *passage house*, with fairly small rooms arranged on either side of a passage. The other is the *centralized house*, in which living-rooms, fire-house, store-rooms, smithy, cow shed etc. were all built together into one connected, rather untidy complex, with passages between the rooms. One of the farms in the so-called Austmannadal in the Eastern Settlement has such a house, with no less than twenty-three rooms.

The *King's Mirror* has a number of items of information of a factual kind, most of which would seem to be reliable. We read there that growing corn was very difficult in Greenland, so difficult that only the noblest of men attempted it. Most of the Greenlanders did not know what

15

bread was – they had never seen it. The passage continues:

'It has been said that there is good pasture in Greenland, and there are great and good farms. The people have much cattle and many sheep, and they make large quantities of butter and cheese. They live chiefly on this and on meat, and they also eat the meat of reindeer, whales, seals and bears; this is the food of the people of that country.' (Holm-Olsen 1983: 30; Halldórsson 1978: 123-4.)

Although this may all be true of life in Greenland, it does not give us a complete picture, for the risks involved in breeding cattle on an arctic island are not even mentioned. For the sheep, grazing out of doors all the year round, ice and deep snow might well be catastrophic. Night frost before the first fall of snow was more common here than in Norway and Iceland, and could result in poor pasturage and little fodder for the winter. Polar bears and probably also wolves represented a very real danger. Nor must we forget that farming and animal husbandry would require more hard work here than in other countries.

The homefields were probably manured, and artificial irrigation was employed in some places, for instance at Garðar, as I have shown (Ingstad 1966: 190), where a network of canals leads down to the fields. But the grass from the homefields was by no means sufficient to see the stock through the winter. Most of the winter fodder must have been gathered on the outfields, just as in Norway and Iceland. Grass growing among stones and thickets was cut, moss and seaweed were gathered. But often this did not suffice either, and when spring came, some of the animals lay dead in their stalls. An average-sized farm seems to have had about five cows, but the cow sheds of the large farms attest to a surprisingly large number of animals: at Brattahlið there

was room for twenty-five heads of cattle, and at Garðar for about a hundred.

The cows, sheep and horses were small and extremely hardy. Some of the sheep were probably milked, as in Iceland. We have seen that butter and cheese were produced. The butter, which was unsalted, would keep fresh for a long time. Another dairy product was *skyr*; a kind of fermented milk which was stored in large vessels. The sources tell us little about the women of Greenland, but their work must have been hard and exacting. Not only were they responsible for many different kinds of work on the farm, but many accompanied the menfolk on the dangerous voyage to the new land in the west. They must have been strong indeed, not least mentally. At home on the farm they cooked the food and looked after the children, they spun and wove materials for clothes and for sails, they prepared hides, sewed boots from seal-skin, and winter clothes from caribou fur. They looked after the cattle and milked the cows, they churned butter and made cheese, they fetched water and fuel, and so on.

There were usually several out-buildings of different kinds on the farms; the ruins of cow sheds, fire-houses, store-rooms, bath-houses and smithies have been discovered, and bog-iron has been found in or near some of the smithies (Nielsen 1930). The process of extracting iron from bog-ore was well known in the Norse region, and iron production was of great importance in Norway. The men who sailed west took their knowledge of this art with them to the new land beyond Greenland. On the Norse settlement site which I discovered at L'Anse aux Meadows in northern Newfoundland, a smithy with a stone anvil has been excavated; close by, fragments of iron, slag, a charcoal kiln and rich deposits of bog-ore were found.

The tools and equipment of the Greenlanders were simple. The iron tools found included axes, knives, scythes, sickles, forging tongs, sledge-hammers, sheep-shears, chisels, awls, spears, arrowheads, tweezers, strike-a-lights, and a few others. For the rest, the people made do with tools of bone or wood. Soapstone was an important raw material, and this occurs in both the Greenland settlements. Pots and pans were made from this, train lamps, bowls, spindle whorls, loom weights, ornaments, etc. As it must necessarily take some time before soapstone deposits are discovered, it seems most likely that the settlers had to make do without this material during the first years of the Greenland colony. No soapstone has, for instance, been found in conjunction with Thjodhild's church, the earliest of the Greenland churches. In this connection we should note that the Norse settlement in Newfoundland has yielded no soapstone fragments, and no object of soapstone other than a spindle whorl made from the base of a pot or a lamp.

We have already seen that the lack of forest from which one might obtain materials for ship-building and other work was a very serious problem for the Greenlanders. But during the Vinland voyages they discovered the great forests of Labrador (Markland), and it seems most unlikely that after this discovery they should not have made use of the timber there. In fact, ships were so vital to the existence of the Norse Greenlanders that it is difficult to imagine their colony surviving for several centuries unless timber for ship-building had been procured not only from Norway, but also from North America.

Fuel constituted another great problem. There was no difficulty during the first years of settlement, for there were large heaps of driftwood along the shore, and there was some birch growing in the country. But with the increase in the population during the following period, so much driftwood was consumed that no appreciable reserves remained. And, just as in Iceland, the small birch woods were ruthlessly exploited, while regrowth was prevented by the grazing

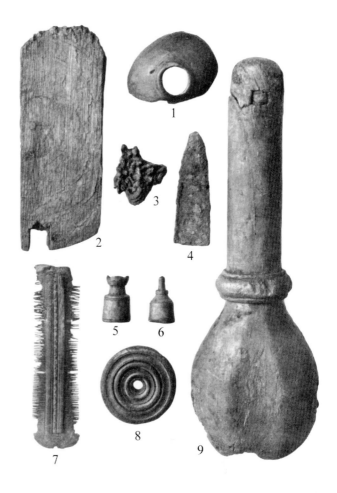

Fig. 13. Norse objects found during the excavations of Eskimo ruins in northern Greenland. From Thule, *c. 77 ° N: 5, chessman, a rook, beautifully turned from walrus ivory. 6, chessman, pawn. 9, wooden case for spoon. 1, a bowl-shaped wooden funnel, probably for straining milk; a straining cloth had been attached to the end of the funnel. From* Marshall Bay, Inglefield Land, *c. 79°N: 7, bone comb. 3, fragment of chain-mail. 4, iron spearhead. 8, checkerboard piece, turned from whale-bone. 2, fragment of an oaken vessel or bottom of a barrel, with incised circles. Photo by E. Holtved.*

cattle. As a result, farms and homefields were exposed to the danger of sand-drift, and in some places, for instance at Vatnahverfi, entire farms were buried in sand. Moreover, the processes involved in the production of iron required a great amount of fuel. After the resources had been exploited in this way for a couple of centuries, the Norse Greenlanders must have shared the fate of the Eskimos with regard to fuel, there was hardly any available except for any heather or withy they might find. They may have eked out this meagre supply with some peat, but the peat of Greenland is thin, and of poor quality.

The returns of hunting, fishing and farming were intended to cover more than the Greenlanders' own requirements. They also had to pay for valuable commodities when ships from other parts of the world came to this arctic island. The natural centre for the Greenland trade was Norway, and Bergen was the regular port of embarcation; sometimes the ships seem to have called at Icelandic ports, but most often they sailed straight to the community in Greenland, a journey of about 1,500 nautical miles. Many such trading expeditions are mentioned in the Icelandic annals, but probably there were more than the sources record. The traffic along this route seems to have been rather irregular. At times several years passed between ships calling in Greenland.

The Greenlanders were very largely self sufficient, but certain commodities such as pig iron, timber, iron pots, nails and rivets, broadcloth, corn, salt and honey were highly desirable. In exchange for these goods they could offer walrus and narwhal teeth, walrus hide, cow, sheep and caribou skins, furs of the white and the blue fox, and of the polar bear, live polar bears, stockfish, train oil, down, and not least the very highly prized white falcons, which eventually made their way to European kings and Arabian princes. In addition they had their farm produce to offer: butter, cheese, wadmal and various craft products. Many excavations have been carried out in Greenland, but only a few of the objects found are certain to be imports.

A different people had also made their home in Greenland; the Dorset Eskimos. According to Ari's *Book of the Icelanders* it seems that Eirik the Red and his colonists never encountered any of these people, but only saw traces of them. Then, around the year 1000, the Thule Eskimos came to northern Greenland from the islands of arctic Canada, and some of them gradually made their way south along the west coast. In the course of time they reached the Norse Greenlanders' northern hunting grounds, then the Western Settlement and finally, towards the end of the fourteenth century, they came to the Eastern Settlement, thus becoming the neighbours of the Norse Greenlanders. Although there must have been some instances of conflict between these two peoples, relations between them seem, on the whole, to have been good.

Most of the Norsemen were still pagan at the time of the settlement of Greenland, shortly before A.D. 1000. A soapstone fragment (*fig. 8*) with an incised Thor's hammer has been found at Brattahli∂. In Iceland Christianity was adopted at an Althing in the year 1000, but Greenland seems to have been converted gradually by Christians, possibly missionaries who came to the country. True, Eirik's Saga states that Leif Eiriksson was commissioned by the Norwegian king Olaf Tryggvason to convert Greenland but, as we shall show below, this is probably a fictive account intended to enhance the prestige of the Church.

In 1961 a Greenlander discovered Greenland's

Fig. 14. Eskimo carvings from Greenland, representing Norsemen: 2, 3 and 4 were found at the Eskimo site of Inugsuk at about 73°N. 1 is from Umiviarssuk, 5 from Austmannadal and 6 from Sandnes, the three last all in the Western Settlement. Photo courtesy of The National Museum, Cpn.

18

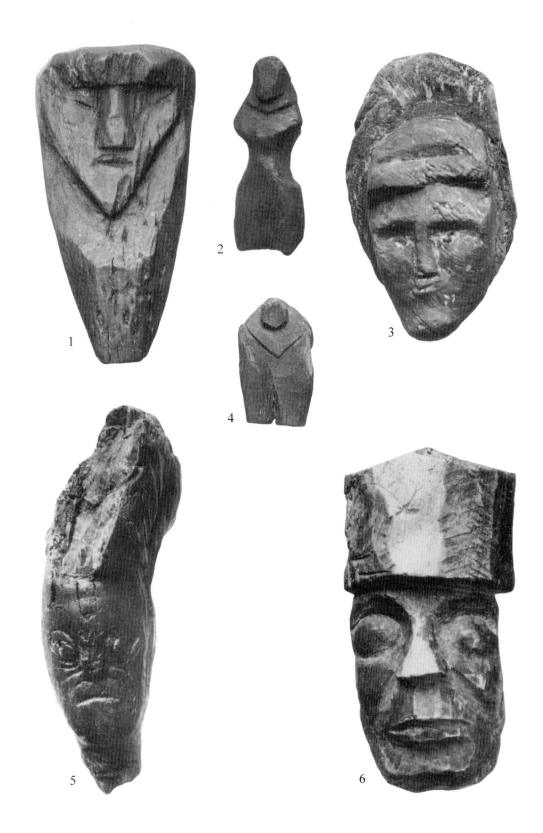

1   2   3

          4

5   6

19

Fig. 15. Thjodhild's church, with church-yard – sketch-plan, 1:100. The turf walls of the church are hatched. Women's skeletons are shown in red, men's skeletons in blue, children's in green. The sex of some of the skeletons could not be determined. The National Museum, Cpn.

first church, not far from the farm Brattahliδ, and this has now been excavated by Danish archaeologists. This must be Thjodhild's church, of which Eirik's Saga tells. According to this account, Eirik was unwilling to abandon his faith, but his wife Thjodhild was baptized and had a church built 'at some distance from the houses' (Sveinsson and þórδarson 1934: 212). This church, which measures only 2 m x 3 m, is built of turf (Meldgaard 1964: 281 ff., Krogh 1967: 19-36). It was surrounded by a church-yard, where 144 skeletons have been excavated. Only very few of these had been buried in coffins; the rest were probably either buried in their clothes or wrapped in a shroud, but no traces of any cloth remain. They all lay facing east. South of the church a mass grave was found, containing a confusion of bones and thirteen skulls. Bundles of human bones occurred in several places; it seems likely that they had been moved to this churchyard from elsewhere.

This material provides unique evidence of the time of the Vinland expeditions and the immediately following years, and it seems likely that some of the people who had taken part in these voyages were buried in this churchyard. Thus the testimony of this skeletal material is of particularly great interest. According to Knud J. Krogh (1967: 37-43), a detailed examination of these skeletons had yielded the following interesting results: of the 144 individuals buried there, twenty-four were children, sixty-five men – twelve of them buried in a mass grave – and thirty-nine women. The sex of sixteen adults could not be securely determined, but there is reason to believe that the majority of them are female. Fifteen of the children were infants; the infant mortality rate conveyed by these figures is very low, but we cannot know whether infants were always buried in the churchyard.

The age at death of these people was as follows: of fifty-three men (this figure does not include the twelve men in the mass grave) one had died at an age of 18-22, fourteen at an age of 20-30, twenty-three at an age of 30-50, while another fifteen had died after the age of 20, but their age at death cannot be determined.

Of the thirty-nine women, two had died at a age of 18-22, ten at an age of 20-30, ten at 30-50, while two lived to be over 50. Fifteen women had lived beyond the age of 20, but their age at death is uncertain.

The sixteen adults whose sex could not be determined include three who were between 20 and 30 at the time of death, one who was over 50 years of age, and nine who were over 20, although their age cannot be determined more precisely than this.

The average height of the women is 156 cm, that of the men 171 cm, but some men were 184-185 cm tall – the latter figures are almost identical with those which apply in Scandinavia today. Most of the men were sturdy, and traces on the bones show that they were muscular. The teeth were good, without any demonstrable traces of caries, and they were considerably worn. The reason for this is, in my opinion, that the Norse Greenlanders used their teeth for all kinds of jobs, just like the Eskimos. Some of the skeletons showed evidence of rheumatic diseases. As we know, rheumatism was common during the Middle Ages, and probably also earlier.

The cause of death could be established in only one case. A man in his thirties had been stabbed with a large iron knife with a wooden handle, which had penetrated deeply into the left side of his chest. This knife was a valuable possession, and there must have been some special reason why it was not removed from the body.

These, then, are the skeletons of the first settlers in Greenland, of the days of Eirik the Red and the Vinland voyages, and probably also of the immediately following years. Suddenly we are confronted with people who up to now were simply names in the sagas and in other sources. But who are they? None of the skeletons can be iden-

Fig. 16. Ruins of Hvalsey church, the Eastern Settlement. Photo by Helge Ingstad.

tified, but according to Grœnlendinga Saga and Eirik's Saga, Thorstein, son of Eirik the Red and Thjodhild, must have been buried here. One of the skeletons may be that of Thjodhild, another that of her son Leif Eiriksson. During the Middle Ages the most prominent persons were usually buried close to the church wall, preferably so close that water from the roof would drip on their graves, or they were buried inside the church. It was thought that such a position would provide the dead with the greatest chances of salvation. A few of the skeletons found in Thjodhild's churchyard lay closer to the church wall than the rest. It seems natural to assume that Thjodhild, Thorstein or Leif Eiriksson may be among them.

The impression conveyed by this skeletal material is one of a strong, a healthy people. It is interesting to note that the natural limit of life seems to have been at about 50 for both men and women. There may be many reasons for this, including the hard struggle for survival, often involving many dangers. This is of particular interest in connection with the information about the death of Eirik the Red in Groenlendinga Saga. We shall return to this below.

Once Thjodhild's church had been established, Christianity gained a stronger foothold in Greenland, but it seems reasonable to assume that the people of this wild, thinly populated country, confirmed adherents of a pagan faith, would not all be converted to Christianity until some time had passed. In 1124 an episcopal see was established in Greenland, under the Norwegian king Sigurd Jorsalfar (the Crusader) (Halldórsson 1978: 103-05, *Dipl. Norv.* XVII B: 281). During the first years of its existence, this formed part of the archbishopric of Lund, and from 1153 part of that of Nidaros (Trondheim). The first Bishop of Greenland was Arriald. He came from Norway and established his see at Garðar, where a bishop's palace and a cathedral were later built. In the course of the centuries he was succeeded by a number of others – it seems possible that Anders, who probably came to Greenland in 1406, was the last bishop there (*Dipl. Norv.* XVII B: 284). Although the Pope consecrated Bishops of Garðar throughout the remaining years of the Catholic era, none of these came to Greenland (*Dipl. Norv.* XVII B: 284-6).

The Church flourished in Greenland after the see had been established at Garðar. A number of churches were built, as well as a monastery and a convent. The position of the Church must have become very powerful. Its demands on the Greenlanders whose toil gave them but little profit in any case must have been oppressive indeed: not only did they have to pay Peter's pence, but a tax for the crusades was also exacted. After some time the Church apparently also became the greatest landowner in the country. According to Ivar Bardarson (Jónsson 1930a: 21-8), the Church seems to have acquired ownership of the best land in the Eastern Settlement, and even the rights to the polar bear hunt on an island off the south-east coast. As a result the economy of the Greenlanders themselves deteriorated, and we must bear this fact in mind when we consider the question of a possible emigration at a later date. The powerful position of the Church must also have led to profound social changes; it is significant that we hear no more about the descendants of Eirik the Red, or of the chieftains who came to Greenland with him, after the eleventh century. One of the last to be mentioned is Thorkel, son of Leif Eiriksson.

One of the basic elements of the traditional Norse society was the importance of the family. The great families were the leaders; they formed, as it were, a society within a society. One was duty bound to protect and avenge one's kin. This aristocratic social order the Norsemen took with them to Greenland, and it is typical that the best land there was taken up by men of great families. In Iceland, blood vengeance was to become a veritable nightmare, but the sources do not mention this blight in connection with Greenland, except for the unreliable *Fóstbrœðrasaga* (ed. þórólfsson and Jónsson 1943). It seems likely that life in Greenland was so hard and survival required such great concentration that internal conflict was at least not as all-pervading as it was in Iceland. Remarkable in this connection is the fact that the great number of excavations have not yielded a single fragment of a shield or a sword. This should be borne in mind in connection with Eirik's Saga's highly coloured account of the multitude of white and red shields raised by the Vinland voyagers when they encountered natives.

The sources are not very loquacious on the subject of the common people. Entertainment was to be had from accounts of the activities and noble deeds of the chieftains, the toil of common men and women was not so interesting. And thus a great deal of the most fascinating aspects of life in Greenland are lost. We hear nothing about daring hunting expeditions far to the north of the west coast of Greenland, nothing of expeditions to Labrador, in order to fetch timber.

It is unthinkable that a Norse community should have existed in a country like Greenland for five hundred years without developing its own distinctive and deep-rooted culture, a culture which included sagas, folk songs, skilful weaving and other crafts. But no sources have survived, and the culture of Norse Greenland disappeared together with the people who possessed and practised it. We shall never know what stories the weather-beaten old men told by the fireside, while the children, with wide-open eyes, sat listening on the earthen floor beside the long hearth. Nor shall we ever find out what song a young Greenland girl might sing when the wild mountains and white glaciers lay bathed in sunshine.

But some few glimpses of the culture of the Norse Greenlanders have survived. Sixty runic inscriptions have been found in Greenland. A small rune-stick looks insignificant, just a few lines on a piece of wood which has drifted across the Arctic ocean from Siberia, and which was worn smooth by the action of the sea. But these spiky lines, cut many centuries ago, have a story to tell: they conjure up the past, and all of a sudden we feel that we know the people who lived so long ago. A Norse Greenlander once held this runestick in his hand. In grave concentration he sat bent over it and carved rune after rune, in the belief that help would come from the gods.

These small, pointed symbols held a mighty force. At the beginning, runes were concealed; they were bound up in life, in the world, they lay in the paw of the bear, in the eagle's beak, on the tooth of the wolf, in the nail of the Norn. But the great god Odin unfettered them, he brought the draught of the scalds down from the wild mountains.

Fig. 17. At the foot of the wild mountains at the head of Ketilsfjord in the Eastern Settlement, there was a small monastery dedicated to St. Olaf and St. Augustine. Photo courtesy of The National Museum, Cpn.

Fig. 18. Kvitserk Rock with compass. Fight with a Greenland 'pigmy'. From Olaus Magnus.

The runes had magic power, they could safeguard human life. They were the key to the secrets of nature, to the place where human fate was forged. When they were used in the right way, they provided protection from disease, from distress at sea, from arrows, swords and hatred, from revenge and other evils; they could also fulfil one's most intense desires. A small rune-stick found under the floor of the ancient Norwegian stave-church at Urnes bore this inscription 'Arne, the priest, wants Inga.'

It is especially interesting to note that some new runic forms were evolved in Greenland, while older forms, which had fallen into disuse in Norway and Iceland at this time, were still current in Greenland. The sources contain references to *Skald-Helga Saga*, to the story about Thordis in this saga, which is likely to have been written in Greenland. The famous *Codex Regius* of the *Elder Edda* moreover contains two poems, *Atlamál* and *Atlakviða*, which are there stated to be from Greenland.

A few other traces of the culture of the Greenland society have been found, for instance some beautiful pieces of wood-carving. We must also note that the Greenlanders must clearly have been very keen chess-players, chessmen have come to light even on a distant farm by the inland ice. When the storms of winter howled round the houses, it must have been a welcome diversion to sit indoors by the light of the train-oil lamp, completely absorbed in the fascinating world of chess. It is by no means uninteresting to note that these polar people set such great store by a game demanding so high a degree of concentration and imagination.

Like Iceland, Greenland was originally a free state, without any constitutional dependence on either Iceland or Norway. We learn from the sources that the Greenlanders had their own laws, their independent Althing, and their own law-speaker in occupied no man's land. In 1261 Greenland voluntarily accepted the rule of Norway, and under the Norwegian king Håkon Håkonson the country became part of the realm of Norway. This included Norway with the Kola peninsula, Iceland, Orkney and Shetland, the Hebrides, the Faeroes and the Isle of Man. On the occasion of the king's assumption of power in Greenland, the scald Sturla Thordarson wrote these verses:

Towards the north your mind was bent,
Your sway to wax over land so cold.
Good men find joy in this,
King under the Pole Star.

No chieftain has ere now
Ruled over so mighty a land,
Radiant blazes your power
Further north than a sun may shine.

The unification of Greenland and Norway was natural for several reasons. The Greenlanders hoped to benefit from a better and fairly regular shipping contact with Norway, a country with which they were closely connected by trade and by church matters. The same motive must have been of importance also to the Icelanders when they reached a similar agreement with the king of Norway in 1262.

In the Eastern Settlement of Greenland the ruins of about four hundred farms, twenty-three churches and two monasteries have been located, as well as those of a bishop's palace. In the Western Settlement the ruins of eighty farms and three churches have been found. In the most prosperous days of the colony, perhaps during the thirteenth century, the population probably numbered about 4,000.

In 1721 Hans Egede, the Norwegian missionary, sailed to the south-west coast of Greenland, and he expected to find Norsemen living in the ancient settlements there. He found no one, only the ruins of farms and churches.

What happened to these Norsemen who lived on this arctic island for almost five hundred years? Why did they disappear so mysteriously? As far as the Western Settlement is concerned we know that Ivar Bardarson, priest at the Bishop's palace in the Eastern Settlement, sailed there in the mid-fourteenth century; he found not a single Norseman, only untended cattle and sheep. This source, as well as others, may perhaps suggest that the people of the Western Settlement had

Fig. 19. Arm of chair, 37.5 cm long. The animal's head measures 7 cm. Sandnes, Western Settlement. The low level at which this piece was found suggests the first period of settlement, as does also the style of the ornamentation. Can this carving be connected with the bishop's see of the Western Settlement, mentioned by Ivar Bárðarson? Photo courtesy of The National Museum, Cpn.

emigrated; they had not, however, come to the Eastern Settlement, from where Ivar had sailed in order to visit them (*see p.* 178).

The last secure item of information about Greenland concerns a ship from Norway, bound for Iceland, which landed there after having lost its way at sea. The crew stayed in Greenland for four years, until 1410. Nothing in this account suggests that the Greenlanders were in any kind of difficulties. Moreover, the clothes and head-wear excavated at Herjolfsnes churchyard show that the Greenlanders followed European fash-ions during the fourteenth century, and until the end of the fifteenth. We must thus assume that there were Norse Greenlanders living in this district until about 1500, and that they were in contact with Europe. In this connection it is of interest to note that the English seem to have rediscovered Greenland around the year 1500.

We know nothing definite about the reasons for the disappearance of the Greenlanders – there are any number of theories, but this is not the place to discuss the many problems involved. The most important of these theories are the fol-lowing: the Greenlanders mingled with the Eski-mos; the Eskimos expelled or killed the Green-landers; the Greenlanders were exterminated by a plague.

An emigration could have taken place for the fol-lowing reasons: the birch forest might have been too heavily taxed, with regrowth destroyed by grazing cattle, and sand-drifts may have turned extensive pastures into waste land. The econom-ic decline in Norway and the failing trade con-nections were in the nature of a catastrophe for the Greenland society. A colder climate may have led to so serious a deterioration in the pos-sibilities offered by the land that is was no longer possible for the Greenlanders to live there. Finally we should also mention E.C. Hansen's

horrific description of the Greenlanders who, according to him, perished as a result of degener-ation. Unfortunately this hypothesis has recurred in many books, even though later scientific inves-tigations have shown that it is quite untenable.

It seems natural to look for the explanation in a concurrency of causes. I have formerly submitted a new point of view, which should not be over-looked. It concerns an account by Niels Egede; in his *Description of Greenland*, of 1769, he gives a report of what an Eskimo had told him. This is a detailed story about pirates who came to Greenland and ravaged the Eastern Settlement, killing the people and setting fire to the build-ings. This straightforward account bears an unmistakable mark of trustworthiness. It accords well with a papal letter of 1448, which tells of foreign ships that came to the settlement, where 'the barbarians ravaged with fire and swords, and destroyed the sacred buildings' (*Dipl. Norv.* VI: 527).

Why the Norse Greenlanders disappeared is only one aspect of this question - but what became of them? If we were to accept one of the theories to the effect that they were either com-pletely assimilated with the Eskimos, or that they died out, there would be no problem. But for various reasons such all-embracing solutions are unacceptable; it seems more likely that the Greenlanders, encountering increasing difficul-ties in their struggle for life, would emigrate, in groups of families and close friends. But where did they go? Norway would be an obvious answer to this question, and so would England, as vessels from the English fishing fleet in Iceland may occasionally have come to Greenland. North America is another possibility, for the route there was known, and we know that a ship from Greenland was in Markland (Labrador) as late as in 1347.

When Norse men and women had settled in Greenland, North America became a neighbouring country. At its narrowest, the Davis Strait which divides them is only about 250 nautical miles wide, and this was a short distance for the Norse seafarers, who time and again crossed the Atlantic from Norway to the community in Greenland, a journey covering about 1,500 nautical miles.

These maritime people from Greenland, who journeyed so far abroad, could hardly avoid discovering North America some time during the centuries of the life of their society. This seems evident even without the testimony of literary sources. But there exist sources which either refer to voyages to new lands west and southwest of Green-land, or which contain more or less concrete information about such expeditions. Some of these sources are fragmentary, others are accounts of the so-called Vinland expeditions: Grœnlendinga Saga and Eirik's Saga.

In the present context a mention of the most important fragmentary sources will suffice. The earliest of these occurs in the fourth book (ch. XXXIX) of *Gesta Hammaburgensis ecclesiae pontificum* (The History of the Archbishopric of Hamburg) by the learned German, Adam of Bremen. It dates from c. 1075 (ed. B. Schmeidler 1918). Here we read that many have discovered an island with grapes which yield excellent wine, and with wild wheat. The earliest mention in the literature of Iceland occurs in *The Book of the Icelanders* (Benediktsson 1968: 13-14), written by Ari the Learned in about 1130. This source merely speaks of the Skrælings, the natives of Vinland. Other mentions occur in Snorri's *Heimskringla*, in the *Large Saga of Olaf Tryggvason* (chs. 86, 95 and 96), written in about 1300. Of great interest is also the mention of Vinland in the introduction to Abbot Nikolaus of Þverá's description of his journey to the Holy Land. The earliest history of Norway, *Historia Norvegiae*, which probably dates from the end of the

THE ANCIENT SOURCES

twelfth century, has no mention of Vinland, but states that there are islands by the westernmost limits of Europe, beyond Greenland.

Grœnlendinga Saga occurs in a vellum manuscript, *Flateyjarbók*, a great codex which was compiled in the late 1380s. It takes the form of interpolations in the *Saga of Olaf Tryggvason*. The saga speaks of Bjarni who was adrift at sea and sighted unknown shores, and of the voyages undertaken by Leif Eiriksson, Thorvald Eiriksson, Thorfinn Karlsefni and Freydis. The latter all followed Bjarni's route, but in the opposite direction. We also hear about Thorstein Eirik's-son's abortive voyage.

Eirik's Saga is preserved in two vellum manuscripts. One of these is *Hauksbók*, but the author, Hauk Erlendsson, a kinsman of Thorfinn Karlsefni's, has 'improved' it considerably. The other version (AM 557 4°) is to be preferred.

In essential respects, the story as it is given in Eirik's Saga differs considerably from that which occurs in Grœnlendinga Saga. In Eirik's Saga, Leif sails from Greenland to Norway, where he meets the king, Olaf Tryggvason, and is commissioned by him to preach Christianity in Greenland. On his way back, he comes to an unknown land where vines and self-sown wheat grow. The same year he returns to Greenland, and we are given an unctuous description of how he brought Christianity to Greenland, and of his work for the Church. Then Leif disappears from the story; in the rest of the saga, the Icelander Thorfinn Karlsefni becomes the hero who sets out on an expedition and finds the Vinland which Leif ostensibly had found far in the south.

Which of these two very different sagas, Grœnlendinga Saga or Eirik's Saga, may we take to be the more historically correct? This question has been much discussed, and a great deal has been written about it. The first to take up the Vinland problem was Arngrímur Jónsson (1568-1648). The work of Thormod Torfæus (1636-1719) and of C.C. Rafn (1837) was also of great

moment. All these scholars preferred Grœnlendinga Saga; for the rest, scholars' views have varied greatly.

During the second half of the nineteenth century Eirik's Saga was generally regarded to be the more reliable of the two sagas. This is not least due to the work of Gustav Storm. He maintained that Eirik's Saga must beyond doubt be regarded as the reliable version, and that everything in Grœnlendinga Saga opposed to the former must be rejected. This preference for Eirik's Saga was accepted by many scholars, including Reeves (1890), Fisher (1902) and Finnur Jónsson (1912a and 1915).

A new view of Grœnlendinga Saga was inspired by Sigurður Nordal and Jón Helgason (Nordal and Helgason 1953: 248-9). They point out that the tradition about Bjarni Herjolfsson's voyage (the essential precondition for Leif's Vinland voyage), must be older and sounder than the story about Leif's discovery of Vinland on his way home from Norway to Greenland, which is given in Eirik's Saga. The late Jón Jóhannesson developed Nordal's view further, and argued along convincing and discerning lines (1962: 54 ff.). He states that the monk Gunnlaug Leifsson (d. 1219) appears to be the original author of the reports given in Eirik's Saga, and continues '... thus Leif did not discover Vinland on his way from Norway to Greenland, and there remains no reason to doubt that the saga of the Greenlanders preserves the original and correct account of the discovery of the new lands in the Western Hemisphere ...' In his opinion, Grœnlendinga Saga is the older of the two sagas, probably dating from c. 1200. He also states that in his view the author of Eirik's Saga not only knew Grœnlendinga Saga, but that he also made use of it in such a way that nothing would conflict with the story of Leif having discovered Vinland in the course of a journey from Norway. Here, Jóhannesson gives some few, but convincing examples to illustrate this point. In my discussion of all of Eirik's Saga (*see pp. 69 ff.*) I return to this matter, and I feel convinced that the author of that saga made systematic use of Grœnlendinga Saga in such a way that nothing must conflict with the story of Leif having discovered Vinland during a voyage from Norway. Below we show important elements of the two sagas in tabular form:

GRŒNLENDINGA SAGA

1. Bjarni Herjolfsson sails from Iceland to Greenland, but drifts at sea and sights unknown shores. Then he finds his way to Greenland. Ch. II.

2. Leif sets out on a voyage of discovery, starting from Greenland, in order to find the land Bjarni had seen. With him he has a crew of thirty-five. He discovers Helluland, Markland and Vinland, where he builds 'large houses'. He remains in Vinland for one year. He finds grapes. He saves a ship's crew on his way back to Greenland.
Chs. III and IV.

3. Thorvald Eiriksson's Vinland expedition, with a crew of thirty. They live in Leif's houses, explore the land from there, meet Skrælings, and Thorvald is killed in the battle. The expedition stays in Vinland for two years. Ch. V.

4. Thorstein Eiriksson's abortive Vinland expedition, with a crew of twenty-five. Ch. VI.

5. Thorfinn Karlsefni's Vinland expedition, which includes sixty men, five women and all kinds of livestock. They settle down in Leif's houses, trade with the Skrælings and fight them. The expedition stays in Vinland for two years. Ch. VIL

EIRIK'S SAGA

1. Leif Eiriksson sails from Greenland to Norway, is commanded by Olaf Tryggvason to preach Christianity in Greenland. On the way home, he drifts at sea and finds a new land with grape-vines. The same year he continues his journey to Greenland, saves a ship's crew, and converts Greenland to Christianity. Ch. V.

2. Thorstein Eiriksson's abortive Vinland expedition with a crew of twenty. Ch. V.

3. Thorfinn Karlsefni's Vinland expedition, which included three ships, 160 people including women, and all kinds of livestock. He discovers and names Helluland and Markland, establishes his headquarters at Straumfjord. Sails south to Hóp, where he finds grapevines and wild wheat. Trades with the Skrælings and fights them. The expedition lasts for three years. Chs. VII-XIII.

6. Freydis's Vinland expedition. With a crew of thirty-five she sails to Vinland, where they live in Leif's houses. At the same time a ship from Iceland, with a crew of thirty, sails to Vinland. She provokes the Icelanders, all of whom are killed in the end. After a year she returns to Greenland. Ch. VIII.

The interpretation of Grœnlendinga Saga and Eirik's Saga presents many problems. The accounts in the preserved manuscripts are based on earlier literary sources which were written down about two hundred years or more after the events they describe, and in the course of so long a period of time much can have been changed, much may have faded. And as these narratives deal with so fascinating a subject as the discovery of a new land far in the west, inhabited by strange beings, and ominous, supernatural creatures, they must obviously have appealed to the popular imagination. No wonder, then, if the subject matter was embellished or changed in the course of time.

Because of their subject matter, the Vinland sagas hold a unique position in the corpus of Icelandic literature. If we are to have a chance of arriving at the historical core on which these accounts are based, we must appraise the problems not only by means of an interpretation of the texts, but also from the point of view of specific, extraordinary circumstances. Here we are dealing with the unparalleled case of a Norse people on an arctic island, and with the discovery of a new world.

Not only must we be critical of the way in which the saga writers many generations later regarded the events; it is also essential that we try to find out what seems to tally with the conditions a thousand years ago. The Vinland voyages started out from Greenland, and the new lands were of importance to the inhabitants of that country. We must therefore try to understand the Greenlanders, the Norsemen who lived on this arctic island. About their way of thinking, their feelings and emotions, we know nothing, but they were no less intelligent than people are today. And they had talents which modern man has largely lost: a fine sense of perception, practical common sense and a boldness engendered by the struggle for survival in close contact with nature.

They were farmers, and they kept cattle, sheep and horses; they were also hunters, fishermen and highly accomplished seafarers. We have already seen that the tools and implements at their disposal were simple, axe, knife, bow and arrow, spear, etc. But that does not mean that they were at a loss for want of better equipment, for they most certainly mastered techniques handed down from generation to generation,

and they were highly skilful with their hands. They must have been a hardy, knowledgeable people, quick to attend to rudder and sail when a storm arose, nimble with their spears when hunting the polar bear. In the hard struggle for life these people had only themselves to rely upon. What supplies an occasional ship from Norway or Iceland might bring were certainly welcome, but by no means vital.

This exacting life must have left its mark on the people – their outlook on life must have been highly realistic. Dangerous voyages in icy waters, arduous work and hardship in the blizzards and deep snow of the wintery mountains, hunting the polar bear, the caribou, seals and walrus, leisure spent in good company by the long hearth in houses built of stone and turf – all these formed part of the daily round, and they saw nothing romantic in it. The discovery of new tracts of land to the north along the west coast of Greenland would certainly be of interest, but such matters would be discussed quite objectively. And in the same way, the accounts about Vinland would also be sober. This was a subject which would be practically assessed with a view to hunting or stock-keeping by people who were experts at dealing with life in the wilderness. And therefore any element of a romantic or a heroic nature in the Vinland sagas must needs arouse our scepticism.

Another point of importance in this respect is the fact that the Greenlanders lived almost in isolation, and their knowledge of foreign lands and their culture must therefore have been very limited. We must also assume that impulses from Europe had barely reached Iceland by the year 1000. Moreover, the Roman alphabet came to the North together with Christianity; it was officially introduced in Iceland during Leif Eiriksson's lifetime. Thus any element in the Vinland sagas indicative of scholarly insight must be considered suspect, as must also points presupposing a knowledge of distinctive features of other, non-Northern countries. This brings us to the significant point of whether the Greenlanders could possibly have known what grapes looked like, so that they could identify them.

Yet another aspect important to the interpretation of the saga and an appraisal of its reliability is the manner in which Christianity is discussed. How important is the difference between a brief, sober mention and a circumstantial, pious discussion? Christianity was, as we have seen, adopted in Iceland by an Althing resolution in the year 1000, but there must have been many who were long loyal to their ancient faith. When Eirik the Red colonized Greenland in 985/986, the majority of the immigrants were presumably heathen. After this, Christianity from Iceland and Norway slowly gained ground, but at the time of the Vinland voyages, some 15-25 years after the colonization, the new faith had hardly taken hold, and thus it would scarcely have been given much space in the original version of the Vinland traditions. A discerning reader must be sceptical when Christianity pervades the account of the Vinland sagas as though it had been generally accepted in the Greenland society, especially when it is expressed by means of edifying features related to later theological contemplations. Another point which should be taken into consideration when assessing the sagas is the fact that people from two different countries, Greenland and Iceland, took part in these expeditions. We know that the Greenlanders had established their own free state, and it appears from Grœnlendinga Saga and other sources that there was a clear distinction between Greenlanders and Icelanders. As Norwegians who emigrated to Iceland became Icelanders, the immigrants to the new state in Greenland became Greenlanders.

The sources tell of various problems in the relations between Greenlanders and Icelanders in the early days, but it does not seem likely that the Icelanders and Greenlanders of the eleventh century should have been so very concerned with whether the credit for the discovery of Vinland should be given to the Greenlander Leif or the Icelander Karlsefni. This question of prestige probably became more important at a later stage; similar, later conflicting priorities with regard to discoveries are also well known from many other countries. There are no extant manuscripts from Greenland, but matters are entirely different as far as Iceland is concerned. From the twelfth century onwards, Icelandic literature entered an age of retrospection, when authors dwelt to a great extent on the national heroes and their achievements. In a matter of contention, Icelandic authors would presumably favour their own compatriots, just as authors of other nationalities also do; in this case, a great and renowned Icelander, Thorfinn Karlsefni. He was, moreover, of noble birth, and his descendants included several prominent bishops. It also seems reasonable to assume that Icelandic authors would have a freer hand when writing about matters dealing with far-distant Greenland and Vinland: they must have felt fairly safe from having all their statements checked. These matters must be taken into consideration when assessing the sagas, bearing in mind that Grœnlendinga Saga deals primarily with Greenlanders.

The discovery of America by Christopher Columbus was a singular event, which ushered in a new era. But the Greenlanders and the Icelanders must have seen the discovery of the new lands in the west in an entirely different light. Not only had they not the slightest idea that these new lands formed part of a continent, but their attitude to discoveries was altogether quite different from that of Columbus and those who came after him. The Norsemen were not searching for gold and other riches. They were simply looking for a goodly land where their families might settle down and live, a place with ample pasture for their cattle, with forest, game and fish. All this they found in Vinland.

Although it seems likely that the discoveries were regarded with considerable interest during the time immediately following the Vinland expeditions, they hardly created the stir conveyed by the sagas. The discovery of new land was no singular event at the time, this was an age of discoveries. We must, moreover, bear in mind that these new lands west and south-west of Greenland were of very little practical importance to the people of Iceland, where the sagas were written – the distance was far too great for that. For the Greenlanders, on the other hand, this was not so, for these new regions were a neighbouring land, where they probably fetched timber for ship-building, and hunted.

Another striking point is the fact that the earliest Icelandic sources have surprisingly little matter about Vinland. *The Book of the Icelanders*, which was finished not long before 1133, merely states that the people (Eskimos) of whom Eirik the Red had found traces in Greenland must have been the same kind of people as the Skrælings of Vinland. The *Book of the Settlements*, whose earliest passages probably date from c. 1130, mentions Vinland in a legendary account of Ari Másson's sea voyage to the so-called *Hvítramannaland*. Leif is also mentioned, as the son of Eirik the Red. We should have expected at least a brief notice about his discovery of Vinland, if this had been considered important, the more so as the *Book of the Settlements* in this connection mentions another supposedly unknown region, the unhistorical Hvítramannaland, stating that it lay near Vinland the Good. The first history of Norway, *Historia Norvegiae*, mentions islands beyond Greenland, but in no way specifies Vinland in spite of the fact that the author made use of Adam of Bremen's work, in which Vinland is mentioned. Secure conclusions can hardly be inferred from the above, but these remarkably scant items of information about Vinland in important early Norse sources may indicate that the discovery of this new land did not attract particularly great attention.

Scholars of most periods have tended to accept the text of the Vinland sagas, their main concern being a study of the philological problems they present. But that is hardly enough. We must approach these texts with an extremely critical mind, for they are not scientific treatises, but popular narratives which may have undergone a great many changes in the course of time. In order to gain a more profound understanding of the Vinland problem one must, moreover, view it in a wider context. A number of specific factors require a close examination: matters concerning ships, navigation, wind, currents, ice conditions, geographical conditions, climate, zoology, botany, ethnology and astronomy.

That Norsemen discovered parts of North America around the year 1000 is made clear by certain elements of the Vinland sagas. The process of stripping the texts of all later additions, so that only the original accounts remain, is a difficult one, which may well prove still more difficult here than in the case of other sagas, since the subject matter of the Vinland sagas is of so singular a nature.

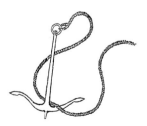

BJARNI IS LOST AT SEA
AND
SIGHTS UNKNOWN COASTS

GRŒN-LENDINGA SAGA

In *Flateyjarbók* we read about Bjarni's father, Herjolf Bardarson, who emigrated to Greenland at the same time as Eirik the Red, and who settled at Herjolfsnes in A.D. 986. His son Bjarni was an esteemed trader, who often sailed abroad in his own ship in order to trade. He sailed from Norway to Iceland the summer his father Herjolf had left Iceland for Greenland, and decided to go on to Greenland in order to stay with his father. He knew nothing about the Greenland Sea. When they had sailed for three days, the wind died down, and then north winds and fog overtook them. They sailed for many days without any idea of where they were. Eventually the sun reappeared and they took their bearings (*deila ætir*), and sailed for another day and night. Then they sighted an unknown land with low hills and forest, but no mountains. Bjarni realized that this could not be Greenland. They left the land to port of them, and let their sheet turn towards the land, and sailed north.

After they had sailed for two days, another land appeared on the horizon. They sailed towards the land, and saw that it was flat and covered with forest. Bjarni did not think that this could be Greenland either, for he had heard that there were great glaciers there. His men wanted to go ashore, to fetch wood and water, but as on the rest of the voyage, Bjarni would not permit this. His men reacted with harsh words.

They sailed on with a south-west wind, and after they had sailed for three days and nights, they sighted a third land, high, mountainous and with glaciers. Bjarni said that this could not be Greenland either, for this was a barren land, good for nothing. Then he sailed south with a strong wind, and after four days at sea he reached Herjolfsnes, his father's farm.

35

Fig. 20. Eiriksfiord, Greenland, near the ruins of Eirik the Red's farm. Photo by Helge Ingstad.

Bjarni is not mentioned in other sources, but that does not imply that he did not exist. He became a Greenlander, and as such he was of little interest to the Icelandic authors. Gathorne-Hardy (1921:115) puts it this way: 'It is the rarest possible exception to hear in Icelandic sagas of the exploits of anybody who had permanently left the country, and whose life never again threw him into contact with the Icelanders.'

The identity of Bjarni's father is perfectly clear. The *Book of the Settlements* describes him as an important man of one of the oldest Icelandic families. Herjolfsnes, the place where he built his farm, is mentioned in several sources; it is located on the south-west coast, not far from the southernmost point of Greenland (Nørlund 1924: 1-267).

With regard to Bjarni's voyage it is important that we realize how easily seafarers might sail past the southern point of Greenland in fog and rough weather, so that they would drift westwards, towards North America. This was an ever-present danger, not least because there might be pack-ice far out to sea off the southern point of Greenland, so that one had to sail far from land. Fog is also very common in these waters. During the centuries of the existence of the Greenland colony, it must have happened several times that ships lost sight of Greenland during storms and fog, so that they sailed past the southern point of Greenland and lost their bearings.

The matter-of-fact, nautical aspect of this account is immediately striking. Here we find no attempt at dramatization, no erudite or religious contemplations. The account keeps strictly to the voyage; it is as sober as a ship's log.

The specifically nautical features are many: we hear of fog, direction and force of winds, times of sailing, and how bearings were taken when the sun appeared. Even technical aspects of sailing are present: the sail is turned towards land, the sail is reefed. The description of the lands seen from the sea includes precisely such essential features as sailors would naturally notice when sailing along unknown shores.

The identification of Bjarni's route, and of the lands he sighted from the sea, is of special significance to an assessment of Leif's voyage. Leif followed Bjarni's route, but in the opposite direction. The first land Bjarni came to was without mountains; there were low hills there, and forest. This description fits northern Newfoundland well, provided we take more recent overworking of the forest and forest fires into consideration. Moreover, Newfoundland is the easternmost region of North America. It seems hardly likely that Bjarni should have reached a more southerly part of North America; he would simply not have been able to carry through such an absurdly long voyage from Norway. The distance from Eyrar in Iceland, from where Bjarni had set out, to Cape Bauld, the northernmost point of Newfoundland, is about 1,250 nautical miles as the crow flies.

We must try to put ourselves in Bjarni's place when he found himself by a completely unknown shore in his small, square-sailed ship. He presumably knew that he was somewhere south-west of Greenland, but he had no means of determining the longitude. Simply setting out in a hit or miss fashion would have been disastrously hazardous. Bjarni's only chance was to sail north along the coast, and this is precisely what he did.

The second land he sighted is described as being flat and forested, not a very detailed description, to say the least of it. However, since we are told that it took him two days to sail to this land, a probable identification is possible. It appears most likely that he came to the flat, forested and highly distinctive part of the coast of Labrador, south of Hamilton Inlet. There are no skerries here, no islands; the long beaches and the forest are visible from far out at sea.

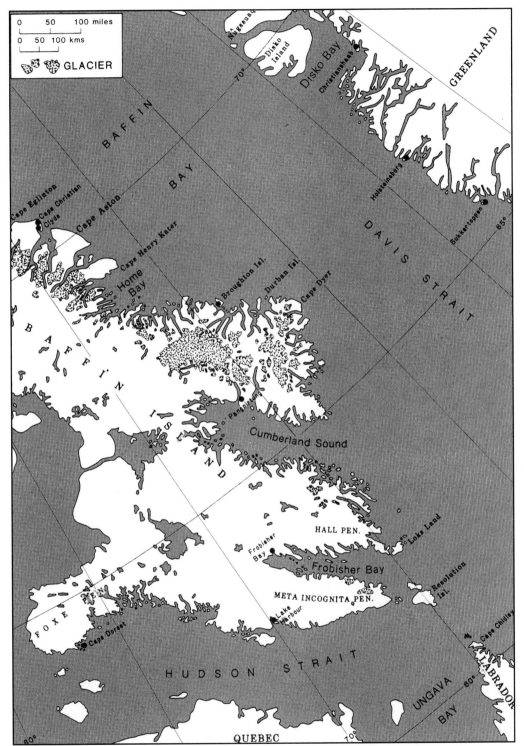

The northern part of the Vinland route, from Disko Island to Cape Aston and along the coast to Labrador.

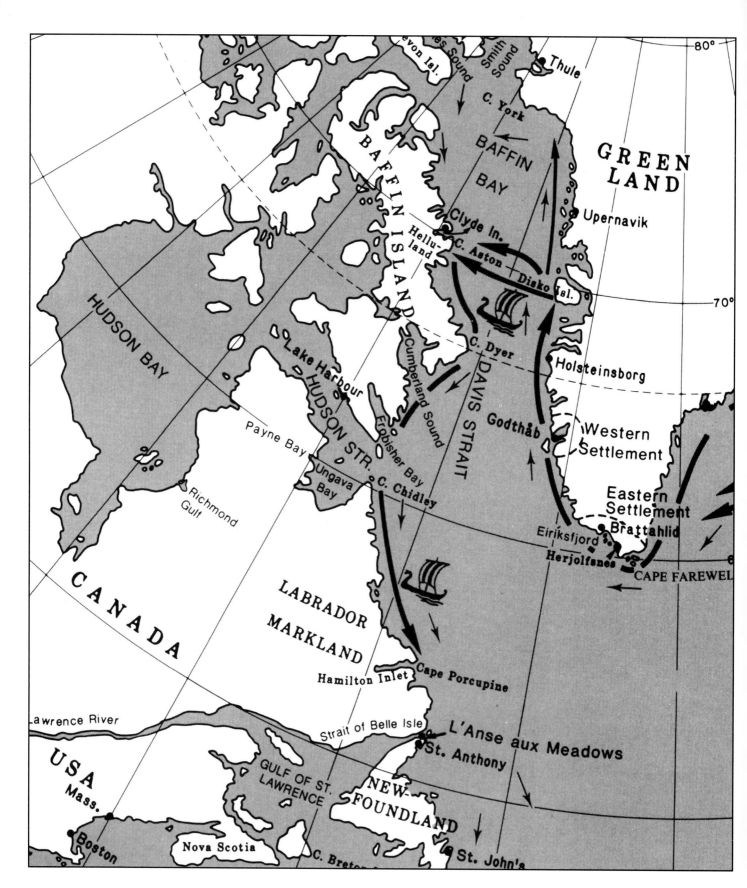

Bjarni tells his men that this land cannot be Greenland either, for he had heard that there were great glaciers in Greenland. This is important: here Bjarni has a genuine geographical element to go by, one that suggests the north. He is on the look-out for glaciers throughout his voy- age. He never goes ashore, and his crew grow angry. But it is easy to understand Bjarni's point of view: he is not an explorer, but a sailor lost at sea. All he wants is to reach his father's farm in Greenland. Time is short, for the autumn storms are close at hand.

Now Bjarni continued to sail north with a south-west wind. After three days he came to a third land, a high land with mountains and glaciers. But it was a barren land, good for nothing, and Bjarni thought that this could not be Greenland. But the description of this third land provides an almost certain basis for identification. Although he must have been on the look-out for glaciers all the time, Bjarni had seen none during the earlier part of his voyage. The reason is obvious, there are no glaciers further south. The most southerly region with glaciers which can be seen from the sea is Baffin Island, and this must be the third land Bjarni sighted.

Then he sailed south, with a strong wind, probably along the coast of Greenland, and came to his father's farm at Herjolfsnes. Here he settled, and took over the farm after his father's death.

LEIF EIRIKSSON DISCOVERS VINLAND

Leif bought Bjarni's ship, and not long after the year 1000 he set out from Brattahlið in Greenland. He followed Bjarni's route, but in the opposite direction, in order to find the unknown coasts Bjarni had seen from his ship. Leif had a crew of thirty-five.

P. 40. Map of the Vinland route from the Norse Settlement in Greenland to America.

Nothing is said about the northward voyage along the west coast of Greenland. All we are told is that Leif came to the land Bjarni had seen last. The saga reports:

'They sailed to the land there, cast anchor and put off a boat, then went ashore, and could see no grass there. The background was all great glaciers, and right up to the glaciers from the sea the land was like a flat stone. The land impressed them as barren and useless. Leif named the land *Helluland* (Flatstone Land)'.

This must, as we have seen, be Baffin Island, but the question is: where, on this huge island, did Leif land after having crossed the Davis Strait? The remarkable description of a landscape would seem to be based on personal observation. In 1970 I undertook an expedition to examine the east coast of Baffin Island. At Cape Aston, which lies at 70° N, at the narrow part of the Davis Strait, we found a most striking landscape, one which agreed as closely as possible with Grœnlendinga Saga's description of Helluland. We were met by a sight which we are

Fig. 21. In 1992, Gunnar Eggertsson was a crew-member aboard the Gaia. The experience prepared him for his epic voyage on the Islendingur, which sailed from Iceland to North America in 2000.

Fig. 22. At Cape Aston on the east coast of Baffin Island, opposite Disko Island in Greenland, the author located a large flat country with a row of mountains in the background, covered with glaciers. This is probably the Helluland (Flatstone Land) of Grænlendinga Saga. Photo by Helge Ingstad.

Fig. 23, p. 43: A display depicts the traditional way of life for a now-extinct people - Newfoundland's Beothuk Indians. Beothuk VRC, Boyd's Cove, Newfoundland. Photo courtesy of Parks Canada; John Sylvester, photographer.

hardly likely to forget: a vast plain, strangely flat, bare and grey as a stone, stretched far towards the magnificent inland ranges of mountains with rows of glittering glaciers. It would be strange if the description of so sensationally distinctive and fascinating a landscape encountered in the course of an important voyage had not been preserved in the tradition of the Norse seafarers. This region by the narrow part of the Davis Strait, which is no more than about 250 nautical miles wide, faces Disko Island off the coast of Greenland. Several factors seem to indicate that

Leif set off from Disko Island when he crossed the Davis Strait, a crossing which would have taken him about one day and one night (two *dœgr*).

The location of Helluland is of essential importance. If this land is identical with the Cape Aston peninsula at the narrow part of the Davis Strait, this would be an important fact in several respects: it would give us a key to an appraisal of the rest of the route to Vinland, and it would make it clear that almost the entire voyage consisted of coastal sailing. Coastal sailing is exactly what we would expect of Norse seafarers sailing in unknown waters without a compass. Moreover, the Vinland expeditions would then have had following currents almost all the way – first north along the west coast of Greenland, and then south along the coast of Baffin Island and Labrador.

When one sails southwards along the coast of Labrador, as Leif probably did, the coastal strip of land appears largely barren. Much of it is hidden by the belt of islets and skerries off the coast. But the scenery changes radically a little south of

Hamilton Inlet. North and south of Cape Porcupine the land is flat and covered with forest, which extends as far as the extensive, white beaches, 30 to 40 km long. This land can be seen from far out to sea.

This accords well with the second land Bjarni had seen during his voyage in the opposite direction, the land which is described as being flat and forested. The beaches are not mentioned in the account of Bjarni's voyage. This may be due to the fact that, unlike Leif, he did not go ashore, and thus he was not in contact with them. He may have been far out at sea when he caught sight of the coast. During my expeditions this region, which is uncommonly beautiful, was explored on several occasions. Cape Porcupine juts out into the sea like a spearhead, with the beaches extending north and south. As the saga tells us, they slope gently down to the sea. The spruce forest all but adjoins the beach, which is very wide, and consists of very fine, white sand. The land seemed to be fairly flat, the result of a river having deposited large quantities of sand in the estuary during the Ice Age; later the sea-bed rose.

No other similarly distinctive area exists anywhere along the whole coast of Labrador. In fact, the topography of the Cape Aston peninsula leaves little doubt as to this region being Leif's *Markland*.

True, Markland was a fascinating land with a virgin stock of wild caribou, bear, fur-bearing animals, walrus, seal and other prey, and the mighty forest must have looked most impressive to anyone, but it must have been quite sensational for the Norse Greenlanders, who had to rely on imported timber for most of their shipbuilding. But one important factor was lacking: there was very little grass, no pasture for their cattle. Grass does not do well in the cold climate of Labrador, which is largely a result of the ice-filled Labrador Current flowing south along the coasts.

What Leif was looking for was a land with good pasture for his livestock, a land which would offer the people from arctic Greenland more favourable conditions of life, a land suited for immigration by people of their culture. He weighed anchor, and continued sailing southwards, along the coast of Labrador, in search of a better land.

After they had sailed for two days with a northeast wind, they caught sight of another land, and steered towards an island which lay north of the land. They went ashore and looked about them, and beheld the unknown coast of the land.

The weather was fine, according to the saga. There was dew on the grass, and when they passed a hand over the grass and carried it up to the mouth, they thought they had never tasted anything so sweet. This beautiful, lyrical description bears witness to the delight of these people when they had found pasture for their animals; nothing was as important to them as grass. During their long voyage they had looked for green pastureland in vain. Now, at last, they had found it. Not only was the island lush and green, there were green meadows on land too.

If we are right in assuming that Markland is the flat, forested land with the long beaches in Labrador, two days' southward sailing would have taken Leif to the north coast of Newfoundland. There was no way of avoiding Newfoundland on a coastal voyage to the south, and it is particularly interesting to note that if he sailed along the coast of Labrador, Leif would have made almost straight for L'Anse aux Meadows, the site of the Norse settlement we discovered. When he had reached the new land, Leif must have covered a distance of rather more than 1,500 nautical miles. We have seen that he would have sailed along the coast for almost all

Fig. 24. The extensive beach north of Cape Porcupine in Labrador (Markland). This must be the long beaches of the sagas. Photo by Helge Ingstad.

the way, and he would have sailed on a following current, first northwards along the west coast of Greenland, and then south along the coasts of Baffin Island and Labrador.

Up to this point the account in Grœnlendinga Saga is sober and makes a reliable impression. Now follows an objective description of how they sailed westward, through a sound lying between the island and a headland which extended north from the mainland. The tide was low when they steered towards land, and the water was shallow for a long way out, so that their ship ran aground. But they were so eager to go ashore that they did not want to wait for high tide, so that their ship would again be afloat. They went ashore, so the saga tells us. A genuine, vivid point: we can practically see Leif and his eager men jump from the ship and run ashore, curious to see what they would find in this new land. I shall later return to a number of elements in this account which accord well with conditions at L'Anse aux Meadows. At present it will suffice to mention the headland which juts out to the north, and the very long shallows of the inlet. But we should take care not to base conclusions exclusively on certain geographical elements given by the saga.

It was essential that houses for about thirty-five people should be built as quickly as possible. This was hard work, for according to the Norse building practice in Iceland and Greenland, the building material was turf. The sagas state that they first built *búðir*, small, temporary turf huts. Once these had been erected, large houses were built.

It was also important that the land be explored. This was done, and Leif gave orders to the effect that those who went out to reconnoitre, must be back by evening and that, moreover, some of the men should always stay by the houses. He probably feared the natives; he never saw them, but an intelligent man like Leif must have found traces of them or observed the natives in the distance.

The saga stresses the fact that the new land was a good land. Again, great interest attaches to the grass growing here, and the good pasture for the Norsemen's livestock is emphasized. The new land lay about 9° south of the central part of the Eastern Settlement of Greenland, and it is easy to see that men from polar Greenland should be delighted by this promising virgin land. The forest was new to them, and of great importance, and there may have been an abundance of wild caribou, fur-bearing animals, plenty of fish in the rivers and the sea, whale and seal and – not least – there was bog-ore from which they could extract iron. As a result of the cold Labrador Current, the climate and the fauna were very similar to what these Norsemen were accustomed to, and their methods of hunting and a good deal else in their way of life fitted in well with this new land. They felt at home here. The saga has an interesting observation of the sun, which may be paraphrased thus: on the shortest day of the winter the sun was visible in the middle of the afternoon as well as at breakfast time (lit. the sun had there *eyktarstaðr* and *dagmálastaðr* on the shortest days). This observation, although presumably historical, does not allow us to fix an exact location.

Leif called the new land Vinland, in accordance with its produce. As the good grazing conditions are so strongly emphasized, it seems most likely that the text refers to cattle farming.

The saga characterizes Leif as follows: Leif was big and strong, of striking appearance, shrewd and in every respect a temperate, fair-dealing man.

One passage of Grœnlendinga Saga differs greatly from the sober tone in the rest of the account. A man by the strange name of Tyrkir is accorded quite an unduly detailed description, he comes from southern parts and speaks German. He is said to have been with Eirik the Red for a long time, and had been Leif's foster-father. We read that he disappeared, and when he was found he was in strangely high spirits. He pulled faces and rolled his eyes as though he were drunk. He spoke for a long while in German. Then he said that he had found vines and grapes. Leif asked him if this was true. Of course it was true; he knew all about grapes as he had been born in a country where grapes grow.

This is undoubtedly a later addition, and Tyrkir is an unhistorical person just like other baroque personalities in post-classic Icelandic sagas. He is presented here as evidence of the presence of grapes in Vinland. But this addition is so clumsy that it is easily seen through; we read, for instance, that grape-vines were cut as a cargo for the ship, and the ship's boat was filled with grapes. It is not easy to understand where they found grapes in spring (*see pp.* 56, 107).

THE VOYAGE BACK
TO GREENLAND

Having spent the winter in Vinland, Leif again set out to sea, heading home to Greenland. While they were at sea and probably in Greenland waters, they found a ship-wrecked crew on a reef, and took them all on board. The captain was a man by the name of Thorir, an Eastman, i.e. a Norwegian. It appears that he had a cargo of timber, which was in great demand in Greenland. His wife, whose name was Gudrid, was also of their company. After Thorir's death, she married Leif's brother Thorstein. After he, too, had died, she was married to Thorfinn Karlsefni, the Icelander.

They reached Brattahlið in Greenland, but that year a plague broke out. Thorir and Eirik the Red both died, as did many others. The matter-of-fact mention of Gudrid in Grœnlendinga Saga is radically different from Eirik's Saga's romantic tale in connection with her arrival in Greenland.

There appears to be no reason for doubting the authenticity of Grœnlendinga Saga's straightforward version.

THORVALD'S VINLAND VOYAGE

In Thorvald's opinion the new land had not been sufficiently explored. He borrowed his brother Leif's ship, and sailed out with a crew of thirty men. Nothing is said about their voyage to Vinland, only that they came to Leif's houses, *Leifsbúðir*, in Vinland.

When spring came, Thorvald ordered some of his men to go west in the ship's boat and to explore the country there in the course of the summer. They found a fair land. The next summer Thorvald sailed first east with the ship, and northwards along the land. Near a headland they were overtaken by a storm. They were driven ashore and the keel of their ship broke. They spent a long time repairing their ship, and then they set the old keel up on the headland, and Thorvald called it *Kjalarnes* (Keelness). They sailed eastwards along the land to a headland that jutted out between two fjords. Thorvald went ashore there and said: 'This place is fair, here I should like to build my farm.'

Then they saw three mounds on the sands up inside the headland. They walked to them and could see three skin-boats, *húðkeipar*, and there were three men under each. They killed eight of the men, but one got away in a boat. On their way back to the headland they saw various mounds higher up by the fiord, and they judged these to be human dwellings, *byggðir*. Then they grew very drowsy. They fell asleep, but a mysterious cry aroused them, saying that if they would save their lives, they must hurry back to the ship. From up the fjord came a great swarm of skinboats towards them. On board their ship, Thorvald ordered his men to raise a lattice of branches in defence along the side of the ship, and that they must defend themselves, but not attack the foe. The Skrælings shot at them for a while, and then they disappeared. Thorvald was fatally injured by an arrow, and he was buried in the place where he had hoped to build his farm. Two crosses were set on his grave, and the place was called *Krossanes* (Crossness). Greenland was Christian by this time, but Eirik the Red had died before the coming of Christianity.

The expedition stayed in Leif's houses that winter; in spring they gathered grapes and vines for their cargo, and sailed back to Greenland.

It appears clear that the purpose of Thorvald's Vinland expedition was the to explore land, with a view to colonization. He himself points out that Vinland had been insufficiently explored, and he wants to find out more about it. There were no women with him, no livestock. We learn that he came to a beautiful place, where he would have liked to build a farm – this suggests that he was thinking of emigrating from Greenland.

This account rings true, and it is indicative of the methodical approach to be expected of the experienced Greenland farmers. The same approach must have been employed as a matter of course also when Iceland and Greenland were settled: first came the discovery, then the land was explored and found to offer a livelihood – only after this did emigration take place.

The methodical approach reported in Grœnlendinga Saga is in clear contrast to the account of Karlsefni's voyage given in Eirik's Saga. This simply has a brief mention of Leif's earlier discovery of a new land whose position, according to the narrative, is more than vague; but in spite of the unreliable information at his disposal, and without any preceding exploration of this new land, Thorfinn Karlsefni is there reported to have set out, with women and cattle on board, on a large-scale emigratory expedition.

Thorvald and his crew of thirty men on board Leif's ship reached Leif's houses, *Leifsbúðir*, where they settled down. In connection with the exploratory westward voyage along the coast, the saga gives a fascinating and detailed description of the land: it is beautiful and well wooded, the forest growing almost down to the sea, there are white beaches, many islands, and extensive shallows. This description accords well with the coast west of L'Anse aux Meadows.

They came across only one single trace of human activity – a wooden container. They thought that it was meant for holding corn, but they must have been mistaken. This container was presumably an object left behind by the natives, and it seems most likely that it was one of the fairly large bark containers which the Beothuk Indians of Newfoundland are known to have made and used (Howley 1915:21, 87).

Of particularly great interest is the voyage of exploration which Thorvald undertook the second year. If we assume that this expedition started from the Norse settlement at L'Anse aux Meadows, his route accords perfectly with the actual topography. Starting from *Leifsbúðir*, he would first have sailed east along the north coast of Newfoundland, then north to Cape Bauld, and north of this cape to the northernmost part of the east coast of Newfoundland, sailing over several fjords bordered by good land on the way. There is nothing unusual in the old keel having been set up on the headland where they had repaired their ship after it had been damaged in a storm: it was a typically Norse custom to raise cairns on headlands and mountains, to serve as beacons, and such landmarks were especially important for those sailing along unknown coasts. Now they could raise a landmark which would be more prominent than a cairn – part of a tall keel.

At the first fjord they came to when they were sailing east of the land, Thorvald and his men went ashore, and this land was so inviting that he

wanted to build his farm there. He would hardly have settled without his family and his livestock; his statement indicates that he was thinking in terms of a future emigration.

Next comes their first meeting with the natives: under each of three skin-boats, three Skrælings were lying asleep. The Norsemen killed them all except one, who got away in his boat. The repeated use of the number three is a suspicious element. It is, however, a fact that American Indians and Eskimos often slept under their boats. The natives' violent attack immediately after this episode also suggests that someone had been killed, for it is typical of Eskimos and Indians to avenge the blood of their dead.

The mention of skin-boats is of importance. Indian canoes were most often covered with

Fig. 25. The Beothuk Indians, who lived in Newfoundland, were exterminated by the white man during the 19th century. Their pointed tents were covered with birch bark, as were also their strange, crescent-shaped canoes. After J. P. Howley.

birch bark, for instance in Newfoundland and Labrador, while Eskimo kayaks and umiaks were covered with hide (Gathorne-Hardy 1921:178). It is most likely that these keen-eyed seafarers, who were particularly interested in boat-building, would be eager to scrutinize these unfamiliar boats quite closely. And they had the opportunity to do so not only when they fought the Skrælings who had been sleeping under their boats, but also later, during the battle, as the natives were paddling towards the ship. Had the Skrælings' boats been covered with birch bark, they would have created more of a sensation, and we should probably have had a different, more detailed description of such extraordinary vessels.

The next item of information, that Thorvald and his men saw a number of mounds, *hæðir*, higher up by the fjord, which they took to be human habitations, is also reminiscent of Eskimos. Seen from a distance their huts, built of stone and turf, look like mounds, unlike the tall, pointed Indian tents. And an Eskimo settlement accords well with the large number of Skrælings in skin-boats, who attacked the ship a little later. This tale is not without an element of superstition: a sudden drowsiness overtakes Thorvald and his men, they fall asleep, and are aroused by a cry warning them of danger. The Norsemen believed firmly in omens; they looked upon them as part of their daily life. This brief description does not look like a literary addition. It may well be an ancient element of the saga.

The battle from the ship against the Skrælings, who came teeming in a great number of skin-boats, would certainly provide any narrator with a tempting motif, and it would not be surprising if later generations had embellished this dramatic event by, for instance, stressing the Norsemen's daring in battle. But instead we have a remarkably matter-of-fact, objective description of the event. The orders given by Thorvald are expedient and to the point: a bulwark is to be raised, the men must defend themselves, but attack as little as possible. There is no mention whatsoever of the kind of heroic conduct described by Eirik's Saga in connection with Freydis during the battle with the Skrælings. The superiority of the Norsemen is not mentioned, and there is no indication that any Skrælings were killed.

Thorvald was hit by an arrow and died, and there is little reason to doubt the authenticity of this statement. True, according to Eirik's Saga

he died in quite a different region, and in an entirely different manner, but that account must for various reasons be considered to be fictitious (*see* p. 97).

Next we read that two crosses were raised on Thorvald's grave at a place called Krossanes, that Greenland was Christian by this time, but that Eirik the Red had died before the coming of Christianity. This statement should be considered in conjunction with the following account, that about Thorstein. There we read that Christianity was still in its infancy at that time, and we have reason to believe that this is correct. That all the people should have renounced their ancient faith at so early a date seems most unlikely. Thjodhild's church had probably been built, and Christianity may well have gained a foothold among some of the people living in the most central parts of the Eastern Settlement.

After two years in Vinland, the expedition returned to Greenland. The saga reports that the men gathered grapes and vines as a cargo for their ship. This reads like a stereotyped copy of the grotesque account of vines and grapes in the account of Leif's voyage, and must be considered a later addition.

THORSTEIN'S ABORTIVE VINLAND VOYAGE AND DEATH

Here we read about the marriage of Thorstein and Gudrid, the widow of Thorir the Norwegian whom Leif had rescued from the shipwreck. Thorstein was bent upon voyaging to Vinland, to fetch home the body of his brother Thorvald. He took a crew of twenty-five men, and his wife Gudrid.

All summer long, storms tossed them about on the ocean, and they did not know where they were. After one week of winter had passed, they reached *Lysufjord* in the Western Settlement of Greenland. Thorstein and Gudrid were invited to stay at the home of a man called Thorstein the Black, a pagan. Christianity was in its infancy in Greenland at that time.

In the course of that winter a sickness broke out, and many people died. Several elements of superstition are woven into the narrative dealing with this pestilence. Thorstein Eiriksson dies, but he wakes up from the dead and predicts Gudrid's future: she will marry an Icelander, their life together will be long, and hers was to be a splendid line. She will leave Greenland for Norway, and then travel to Iceland to make her home there, and she will outlive her husband. She is, moreover, to make a pilgrimage to Rome, and then she will return to her home in Iceland. There a church will be raised, where she will take the vows of a nun, and where she will die. After he had made this prophecy, Thorstein died for the second time.

Thorstein the Black then sailed to Eiriksfjord together with Gudrid, and they took the bodies of those who had died, and they buried them at the church there. Gudrid stayed with Leif Eirik's-son at Brattahlið, and Thorstein the Black made his home at Eiriksfjord, where he lived for the rest of his life.

Of interest in this narrative is the fact that Gudrid's first marriage, to Thorir the Norwegian, is mentioned again, while her new marriage, to Thorstein, is accorded the briefest possible mention. Just as in the account of Leif's voyage, no particular attention is drawn to her. This is very different from the description of her given in Eirik's Saga, where she appears as a wonderful heroine and a very important woman. The statement to the effect that Thorstein went to Vinland in order to bring home the body of his brother Thorvald may well be authentic, but it seems likely that he also wanted to explore the new land. It was important that the dead were buried in consecrated ground, as their salvation depended on a Christian burial.

This belief is well illustrated by a story in *Flateyjarbók* (*Grønl Hist. Mind.* II: 686 ff., *Halldórsson* 1978: 103-16), which tells of the hunter Sigurd Njalsson finding a ship-wreck off the east coast of Greenland, while the bodies of those who had perished lay in a hut close by. As it was hardly possible to transport the bodies all the way to the settlement, they were boiled in cauldrons until they dissolved, and then the bones were taken to the church. In an Icelandic seventeenth-century manuscript (*Grønl. Hist. Mind.* II: 656-7, Halldórsson 1978: 56-7) we hear of a Greenlander by the name of Lika-Lodin (Corpse-Lodin). He had been given that name because he transported bodies he found in caves etc. in the uninhabited parts of northern Greenland to church for burial. They were the bodies of men who had drifted there on ice floes or after having been ship-wrecked, and some had cut runic inscriptions telling about their fate.

Lysufjord, where Thorstein landed after having been tossed about on the ocean, is probably identical with the Ameralikfjord in the Western Settlement of Greenland. Highest up in the fjord lie the ruins of quite a large farm, at a place which is now known as Kilaussarfik. This is probably the Sandnes of the sources, and the ruins of a church built after Thorstein's lifetime have also been found near the farm. The upper part of the fjord has yielded the ruins also of other fairly large farms. It seems likely that Thorstein, a member of so prominent a family, would make his way to one of these farms, where the wealthiest farmers of the settlement must have lived.

Eirik's Saga has a very different story about Thorstein. It states, for instance, that he owned half of a farm in the Western Settlement, and that he moved there together with Gudrid, his wife. It seems very unlikely that the son of Eirik the Red, the chieftain, should have owned no more than half a farm in the far-off, much less favourable Western Settlement. It is probable that he had full ownership of a farm in the fertile

Eastern Settlement, a farm corresponding to his social status.

The information about a fatal pestilence at the Western Settlement is probably historically correct. Such a tragedy in a small, almost isolated community far away in the wilderness would certainly be remembered by future generations. The preceding sickness at the Eastern Settlement, where many also died, lends support to this account. The epidemic was probably transmitted from there to the Western Settlement. It is unlikely that an epidemic in the true sense of the word should occur in an almost isolated arctic community, except through infection from the outside world. In the Eastern Settlement this sickness, as we have seen, broke out when Thorir and Gudrid came to Greenland from Norway. We hear that Thorstein died, and many others also. That may be historical fact, but many elements of superstition are also present in this narrative. Such superstition may easily arise from the hard and perilous existence of an isolated people living in an arctic land of wild mountains, glaciers and drift-ice, a world where men were small in the presence of the enormous forces of nature. Superstition became a reality.

The glorification of Gudrid, on the other hand, is an entirely different matter, a suspect point. Here we have a very detailed prophecy, which depicts a number of points in her brilliant future, a future which spans from Greenland to Norway, to Iceland, Rome, and back to her Icelandic home. It seems remarkable that Gudrid, who earlier in the saga is briefly given a sober mention as one who happened to come to Greenland, should suddenly become one of the principal figures. Moreover, this prophecy not only includes a number of unhistorical features, but in the last part of Grœlendinga Saga it is fulfilled in every detail. A more exhaustive analysis of this prophecy finds its natural place in connection with the later account, in which it is fulfilled (*see p. 60*). The fact that Eirik's Saga contains a sim-

ilar prophecy is also liable to arouse suspicion. The last lines of this chapter tell of Thorstein and the other victims of the pestilence being taken to Eiriksfjord, where they were buried, This is an interesting point, which may well be historically correct. Thjodhild's church, which was built during Eirik the Red's lifetime, has been found; this must be the church referred to here. It is likely that Thorstein's grave is among those that have been excavated in the graveyard of this church.

THORFINN KARLSEFNI SAILS TO VINLAND

The summer when Gudrid returned to the Eastern Settlement, a ship from Norway arrived in Greenland. Her captain was Thorfinn Karlsefni, a wealthy Icelander. He stayed with Leif at Brattahlið, fell in love with Gudrid, and with Leif's consent they married that winter.

There was much talk about Vinland, and the following summer Karlsefni set out on a voyage there, with a crew of sixty men. He had five women on board, one of them being Gudrid; he also took livestock of all kinds. They planned to settle in the new land. Karlsefni wanted to buy Leif's houses in Vinland, but Leif would only lend them to him. They agreed that the profits of the expedition were to be shared equally among those taking part.

The expedition reached Leif's houses. Soon they had plenty of food, for a large rorqual was stranded there. The males among their livestock became somewhat unmanageable. Karlsefni gave orders to have timber felled and dressed, and to lay it on a rock to dry. They exploited the resources of the country: they gathered grapes, hunted, fished and so on.

Fig. 26. Aerial photograph of Southern Greenland with Cape Farewell. Photo Copyright: The National Survey and Cadastre, Denmark.

53

Next summer a crowd of Skrælings came out of the forest. When the bull started to bellow, they were frightened and ran to Karlsefni's houses with their bales of grey furs, sable and skins of all kinds, but Karlsefni would not let them in. The Skrælings wanted weapons in exchange for their goods, but Karlsefni would not allow this. He told the women to carry out butter or cheese, *búnyt* and then the Skrælings wanted nothing else in exchange for their furs. What they had bought, they carried off in their bellies.

Karlsefni had a strong stockade raised around his farm. Gudrid gave birth to a son whom they named Snorri.

The following winter a still bigger crowd of Skrælings came, and they traded with them just as they had the first winter. Gudrid was sitting in the doorway by the cradle, and she had a vision: a woman in close-fitting garments, *nám-kyrtill*, and with a band around her head, appeared. Her hair was brown, her face pale, and her eyes were bigger than those of other people. She said her name was Gudrid. When she was asked to sit down, there was a loud crash, and she disappeared. At that moment, one of Karlsefni's men killed a Skræling who had tried to steal weapons. The Skrælings fled, leaving their clothes and their furs behind.

Karlsefni assumed that when the Skrælings returned for the third time, hostilities would break out. Ten men were to go up on the cape, so as to be clearly visible, the others were to clear a passage in the forest, where they might drive the cattle. When the Skrælings came out of the forest, the bull was to be led out, at the head of the Norsemen. The Skrælings came to the very place Karlsefni had foreseen, battle was joined, and many of them were killed. During the battle, one of the Skrælings picked up an axe, looked at it for a while, and then killed one of his comrades with it. A big and handsome Skræling picked up the axe and threw it into the water, then they all fled into the forest.

Karlsefni did not want to remain in Vinland any longer; next summer the expedition returned to Greenland, with a valuable cargo of vines, grapes and furs. They came to Eiriksfjord, and spent the winter there.

Karlsefni had organized this expedition with a view to settling in the new land, he intended to establish a colony there. This attempt at emigration was the final stage of a process of development that had started with Leif's discovery and continued with Thorvald's exploration and which had made it clear that Vinland was a good land. Karlsefni's expedition consisted of sixty men, five women, and all kinds of livestock. Only one ship is mentioned, but with so heavy a load it seems more likely that two ships were used. Not only were there sixty-five people; an expedition intending to settle in the new land must presumably have had with them horses, cattle, sheep and possibly also goats. They had to have provisions, hay, tools and other equipment. An overloaded ship crossing the drift-ice of the Davis Strait would constitute a great danger.

In this connection we should note that Leif's ship had thirty-five people on board, Thorvald's twenty-five and Thorstein's thirty, roughly half the number of those taking part in Karlsefni's expedition. Crews of a similar number are known to have taken part in other ocean voyages; the ocean-going Gokstad ship, which has been excavated in Norway, had thirty-two oarsmen.

The agreement which was reached before the voyage that all profit should be shared equally seems authentic. It testifies to practical knowledge of a matter of particular interest to those taking part in the expedition: clearly they would want to know what their share would be, before they left their homes and embarked on so hazardous an adventure.

The fact that Leif would not sell his houses in Vinland to Karlsefni, merely let him borrow them, opens an interesting vista. The houses were a symbol of his landfall, and we may assume that he had secured the area where they lay for himself and his family. This may be compared with the first settlement of Iceland and of Greenland, where the original settlers took up large districts. Moreover, the text seems to imply that Leif had not given up the idea of returning to Vinland.

The information about a rorqual, *reyðr*, being stranded in Vinland, and providing the expedition with plenty of food, seems genuine. This matter-of-fact account is very different indeed from the dramatic and incredible story in Eirik's Saga, which also tells of a whale that had been stranded during Karlsefni's expedition. The very fact of the genus of whale being specified adds to the impression of authenticity. The rorqual (*Balaena mysticetus L.*) is about 18-20 m long, and lives in the Greenland Sea, also migrating along the coast of North America. During my expeditions to L'Anse aux Meadows, which covered a period of eight years, whales were stranded on the coast of Newfoundland several times. Interesting in this connection is a list of whales etc. in the *King's Mirror*: here the rorqual is described as 'the best food of all kinds of fish'. Trustworthy, too, seems another practical piece of information: the timber which had been felled was also dressed and laid on the rocks to dry. This is exactly what experienced sailors would do, for in this way they could carry the maximum possible cargo.

Next comes the first meeting with the Skrælings. We learn that the roaring bull so frightened these natives that they fled to Karlsefni's houses – this may be historical. Meeting a roaring bull can be a fearsome experience for us today, but these natives had never seen this large beast. Such an extraordinary event – the first meeting with the Skrælings, and their being frightened by the terrifying bull – would be remembered, and it seems quite natural that

such an occurrence would be preserved in tradition.

It is interesting to note that Karlsefni gave the Skrælings butter or cheese in exchange for their furs, and that the natives greedily devoured these, being perfectly happy with the deal. For many primitive peoples, specially those of northern regions such as Canada and Alaska, fat was the most valuable of all commodities, and they could hardly get enough. My own experience may serve to illustrate this point. For many years I lived among the Indians of Northern Canada (*the Caribou Eaters*) and among the inland Eskimos (*Nunamiut*) of Northern Alaska. These peoples are caribou hunters, and they live almost exclusively on caribou meat.

Fat was always a great problem, and a hunger for fat often made itself felt. When an animal had been killed, every slightest bit of fat was carefully utilized; the fat across the back, that surrounding the stomach, behind the eyes etc. The bones were boiled, and the fat skimmed off. This was an ancient practice. On one occasion during these years I was on a long journey by sledge to a Hudson Bay outpost by the Great Slave Lake, and my need for fat became so great that I ate almost half a pound of butter in one day. Never had I tasted anything as delicious!

Thus it is easy to understand that the Skrælings thought they had done well in their deal with the Greenlanders. The latter, however, were amused, as we can see from the glimpse of humour provided by the phrase about the Skrælings carrying away what they had bought in their bellies. The very nature of this rough humour from the first meeting with the Skrælings seems to ring true, and it is of just the kind which would lead to merriment when the story about the Skrælings was told in Greenland, by the long hearths in houses of turf and stone.

Karlsefni must have made an excellent deal when he acquired furs so cheaply. Fur was of very high value on the European market at that time, and it was an important article of export from Norway and from Greenland. The saga mentions grey furs, sable and furs of all kinds. Grey furs may be those of the grey squirrel; sable, on the other hand, is not found in America, and thus this must refer to fur of the marten – there was much marten in Canada and other parts of North America. The marten of these dense forests can be very dark and closely resemble sable.

The second meeting with the Skrælings leads up to dramatic events: first we hear about Gudrid's vision, her meeting with the pale-faced woman with the big eyes, who was her namesake.

Gudrid's vision is clearly connected with the immediately ensuing event: a Skræling is killed, apparently an ominous occurrence. The danger is further emphasized by the next sentences, which make it clear that Karlsefni now fears that the Skrælings will attack them.

Unlike Eirik's Saga, Grœnlendinga Saga gives a motive for the clash with the Skrælings, and this is an important point. Throughout the ages we see time and again that Indians and Eskimos as a rule tend to be peaceful at their first meeting with Europeans. But when the white man was brutal, when he killed or abducted natives, they lost their trust in him, and often such a breach of confidence would lead to bloodshed. Revenge was as important to the Indians and the Eskimos as it was to the Norsemen.

The third meeting with the Skrælings resulted in battle. Little is said about the actual battle. As there is no mention of a single Norseman being killed, and as we must assume that the quick, nimble natives with just about equally good weapons were no less skilled in battle than Karlsefni's men, it seems most likely that this was only a minor skirmish. The episode of the Skræling who picked up an axe during the battle, stared at it, swung it at one of his comrades and killed him, and of the big and fine-looking Skræling who threw the axe out into the water, is interesting by virtue of its absurdity. It may indicate that the scribe tried to follow the original quite faithfully, but that the manuscript was difficult to decipher, so that he misunderstood the text of this particular passage. A similar episode occurs also in Eirik's Saga, and is probably a loan from Grœnlendinga Saga.

Were the Skrælings whom Karlsefni met Eskimos or Indians? The saga contains some interesting points which may throw light on this question. The Skrælings whom Karlsefni encountered had obviously hunted fur-bearing animals of the forest, and we are told that the natives came from the woods, into which they again disappeared. There is no mention of skin-boats, such as those from which the natives had attacked Thorvald; such boats are typical of the Eskimos. We have good reason to believe that the natives whom Karlsefni met were people from the forest; Indians.

Thus there are strong indications suggesting that Thorvald, as we saw above, had met Eskimos, whereas the Skrælings encountered by Karlsefni were Indians. As we shall show below in greater detail, there were Indians and Dorset Eskimos living in Newfoundland at the time of the Vinland voyages, when the Norse settlement at L'Anse aux Meadows was built and occupied. Moreover, Eskimo territory never extended farther south along the east coast of North America than Newfoundland.

After two years in Vinland Karlsefni decided to return to Greenland. The saga gives no reason for his abandoning his plans to colonize the new land, but it seems likely that this decision was due to a fear of the natives.

This chapter, too, ends with an account of the Norsemen loading their ship with vines and grapes when they leave Vinland in spring, but mere repetition does not make this statement any more plausible (*see p. 47*).

56

FREYDIS SAILS TO VINLAND

The same summer that Karlsefni returned to Greenland, a ship came there from Norway, commanded by the Icelandic brothers Helgi and Finnbogi. Eirik the Red's daughter Freydis, who was married to the weak Thorvard of Garðar, went to see the Icelanders, and it was agreed that they should together undertake a voyage to Vinland. Any profits were to be shared equally. Each ship was to take a crew of thirty, in addition to the women, but Freydis broke the agreement right from the start, and secretly she took another five men.

The Icelanders reached Vinland first, and moved into Leif Eiriksson's houses, but when Freydis arrived, she demanded to live there. After an exchange of harsh words, the Icelanders moved out and built a house by a lake, farther away from the sea. Relations between the Icelanders and the Greenlanders grew tense in the course of the winter, and in the end there was no contact between them at all.

Early one morning Freydis went barefoot over to the house of the Icelanders. She called to Finnbogi to come outside, and told him in so many words that she wanted to change ships with him, because his was the bigger. Finnbogi agreed to this. When she returned to Thorvard her husband, she told him that she had offered to buy the Icelanders' ship, but that they had abused and maltreated her. She baited him to take revenge, and threatened to divorce him.

In the end Thorvard gave in. He roused his men, who then took the sleeping Icelanders by surprise, bound them and led them outside. All of them were killed. Freydis herself killed five women, for no one else was willing to do it. Freydis, content with the turn of events, said to the crew that if any of them on their return to Greenland talked of what had taken place, they would be killed.

Early in the spring they loaded the Icelanders' ship with all the produce of the land they could lay their hands on, and then they sailed to Eiriksfjord in Greenland. Karlsefni was still there, waiting for a good wind, and it was said that no ship had ever sailed from Greenland with a more valuable cargo.

This version of Freydis's voyage is entirely different from that given in Eirik's Saga. There she is shown as a heroic figure, who terrifies the Skrælings and saves Karlsefni and his men when she whets her sword on her breast. This must be fiction.

Is this dreadful story historical in the main, or does it at least have a historical core? Interesting in connection with this question is the fact that certain elements of this account correspond with information contained in the story of Bjarni. There Freydis is described as an arrogant woman, her husband Thorvard more or less as a nonentity. She married him for his money, and according to the saga they lived at Garðar, 'where the bishop's seat is now', a description which gives an impression of reliability. Women of Freydis's type, domineering and ruthless, are well known in the sagas, for instance in *Njáls saga*.

These two expeditions, that of Freydis and that of the Icelanders, aim neither at exploration nor at settlement, their purpose is that of profit. They must have been interested in valuable commodities such as timber, furs, hides, walrus ivory, blubber, down and falcons. The account contains almost no information of interest from the points of view of geography or botany; it is concerned with the people and their fate, primarily with the atrocious crime committed by Freydis. It is evident that the saga differentiates clearly between Icelanders and Greenlanders. It seems natural that the Greenlanders considered their community in a new land to be a free, independent state, just as the immigrants to Iceland had done, but rivalry might easily arise. In this particular case the very core of the account concerns bitter controversy.

Freydis provoked the Icelanders right from the start. She took more men than they had agreed upon, she threw the Icelanders out of Leif's houses and moved in herself, she demanded their ship in exchange for her smaller one, a request to which the Icelanders agreed, and finally she had the Icelanders killed, murdering their women herself. No Icelandic author would have shown his own compatriots in so sorry a light, and there can hardly be any doubt about this saga having its origin in Greenland, a point to which I shall return at a later stage (*see pp. 163-7*).

It is important that we also appreciate the mental stress involved when a group of people spend an entire winter in a distant wilderness, completely cut off from the outside world. When, as in this case, two groups from different countries are involved, the strain of the situation must increase, resulting in conditions liable to lead to animosity, to downright hatred. Throughout the ages ruthless discord is well known to have arisen during such expeditions; there are reports of murder, mutiny, and cannibalism. Members of expeditions like Hudson and his son are known to have been left behind to die in a remote wilderness.

There can be no doubt that certain elements of this account are highly dubious. The lengthy description of Freydis getting out of bed early in the morning, and going barefoot over to the Icelanders demanding to trade ships with them, is obviously a literary element. Her request is immediately complied with, without any difficulty at all. But even though she is promised the larger ship, she goads her husband into avenging her.

There are good reasons for assuming that the author was somewhat ignorant about the actual events in the far distant wilderness. He may have known that all the Icelanders disappeared,

without being aware of how this happened.

The fact that such great importance is accorded to the ship and to the exchange of ships may perhaps be a reminiscence indicating a different, more natural course of events than that so illogically described in the saga. The Greenlanders' ship may have been wrecked, so that they were in quite a hopeless situation. Under such conditions an arrogant woman like Freydis would hardly think twice about attacking the Icelanders, seizing their ship and setting out with it. Some Icelanders would lose their lives in the process; others might have been able to escape into the wilderness, only to die there.

It would become known that the Icelanders did not return; contemporary Greenland would probably gain an approximate knowledge about the actual events. But the only witnesses to the tragedy were the members of the expedition, and they were hardly interested in talking too much about the matter, thus taking the blame on themselves. In the course of time the same may have happened here as in the case of other appalling tragedies in distant wilds, popular imagination transforming the actual course of events, and providing a new explanation of the disappearance of the Icelandic crew.

THORFINN KARLSEFNI SAILS TO NORWAY AND ICELAND

On her return to Greenland, Freydis gave lavish gifts to all the members of her crew, so that they would say nothing about the murder of the Icelanders. But Leif heard rumours about what had happened, and he tortured three members of the crew until they confessed everything. Leif was not willing to punish his sister Freydis, but he predicted misfortune for her family and her descendants, and from that time on, everyone thought ill of her.

It seems most unlikely that Freydis would have

thought that lavish gifts could silence her crew completely. There were more than thirty men and women, and Freydis would hardly have been so naive as to imagine that all these people would refrain from telling the sensational news of the murder of the entire Icelandic crew. It also seems unlikely that Leif should not have been able to make the sailors talk by virtue of his authority, that he had to employ torture instead. Leif's mild reaction to the misdeed, and his prediction about the misfortunes that would befall Freydis and her descendants, read like a text from the Bible.

The main part of the chapter deals with Karlsefni's and Gudrid's return to Norway. He spent the winter there and sold his wares, and they were honoured by the most notable people in the country. When he was preparing to sail to Iceland the following spring, a German from Bremen came to him, and for half a mark of gold he bought a carved *húsasnotra*, a weather-vane, which had been in use as an ornament on Karlsefni's ship. It was made of a kind of wood called *mǫsurr*, probably the knotty protuberance sometimes found on birches, and it was said to have come from Vinland.

Karlsefni and Gudrid then sailed to Skagafjord in Iceland. He bought land in Glaumbær, and farmed it for the rest of his life. He was a man of great distinction and nobility, and from him and Gudrid sprang a notable, numerous and splendid line. After Karlsefni's death, Gudrid and her son Snorri, who was born in Vinland, took over the farm. Gudrid made a pilgrimage to Rome, and when she returned home, her son had built a church at Glaumbær. There she spent the rest of her days as an anchoress.

This account is followed by information about the descendants of Karlsefni, and his line is stressed. Finally we are told that it was Karlsefni who gave the fullest report about all these voyages, and that some account of this has now been given.

This end of the Grœnlendinga Saga is an unexpected conclusion, a conclusion which implies a radical break with the rest of the saga text in the matter of content as well as that of the style of the narrative.

Suddenly the Icelanders Karlsefni and Gudrid are shown as the main characters of the story. Special prominence is several times given to them and to their progeny, with the greatest possible emphasis. Elements connected with Christianity, earlier merely touched upon, now make their appearance: we read about Gudrid's pilgrimage to Rome, the building of a church, her becoming an anchoress. Leif, who had discovered Vinland, is not mentioned at all, nor are any of the other Greenlanders who had voyaged there.

This does not accord at all well with the rest of Grœnlendinga Saga. In the main text, the Vinland voyages undertaken by Greenlanders occupy a central part of the story. There are as many as four of these, undertaken by Leif, Thorvald, Thorstein and Freydis, and Leif is depicted as the discoverer of Vinland. The description of Karlsefni's voyage is as objective as the others, without any form of panegyrics. Gudrid is introduced briefly as a newcomer to Greenland, married to a Norwegian, and no particular prominence is given to her, except in the unhistorical addition dealing with the prophecy in the account of Thorstein's voyage. Christianity is mentioned briefly, and obviously correctly. The manner of narration is matter-of-fact, and seems authentic on all essential points; there is no attempt at promoting any particular point of view. In fact, this narrative describes the events in a straightforward, simple fashion.

This and other aspects, including a number of unhistorical elements, indicate that the final part of the saga does not have any natural connection with the rest. In my opinion it is a later addition. In the following analysis of the text, this will be dealt with in greater detail.

Already at the beginning of this passage the leit-motif of this text, the splendour of Karlsefni and Gudrid, is emphasized, in that they were honoured by the most notable people of the country during their stay in Norway.

The sale of the *húsasnotra*, the carved ornament for a ship or house said to have been made from *mǫsurr*-wood from Vinland, to a German from Bremen for half a mark of gold, seems highly suspicious. It is reminiscent of later days, of the German merchants who settled in medieval Bergen. Moreover, this German came from Bremen, the native city of Adam of Bremen. *Mǫsurr* is a hard, tough wood, and often has a beautiful wavy grain.

The rather rare term *húsasnotra* also appears in the introduction of Nikolaus of Þverá's description of the route to the Holy Land, which was written in the mid-twelfth century. Here we read: 'It is said that Thorfinn Karlsefni felled a tree for a *húsasnotra* and then he set out to find Vinland.' In connection with this important event, Karlsefni's departure for Vinland, the mention of the *húsasnotra* seems natural and confidence-inspiring. Gustav Storm (1888a: 25) is probably right in maintaining that the story in the saga is merely a corrupted version of this source.

An important aspect of the information about *mǫsurr*-wood would seem to be the fact which is emphasized – that it came from *Vinland*. Obvi-ously the intention is that this wood should serve as proof of Karlsefni actually having been there. This must be viewed in the context of Eirik's Saga's account to the effect that Leif, during his (unhistorical) voyage from Norway to Greenland was lost at sea and discovered an unknown land; there, not only vines and self-sown wheat grew, but also trees which were called *mǫsurr*. In both cases the discovery of Vinland is connected with the finding of *mǫsurr*, which can only be interpreted as showing that the author of the final part of Grœnlendinga Saga made use of Eirik's Saga.

The passage then continues with Karlsefni's voyage from Norway to northern Iceland, where he bought the farm Glaumbær, and lived there for the rest of his days. This is presumably unhistorical. No other source says anything about this farm belonging to Karlsefni's line (Hermannsson 1966: 65, Storm 1891: 73ff.).

Next we have a new laudation of Karlsefni and of his and Gudrid's progeny. With regard to the following account, which is concerned with Gudrid's pilgrimage to Rome, with a church being built at Glaumbær, where she was to become a nun and a recluse, we must realize that this is not only unhistorical, but also an anachronism. In about the year 1000 there was no church, no convent at Glaumbær (nor at Reyni-staðr). The first convent in Iceland was built on the farm Þingeyrir in the district of the Húnavatn Þing during the twelfth century (Helgason 1925: 74).

The story of Gudrid must be rejected also for an entirely different reason. It was clearly composed in order to prove that the prophecy about Gudrid in the account of Thorstein's voyage was fulfilled. This prophecy runs as follows:

'I am anxious to tell Gudrid what lies ahead of her, that she may bear my death more resignedly, for I have come to a good resting-place. What I have to tell you, Gudrid, is this, that you will be given in marriage to an Icelander, and long shall be your life together. Many descendants shall spring from you and him, vigorous, bright and noble, sweet and of good savour. You shall leave Greenland for Norway and Norway for Iceland, and in Iceland make a home. There you will live, the two of you, for a long time, and you shall live longer than he. You shall go abroad, and make a pilgrimage south to Rome, and return to Iceland to your own place, whereupon a church shall be raised there, where you will live and take the vows of a nun, and where you will die.'

Every single point of this prophecy is fulfilled in the final chapter of the saga: the journey to Norway, the years spent living in Iceland, Karlsefni's death before Gudrid's, her pilgrimage to Rome, a church being built at her home, Gudrid becoming a nun, and finally her noble progeny. In the prophecy her descendants are described with several panegyrical adjectives. In the final chapter of Grœnlendinga Saga, this praise is repeated in various ways, and Karlsefni is described as 'a man of great distinction and nobility'. It is of particular interest that the prophecy has much in common with the prophecy about Gudrid in Eirik's Saga.

The excessive praise of their descendants refers to a number of bishops of Karlsefni's and Gudrid's line: Thorlak Runolfsson (1119-33), Bjorn Gilsson (1147-62), Brand Sæmundarsson (1163-1201) and Brand Jonsson (1263-64).

As I showed above, the contents and the style of the final part of Grœnlendinga Saga differ so greatly from the rest of that saga that there would seem to be reason to believe that we are confronted with a later addition. As it includes so many elements characteristic of Eirik's Saga, a conclusion to the effect that Eirik's Saga – or a related account – must have been an important source for this addition, would seem to be justified.

The final chapter of Grœnlendinga Saga ends with yet another merit being accorded to Karlsefni; we read: 'It was Karlsefni who gave the fullest report about all these voyages, some of which are described here.' And thus Karlsefni is also credited with being the source of Grœnlendinga Saga. Bearing in mind all the praise previously accorded to him, and also the fact that the final chapter of the saga is permeated by so many unhistorical elements, this new credit to Karlsefni may also be assumed to be unreliable. Moreover, the authors of the Icelandic sagas are, as a rule, unknown.

Gustav Storm's opinion (1888a: 25) about this final part of Grœnlendinga Saga may be right: he does not believe in Karlsefni's voyage to Norway. According to Storm, this entire story was composed simply in order to provide a frame for Karlsefni's vane of mǫsurr-wood, said to have come from Vinland, and to have been sold to a German from Bremen.

SUMMARY

This saga is mainly concerned with Greenlanders. We hear about Eirik the Red and his children, Leif, Thorvald, Thorstein and Freydis, and about Bjarni, who lost his way at sea, sighted a new land, and then settled in Greenland and became a Greenlander. We are also told about the Icelander Karlsefni and his wife Gudrid (who was first married to Thorir, a Norwegian); they appear as visitors to Greenland, and return to Iceland.

The accounts of the Vinland voyages are given in a logical sequence similar to those well known from other discoveries: first comes a chance discovery, then a systematic exploration of the country and its produce, and finally an expedition of emigration takes place. This includes women, livestock and equipment.

The language is plain. There is no indication of learning on the part of the author, we find no traces of European literature. Christianity, which occupies an important place in Eirik's Saga, is here simply mentioned briefly as something new, which may accord well with conditions during the Viking Age.

There is no cult of personalities like that of Eirik's Saga. Greenlanders and Icelanders – Karlsefni and Gudrid – are treated in the same, objective manner; there is no trace of any tendency to side with any of the persons. This does not, however, apply to the last chapter, whose one-sided glorification of Karlsefni and Gudrid, combined with the great number of unhistorical elements and the general presentation of the material as such, renders it so different from the rest of the saga that it must be taken to be a later addition.

Grœnlendinga Saga was probably written down about two hundred years after the events it describes had taken place. Like all sagas, it has certain weaknesses, the most important being the story dealing with vines and grapes, which must have been added at a later date (*see pp. 105-6*). But none of these factors can overshadow the generally authentic character of this plain, straightforward narrative. Typical, too, is the fact that the remarkable observation of the sun taken in Vinland should occur in this saga; practically all authorities consider this to be historical.

Of particular significance are Grœnlendinga Saga's descriptions of sailing times, geographical matters and, not least, of landmarks. We have seen that Leif followed Bjarni's route, but in the opposite direction; after he had sailed north along the west coast of Greenland, it was presumably fairly simple to find the land which Leif called *Helluland*. There can hardly be any doubt as to this land being identical with a part of Baffin Island: Bjarni had been on the outlook for a land with glaciers, which he knew were to be found in Greenland, and Baffin Island is the first glaciered land he could possibly have come to during his northward voyage along the east coast of North America. In this connection I would point out that at Cape Aston in Labrador, which faces Disko Island, I found a region which corresponds as closely as possible to Leif's fascinating description of Helluland.

The course of his further voyage south to Vinland may well be described as being inevitable – there was little more to it than first following the coast of Baffin Island and then that of Labrador. In connection with Labrador (*Markland*) landmarks are mentioned, the strange, long beaches and the forest. Finally we read that it was two days' sailing from the long beaches to Vinland, and this corresponds well with the time it takes to sail from Cape Porcupine in Labrador to the north coast of Newfoundland. Sailing south along the coast of Labrador, Leif could hardly avoid making straight for L'Anse aux Meadows, the place where the Norse settlement lies. Some scholars have maintained that it would be quite absurd to imagine that later expeditions would be able to find Leif's settlement on the extensive coast of North America, but this is not so. On the contrary, the coastal route described in the sagas is so straightforward that the later voyagers could have reached L'Anse aux Meadows by following an account given by Leif Eiriksson at home at his farm Brattahlið in Greenland, unless something really unforeseen should have occurred.

When did the Vinland voyages take place? Several factors would seem to indicate that Leif Eiriksson's expedition took place shortly after A.D. 1000. The C^{14} analyses of material from L'Anse aux Meadows would also appear to indicate such a date. We shall return to these dates below; here I shall merely point out that the mean result – A.D. 990 ± 30 – is given with a limit of error of one standard deviation. This means that there is about a 70 per cent probability of the true age lying between A.D. 975 and A.D. 1020.

These dates accord well with the result reached by Gathorne-Hardy by means of dates of the descendants of Karlsefni's son Snorri, who was born in Vinland. He arrives at the conclusion that Karlsefni undertook his Vinland voyage in about A.D. 1020, which would seem to imply that the expeditions undertaken by Thorvald and Thorstein took place between c. A. D. 1000 and 1020, and that Freydis's expedition should be dated to shortly after A.D. 1020.

It is strange that a society as restricted as that of Iceland, where it was customary to narrate sagas at home and at the meetings of the Thing, and where there was close and frequent contact between the different families, should have given rise to two highly dissimilar sagas about Vinland, Grœnlendinga Saga and Eirik's Saga.

It is also remarkable that the basic motif of the comparatively unreliable, and probably the more recent of these two sagas, Eirik's Saga, should have been accepted and followed in some of Iceland's most eminent literary works, such as *Kristni Saga*, the *Large Saga of Olaf Tryggvason* and *Heimskringla*. They, too, speak of Leif's voyage to Norway, his discovery of a new land when he was on his way home, and of his having brought Christianity to Greenland.

Grœnlendinga Saga in *Flateyjarbók*, on the other hand, is entirely detached from other Icelandic sources, even though its version of the Vinland voyages would appear to be the most reliable. It differs greatly from Eirik's Saga on essential points, such as Leif's discovery of Vinland which, in Grœnlendinga Saga, was the result of a planned expedition of discovery, which set out from Greenland.

It has generally been tacitly assumed that both these sagas are of Icelandic origin, but this is a point requiring a more detailed examination. It seems clear that Eirik's Saga must be of Icelandic origin, but a number of elements would seem to indicate that Grœnlendinga Saga must derive from a Greenland source. To the best of my knowledge, this view is shared only by Gathorne-Hardy (1921: 139 ff., 1970).

From the Icelanders' point of view, the discovery of Vinland and other regions far in the west was a remote event, without practical importance. Moreover, the tradition concerning the discovery can hardly have been so firmly rooted that popular knowledge would act as a control in the matter of preserving essential historical elements. How weak this tradition was is illustrated

THE ORIGINS OF GRŒNLENDINGA SAGA

by the fact that the earliest Icelandic sources, the *Book of the Settlements* and the *Book of the Icelanders*, make no mention of the discovery of Vinland, either by Leif or by others.

But the Greenlanders were in an entirely different position with regard to the tradition about Vinland and other regions in the west and the south-west. These were matters of paramount concern to the people. The story of the founder of the Greenland colony, Eirik the Red, and of members of his immediate family, who had discovered an immense, strange new land in the west must have been one of the most important elements in the history of the Greenlanders. Moreover, the tradition concerning this discovery was closely connected with facts which were to become highly important to the Greenlanders. I am here particularly thinking of the forests of Labrador, where one came when following the Vinland route from Greenland; it seems very probable that the Greenlanders fetched materials for ship-building there in the course of the centuries. And it seems likely that they made for hunting grounds once this route was known, for instance those off the coast of Baffin Island, where walrus, whale, seal and other marine animals must have abounded.

Under these circumstances we have reason to believe that the stories about the Vinland voyages must have been a living tradition in Greenland, and that essential elements of this tradition must have remained largely unchanged through the ages.

We saw above that the Icelandic sources dealing with Greenland are very sparse, and that they give practically no information about the culture and way of life of the Greenlanders. And not a single document from Greenland has come down to us, but we know that Greenland was a country of the Norse culture, and we gather from occasional mentions in the sources that the art of saga-telling lived on. Some of the Greenlanders' sagas may have been written down. The dearth of source material has influenced our idea of the culture of Greenland, and it may be partly responsible for the fact that Grœnlendinga Saga is as a rule ascribed to Iceland, the sagaland beyond compare.

Gathorne-Hardy emphasizes a unique characteristic of *Flateyjarbók*, the only text to include Grœnlendinga Saga, that the library from which it was derived was evidently rich in literature treating of Scandinavian colonies which existed outside the confines of Iceland. He adds: 'It is therefore precisely in such a work as the *Flatey Book* that we might expect to find incorporated a saga derived from an outlandish source ...' Vigfússon, in the preface to *Orkneyinga Saga* (Icelandic Sagas I: XXXII, 1887), writes about *Flateyjarbók*:

'Its pages preserve more than half of all we know of the older history of the Orkneys, the Faroes, Greenland and Vineland (America). Indeed, John Haconson and his two scribes seem for some reason, now unknown, to have paid particular attention to gathering up every scrap relating to these neighbour-lands of Outer, or Colonial, Scandinavia.'

These general points of view provide a vista which should lead to an investigation of whether Grœnlendinga Saga contains elements which might point to its origin. When appraising the text, it is of importance to note any features which might be thought to be of particular interest either to Greenlanders or to Icelanders, elements with which an author from Iceland, or one from Greenland, would not have been familiar, or such as would obviously be in conflict with an Icelander's or a Greenlander's way of thinking.

It is, in the first place, appropriate to repeat that when Karlsefni, at the end of Grœnlendinga Saga, is given credit also for being its original source, this statement must be unhistorical, like the greater part of the last chapter (*see p. 59*).

A conspicuous element of Grœnlendinga Saga, as opposed to Eirik's Saga, is that the discovery of Vinland not only takes place in a different way, but that we are given accounts of the Vinland expeditions undertaken by the children of Eirik the Red: the Greenlanders Leif, Thorvald, Thorstein and Freydis. All these are described separately. The expedition undertaken by Karlsefni, the Icelander, is also included, but the Greenlanders dominate the saga, and in fact the term 'Greenland family saga' would seem to describe it admirably.

It seems hardly likely that Icelandic sources would devote so much attention to four Greenlanders who were either unknown in Iceland, or at least of little interest to the people of that country. Halldór Hermannsson (1936, 1966: 27) puts it this way:

'When we scan the saga literature, it is noticeable how little is to be found there about the history of Greenland. Only those episodes of that history are recorded in which Icelanders had a part, and who afterwards brought the story to Iceland.'

In Grœnlendinga Saga (ch. VI) we read: 'Christianity was still in its infancy in Greenland at this time.' This is probably a correct description of conditions in Greenland around the year A.D. 1000. In Eirik's Saga, on the other hand, we have an absurdly unctuous, clearly Christian account of Christianity in connection with the first years of the colony. It must be reasonable to assume that the correct information concerning so important an event as the introduction of Christianity in Greenland would come from a Greenland source.

In this connection we must bear in mind that Greenland was an independent republic. The Icelandic sources call the people of that country Greenlanders, thus distinguishing between them and Icelanders, Norwegians and others. And it appears that they, on certain occasions, came into conflict with Icelanders.

Grœnlendinga Saga (ch. VI) gives an account of how Leif Eiriksson rescued Gudrid and her husband Thorir the Norwegian, who were stranded on a reef, and were taken to Brattahlið. There is a brief mention of Gudrid's arrival in Greenland, without any kind of emphasis on her person; she was simply a casual new arrival to the country. Later, when she marries Thorstein, the account is also brief and to the point. I am here disregarding the passage in chapter VI where Thorstein's prophecy suddenly lets her appear as a remarkable, a wonderful woman. This must be an interpolation.

Grœnlendinga Saga's cursory mention of Gudrid is greatly at variance with the extravagant and high-flown description accorded to her in Eirik's Saga – there Thorir, the Norwegian, is not mentioned at all. The brief mention of Gudrid's fortuitous arrival in Greenland would seem to be exactly the reaction to be expected from a Greenland author. Eirik's Saga's glorification of her, on the other hand, would seem to indicate an author who embellished his material with an eye to an Icelandic public.

Gathorne-Hardy notes Grœnlendinga Saga's description of Freydis, a Greenlander, and Thorvard, her insignificant husband, whom she married because of his wealth; he also calls attention to the information that 'they lived at Garðar, where the bishop's seat is nowadays' (ch. II). He is probably right in assuming that this precise location of their home must be of interest to Greenlanders, but not to Icelanders, and that it may indicate a Greenland origin. Here we must add that the description of Thorvard as a rich man accords well with the location of his farm at Garðar, one of the best agricultural districts of Greenland. Greenlanders would know this, but the implication would have been lost on most other people.

Further on in Grœnlendinga Saga (ch. VII) we read that Freydis entered into an agreement with the Icelandic brothers Helgi and Finnbogi, who then sailed to Vinland in their own ship, taking part in her expedition. Freydis's crew consisted of Greenlanders, the other ship was manned by Icelanders. It appears clear throughout the account of this expedition that Freydis deceived, affronted and humiliated the Icelanders, and finally had all of them killed. She herself killed their women. The Icelanders were the first to reach Vinland, and they installed themselves with all their gear in Leif's houses. But when Freydis arrived, she demanded that the Icelanders move out, so that her ship's company could take over the houses. The Icelanders complied immediately, and had to build a new house for themselves. Later Freydis demanded that Finnbogi should change ships with her, since his was the larger; quite an unheard-of demand, and one which one would expect a skipper with any pride in his vessel to refuse point-blank. But once again the Icelander complied. Then Freydis incited her husband and her crew to murder all the Icelanders. They were overpowered and killed and there is not a word about any Icelander with sufficient courage to resist, even though their numbers were roughly equal: there were about thirty Icelanders and thirty-five Greenlanders as well as some women.

In the entire literature of old Iceland, Icelanders are hardly depicted as such sorry wretches. As a rule we find the opposite. It is typical of the Icelandic authors that they glorify their compatriots' activities abroad. There are many examples of this, and in not a few cases there seems to be rather too much glorification. They meet kings and other great men, honours are bestowed on them, they engage in battle with dangerous berserks whom all others fear, and emerge victorious. They do not put up with humiliation, but take vigorous revenge, in fact, they appear as glorious representatives of Iceland. This may be said to be a set pattern in saga literature. But when we read this account about Freydis, which is not only in clear contrast with this pattern, but moreover depicts the Icelanders as such utterly abject creatures, I have no hesitation in maintaining that such an account cannot have been written by an Icelander, it must be the product of a Greenland tradition.

Seen in conjunction with the other factors discussed above, this aspect indicates that Grœnlendinga Saga has sprung from a Greenland milieu.

This view is corroborated by the plain style in which the saga is written, and also by the fact that Grœnlendinga Saga must, unlike Eirik's Saga, be assumed to be essentially reliable. We have already seen that one of the reasons why authentic elements of the narrative were preserved may be the fact that the subject forms an important part of the history of the Greenlanders. Gathorne-Hardy has pointed out that the Greenlanders were not influenced by foreign literature and other impulses from abroad to anything like the same extent as the Icelanders, and this may also have played a decisive part. By the end of the twelfth century contact with Iceland had all but ceased, for the latter country had, as Jón Jóhannesson has shown, practically no ocean-going ships at that time. The shipping route, which was very irregularly frequented, ran between Greenland and Norway (Bergen), and several years might pass between ships calling in Greenland.

If Grœnlendinga Saga really originated in Greenland, we are confronted with the problem of explaining how it found its way into the Icelandic *Flateyjarbók.* It seems very likely that some Greenlanders in the course of time settled in Iceland; they probably had much to tell about their native land. This is not merely conjecture; in *Sturlunga Saga,* Styrkar Sigmundarson from Greenland is mentioned: he is described as a great and truthful saga-teller, *sagnamaðr mikill ok sannfróðr.* One of his stories is quoted, and it testifies to a detailed knowledge of matters concerning Greenland. It deals with a ship-wreck in the wilderness, off the south-east coast of Greenland. A dispute arose among the wrecked crew, and three men, including Einar the Icelander, left the others and went over the glaciers in order to try and find the settlement. They lost their lives, their bodies being found the following year only a day's march from Herjolfsnes, where they were buried. This must have happened some time during the twelfth century, as Einar's father, according to the Icelandic annals, died in 1169.

Styrkar Sigmundarson must evidently have been a highly renowned man in Iceland, since the sources refer to him in such respectful terms: a great and truthful saga-teller. Even though only one of his stories is included in the saga, his reputation must presumably imply that he told considerably more about Greenland. Events in this strange, polar land were largely unfamiliar to the Icelanders, and must have been so fascinating as to compel their interest. The Greenlanders must have had their own sagas, as we have seen, and it would be most strange if this Greenland saga-teller had not related so important and spectacular a part of the history of Greenland as that concerning the children of Eirik the Red: Leif, who had discovered a new and promising land in the south-west, where he had built large houses, and his brothers and sisters. The authors of *Grønlands Historiske Mindesmærker* state the following about Styrkar Sigmundarson (II: 755): 'About this remarkable man who apparently lived in Iceland in his old age, and to whom many of the stories contained in this volume may presumably be attributed, we know nothing, unfortunately, apart from what little is said here.'

It seems highly probable that other Greenlanders also settled in Iceland in the course of the years, and that they could tell much about the society of Greenland. The Norwegian *King's Mirror* contains an interesting parallel to the above: the author states that he had on several occasions met Greenlanders who had lived in their native land for a long time, and that he had listened to what they had to tell. It seems evident that most of the material on which he bases his excellent description of conditions in Greenland originated with these Greenlanders.

Thus it is not surprising that a Greenland saga should have been preserved in Iceland; as not a single document from Greenland has come down to us, it is understandable that this saga has also been assumed, although incorrectly, to derive from Iceland. We must remember that the society of Greenland developed its own independent and distinctive culture in the course of the centuries. Greenland had its own legal system, its own churches and much else peculiar to their own society. Their culture must undoubtedly also have included poetry and sagas. In my mind's eye I can see the Greenland bishop in his study at Garðar, where sagas, painstakingly written down on vellum, formed part of his library.

Nanuk at Saglek. *Photo by Ray Fennelly.*

68

EIRIK'S SAGA

INTRODUCTORY REMARKS

The discussion below is based on the so-called *Skálholtsbók* (AM 557 4°), the most reliable source. The chapters of this manuscript have no headings.

Jón Jóhannesson (1956, 1962) has, as we have seen, given convincing grounds showing that Grœnlendinga Saga is the elder of the two Vinland sagas, and that there is no reason to doubt the reliability of its account of the discovery of the new lands in the west. According to this, Leif discovered Vinland as the result of a planned voyage of discovery starting from Greenland. This is radically different from the version in Eirik's Saga, which most other scholars accept; here Leif, who had been in Norway, lost his way at sea on his return voyage to Greenland, and found a land where grapes grew.

Jóhannesson has, moreover, shown that the author of Eirik's Saga not only was familiar with Grœnlendinga Saga, but that he also made use of it. He used the text of the other saga in such a way that nothing would conflict with the version according to which Leif had discovered Vinland on his return from Norway.

Jóhannesson's article is brief, and he gives only a few convincing examples of this practice. In the following examination of the entire text of Eirik's Saga, we shall systematically investigate whether, and to what extent, the author made use of Grœnlendinga Saga.

GUDRID'S LINE
Eirik's Saga I

Olaf the White, who was of royal Norwegian blood, conquered Dublin and other parts of Ireland. He fell in battle there, and his wife Aud the Deep-minded and his son Thorstein the Red journeyed to the Hebrides. Together with Earl Sigurd, Thorstein conquered much of Scotland, where he reigned as king until the Scots killed

him. Aud then sailed to Iceland, with twenty freemen on board her ship. She took possession of Dalir, and made her home at Hvamm. One of her men was called Vifil; he was of high birth, but was a slave until Aud set him free. She gave him land on which to settle, Vifilsdal. He married and had two promising sons, Thorgeir and Thorbjorn, the father of Gudrid. Much of the text in this chapter comes from the *Book of the Settlements (Landnámabók)*.

EIRIK THE RED EMIGRATES FROM NORWAY TO ICELAND – HE COLONIZES GREENLAND
Eirik's Saga II

Thorvald and his son Eirik had to leave their home in Jæren in south-western Norway because of some killings, and they sailed to Iceland. They settled in Hornstrandir, in the northwestern part of the country. Thorvald died, and Eirik married Thjodhild. They moved south, first to Haukadal, and then to Breidafjord. He came into conflict with mighty Icelandic families, and finally he was outlawed at the Thorsnes Thing. In secrecy he equipped a ship, and sailed west in order to find the land Gunnbjorn was said to have seen. He came to south-western Greenland, and spent three years (982-85) exploring the land. Then he sailed back to Iceland, spent the winter there, and made peace with his enemies. The following summer (986) he set out to colonize the land he had discovered. He called it Greenland, as he thought that such a name would attract settlers.

Most of this chapter also comes from the *Book of the Settlements*. In the information about Greenland which follows the above passage in that source, however, the author has omitted the names of the most prominent among the first settlers. One of these was Herjolf, who settled at Herjolfsnes. This is of interest in connection with the next chapter, where a man named Thorkel is, oddly enough, presented as the owner of Herjolfsnes.

GUDRID SAILS TO GREENLAND
Eirik's Saga III

Vifil's two sons, Thorgeir and Thorbjorn, married the daughters of Einar of Laugarbrekka. Thorbjorn made his home at Hellisvellir, and he is described as a prominent man. His daughter was Gudrid; she is said to be most beautiful, and an excellent woman in every respect. Next a man by the name of Einar comes into the story; he is a well-to-do, accomplished merchant, the son of a freed slave. He fell in love with Gudrid and wanted to marry her. He asked his friend Orm to plead his cause with Thorbjorn, Gudrid's father. Orm did as he had been asked, but Thorbjorn replied bluntly that he would not give his daughter in marriage to the son of a slave. The following spring Thorbjorn prepared a feast, and astonished his friends by announcing that his economic difficulties were so great that he had decided to emigrate to Greenland, where he expected to obtain help from Eirik. He sold his land and set out for Greenland. There were thirty people on board his ship, including friends as well as Gudrid, his daughter. They ran into persistent storms, were tossed about on the sea for a long time, and did not reach Greenland until the start of winter. They came to the farm Herjolfsnes, said to belong to a man by the name of Thorkel, who received them well. Here they spent the winter.

Unlike that of the preceding chapters, the text of the present chapter does not derive from the Book of the Settlements, nor does it, to the best of my knowledge, occur in any other source. In other words, we have only the text written by the author of Eirik's Saga, a factor of great importance to an assessment of the saga.

The present version concerning Gudrid differs radically from the account given in Grœnlendinga Saga, according to which she was married to Thorir, the Norwegian, and they were both saved from a shipwreck by Leif Eiriksson during the latter's return to Greenland from Vinland – a land he had discovered as the result of a planned expedition.

According to Eirik's Saga, the owner of the farm Herjolfsnes in Greenland, which Gudrid came to, was a man by the name of Thorkel. This is an extremely suspect item of information, which no one has as yet been able to explain. It is quite obvious that the author of the saga was acquainted with the Book of the Settlements, since this work forms the basis of most of the two preceding chapters. Here Eirik the Red and his colonization of Greenland are discussed, but the other chieftains who took land in Greenland together with Eirik are not mentioned. One of these was Herjolf Bardarson, who took land by the Herjolfsfjord and settled at Herjolfsnes, according to the account given in the Book of the Settlements. The well-informed author of Eirik's Saga can hardly have been ignorant of such an important historical fact. But he prefers not to give Herjolf as the owner of the farm at Herjolfsnes, letting a man by the name of Thorkel own it instead. And in the account of Eirik's colonization of the land, he chooses not to mention the fact that the chieftain Herjolf settled at Herjolfsnes, for this would have conflicted with his assertion that Thorkel owned that farm.

We have seen that there is good reason to believe that the author of Eirik's Saga was acquainted with Grœnlendinga Saga, which also states that Herjolf settled at Herjolfsnes. Moreover, according to that saga Herjolf's son Bjarni lost his way at sea and sighted unknown coasts, a discovery on which Leif's later Vinland voyage was based. Bjarni made his home at Herjolfsnes, and took over the farm after his father's death.

The reason for omitting to mention that Herjolf, and also his son Bjarni, was the owner of Herjolfsnes, substituting a man by the name of Thorkel instead, must be that the author wished to avoid anything which might be reminiscent of Grœnlendinga Saga's account of the Vinland voyages, which differs so radically from that which he himself was writing. Below we shall show that he employed this method throughout the entire text of Eirik's Saga.

GUDRID AND THE PROPHETESS
Eirik's Saga IV

When Thorbjorn and Gudrid came to Herjolfsnes, there was a famine in Greenland. The saga continues with an account of a strange séance held by Thorbjorg, a prophetess who was known as the Little Sibyl. Once she had had nine sisters, but now she alone was alive. Thorkel invited her to his farm, and we are given a very detailed description of her clothes, shoes, jewellery and other accoutrements, which included a staff with brass ornaments. Great honour is shown to her, and Thorkel leads her to a high seat with a cushion filled with hens' feathers. The extraordinary food she was served is described, as are her eating utensils: her spoon was of brass, and her knife had a handle of walrus ivory, wound with copper.

The séance took place the following evening, and she had all the apparatus she required. But in order to attain contact with the spirits she needed the assistance of a woman who knew the magic lay Varðlokur. Gudrid was the only one familiar with this lay, but she was unwilling to recite it, since she was a Christian. But Thorkel and Thorbjorg persuaded her to recite the lay, and then she said it so beautifully that no one had ever heard the like. After this, the prophetess said that many spirits were coming to her, and that much was revealed to her. She prophesied that the famine would soon be over, and the sickness would also come to an end. Then she predicted that Gudrid would make a most distinguished marriage in Greenland, but she would not stay there for long. Her ways led to Iceland, where a great and splendid line would spring from her, and a bright light would shine over her progeny. The famine came to an end as the seeress had predicted. Then Thorbjorn and Gudrid sailed to Brattahlið, where Eirik the Red welcomed them and gave them land at Stokkanes.

Here the author gives so many elaborate details relating to cultural history that his account reads like a scientific report rather than popular tradition. His literary skill is evident, the dramatic motif being brought to its climax with considerable stylistic talent.

Improbabilities are not few in this passage, such as, for instance, that the prophetess is the only one of ten sisters who is still alive. The brass ornamentation and the brass spoon suggest the Middle Ages, it was not until the end of that period that brass became a common metal in the North (*Kult. Leks.* XII:col. 179). We are told that Thorbjorn did not attend the séance because he was a Christian; yet Gudrid, who was also a Christian, becomes an important participant, invoking the spirits by means of the lay *Varðlokur*. The situation becomes still more illogical as a result of Thorkel's urging Gudrid to participate, from highly questionable motives.

The prophecy refers to Gudrid's later marriage to Karlsefni, and the splendid progeny must be the famous bishops of her line. This lengthy séance, which culminates in the prophecy, does not in any way form a natural part of the story. More-over, not only does the text contain suspect features, the accumulation of highly special elements, combined with the stylistic composition employed, leaves the reader with a strong im-pression of being confronted with a literary product. The glorification of Gudrid would seem to be the aim of the entire elaborately constructed text.

Dag Strömbäck (1935: 49-60, 1940) maintains that this account does not form part of the saga, that it is a literary product of a fairly late date, written by a talented author who knew his subject well. He shows that Gudrid and her line are systematically glorified in the earlier parts of the saga, and explains this by saying that 'she is the ancestress par préférence of the Icelandic bishops'. This aspect is enhanced by the prophecy in the present chapter, and he concludes that the entire passage was composed by the author, in order to glorify Gudrid. According to him, the prophecy is fully comprehensible if we regard Gudrid as biskupamóðir; then it falls naturally into place in the sphere of legend and of historical chronicles with a religious bias.

There is also another aspect to this matter, and this is illustrated by Jón Jóhannesson (1956, 1962: 58). Grœnlendinga Saga, as we have seen, has a similar prophecy about Gudrid; this must also be a later addition, written by an author who must have been familiar with Eirik's Saga. In the chapter dealing with Thorstein's voyage, he makes a prediction, on his death-bed, which includes the following words:

'What I have to tell you, Gudrid, is this, that you will be given in marriage to an Icelander, and long shall be your life together. Many descendants shall spring from you and him, vigorous, bright and noble, sweet and of good savour.'

In Eirik's Saga, the prophetess announces, on Gudrid's arrival in Greenland:

'As for you, Gudrid, I shall repay you here and now for the help we have derived from you, for your future is now an open book to me.
You will make a match here in Greenland, the most distinguished there is, yet it will not prove of long duration; for your ways lie out to Iceland, where there will spring from you a great and goodly progeny, and over this progeny of yours shall brighter rays shine than I am able to see clearly.'

Jóhannesson rightly maintains that it would have been a strange coincidence indeed if two such similar prophecies should have made their appearance independently in the work of two different authors. He further notes that the author of Eirik's Saga also has a prophecy about Gudrid in the chapter about Thorstein; that prophecy is, however, quite brief, probably in order to avoid a repetition of the sibyl's rather long prediction. According to Jóhannesson the fact that the prophecy recurs in the chapter about Thorstein can be explained in one way only: the author of Eirik's Saga must have been familiar with Grœnlendinga Saga, or with some other, similar source, and he has here preserved a relic of this earlier work. It probably suited his purpose best to have the detailed prophecy at an earlier stage, and for this reason he must have invented the episode with the prophetess.

In fact, it seems quite clear that the account dealing with Gudrid's stay at Herjolfsnes is so influenced by fables, other unreliable features and irrelevant folklore, that there can be no doubt of its being fiction. Had Gudrid really been such a brilliant and renowned woman at that time, it seems strange that no other source should contain as much as a mention of her stay at Herjolfsnes, where these sensational things are said to have taken place.

LEIF EIRIKSSON'S VOYAGE TO NORWAY – HE DISCOVERS NEW LAND – BRINGS CHRISTIANITY TO GREENLAND
Eirik's Saga V

Eirik was married to Thjodhild, and they had two sons, Thorstein and Leif. Thorstein, who is here described as the most promising man in Greenland at that time, was at home with his father, while Leif was in Norway. On his way there, he had drifted off his course. He came to the Hebrides, where he fell in love with Thorgunna, a woman of noble birth. There was something strange about her.

When he was preparing to sail away, she said that she wanted to come with him, but Leif replied that he thought it little fitting to take so high-born a woman to a strange country, where there were so few people. She then told him that she was carrying his child, and if it should prove to be a boy, she would send him to Greenland. When the child was born – and it was a boy – he was called Thorgils, and it was said that he came to Iceland the summer before the so-called 'Froda-marvels'. He then went to Greenland. There was always something strange about him. When he left Thorgunna, Leif gave her a ring of gold and other gifts.

Leif came to Norway in the autumn, and proceeded to the court of Olaf Tryggvason, where many honours were accorded him. The king bid him be his missionary, and to preach Christianity in Greenland. Leif pointed out that this would not be easy, but was willing to do as the king had bid him.

On his way to Greenland, Leif ran into a storm, and he was tossed about on the ocean for a long time. Finally he lighted on an entirely unknown land. Here there were fields of wild wheat, vines, and trees of the kind known as mǫsurr. They took with them samples of these things. On the voyage back that same year, Leif rescued a ship-wrecked crew, and he took these men back to Greenland with him. Therefore he was from then on known as Leif the Lucky.

Soon he was preaching the Catholic faith of Christianity throughout the country, and Leif's unique accomplishment, fulfilling the mission with which King Olaf had entrusted him, is accentuated with as much piety and force as can be.

Eirik did not take well to the idea of the new faith, but Thjodhild was baptized and had a church built, not over near the farm.

This account of Leif's journey to Norway, of the mission with which King Olaf entrusted him, the discovery of new land on the journey back to Greenland, and the conversion of all the Greenlanders is of fundamental importance to an assessment of all the subsequent chapters of Eirik's Saga. Is this account historical?

At the beginning of this chapter, we hear that Eirik and Thjodhild had two sons, Thorstein and Leif. In Grœnlendinga Saga, the number of their children is given as four, in this order: Leif, Thorvald, Thorstein and Freydis. It is surprising that the author of Eirik's Saga does not mention Thorvald and Freydis at all, even though they make their appearance later in this same saga. Strange, too, is the fact that Leif is overshadowed by Thorstein, who is described as the most promising man in Greenland.

The story of Leif's stay on the Hebrides, when he fell in love with Thorgunna, is most romantic. We are told that she belonged to a noble family, and that she was versed in the art of magic, that there was something strange about her son, and a connection with supernatural events in Iceland is also indicated. Moreover, Leif is extremely chivalrous, and would not carry off so high-born a lady. When he left her, he gave her costly gifts, including a gold ring. In this connection it is worth noting that during all the excavations of Norse settlements in Greenland, only one gold ring has, to the best of my knowledge, come to light, it was found on a bishop's finger.

The statement to the effect that Thorgils, the son she bore Leif, came to Iceland the summer before the so-called 'Froda-marvels' cannot be correct. According to *Eyrbyggja Saga* (chs. 50-55), these supernatural, sinister events took place immediately after the death of a witch by the name of Thorgunna, who had also come from the Hebrides. Clearly the author of Eirik's Saga is trying to identify her with the Thorgunna Leif was said to have met, but according to

Eyrbyggja Saga, Thorgunna the witch came to Iceland in the year 1000, about the time of Thorgil's, birth – thus the chronology does not check at all. Moreover, she is said to have been nearly sixty when she came to Iceland, a big woman, fat and swarthy. The romantic story about Leif's stay on the Hebrides does not include a single element of any historical value. After having spent the winter on the Hebrides, Leif is said to have come to Norway, presumably to Nidaros (Trondheim), where he met the Norwegian king, Olaf Tryggvason. According to the text, the time of this meeting would be about A.D. 999, the year before King Olaf fell at Svolder.

The following summer Leif set sail for Greenland, but his ship was storm-tossed on the ocean, and he drifted to an entirely unknown land. The account of the actual sailing is as brief as it can possibly be, and the same applies to the discovery of the new land. There are just a few lines about this, stating that there were fields of self-sown wheat (*hveitiakrar sjálfsánir*) and vines (*vinviðr*), as well as trees known as *mǫsurr*, and that Leif and his men took samples of these with them. Such a brief, vague account of so remarkable a discovery must be unique.

It seems strange that not a single feature of interest to seafarers is recorded, such as matters concerning the ocean, the coast and, not least, typical features of the land, which would have been quite invaluable for any future voyage there. For seafarers who came to unknown lands it was a matter of course that they would be most particular about noting and remembering useful landmarks. It is of interest in the present connection that this point is confirmed in Grœnlendinga Saga, where the different lands are identified by means of low hills, no mountains or high mountains, glaciers, large plains, forests or long beaches.

The saga mentions vines, but why not grapes?

They must have been ripe at that time of year. We should also have expected a mention of the name Vinland here, in connection with the discoverer of that country, but the first mention of that name occurs in the account of Karlsefni's voyage.

Mǫsurr is, as we have seen, the term applied to knotty protuberances on birches, or to wavy-grained, knurled birch-wood, which is used for making bowls or tools. Why should such a common type of Norwegian wood be mentioned in connection with the discovery? Fields of wild, self-sown wheat do not exist in North America, and the statement that vines should also have been found must also be assumed to be fiction (*see pp. 62, 156*).

Eirik's Saga's statement to the effect that, on his return to Greenland, Leif rescued some people from a shipwreck and was therefore known as Leif the Lucky from that time on, seems more than a little suspect. The same item of information occurs in Grœnlendinga Saga, in connection with Leif's voyage home from Vinland, but here the circumstances are entirely different. According to the latter saga, he was on an entirely different voyage, and had found a Vinland quite different from that described in Eirik's Saga. As elsewhere, the explanation must be that the author of Eirik's Saga here made use of Grœnlendinga Saga.

Eirik's Saga does not contain any description of Leif's voyage from the new land with vines he had discovered in the far south, and home to the colony in Greenland. This suggests that the journey was so simple and straightforward that it was not worth describing – but simple it cannot have been. On the contrary, it would have been attended by such great hazards that it seems difficult to believe that it could have been possible to carry through this long and dangerous voyage at all. A more detailed assessment is called for if we are to form an opinion about Leif's entire voyage from Norway to an unknown land in the south, and from there to Greenland.

We must assume that Leif, if the account is to be believed, sailed from Nidaros (Trondheim), the royal residence at that time. As was customary when sailing to Greenland, he would have tried to follow the same latitude, about 61° N., all the way, in order to make sure that he would sight the east coast of Greenland, somewhat north of the southernmost point, and not run the risk of sailing past the island. As he must have been fully aware of the difficult ice conditions off Greenland early in summer, it seems most likely that he would not set out until the beginning of August, the time of year given as the safest by some sources.

According to the saga, Leif's ship was storm-tossed off this northerly route for a long time, and finally he is said to have reached a land with vines. The northern limit of vines on the coast of North America runs through Massachusetts, at about 45° N. This means that the ship must have drifted at least about 17° to the south, perhaps more, and that does not seem very likely.

The distance from Trondheim to Massachusetts or New York is more than 3,000 nautical miles as the crow flies, but if the ship was storm-tossed for a long time, the actual distance covered would naturally be considerably longer. We might compare Leif's voyage with that Magnus Andersen undertook in 1893, when he sailed the Gokstad replica from Norway to Massachusetts, a voyage which took forty-three days. Andersen had encountered no particular difficulties on the way, but Leif is said to have been storm-tossed for a long time; thus his voyage must presumably have taken considerably longer than Andersen's, and he would not be likely to have reached the land with vines until some time in September.

His situation must have been desperate by this time: he did not know where he was, he had not even any idea of whether he was east or west

75

of Greenland, since he had no instruments for measuring the longitude of his position. His situation was far more dangerous than that of Bjarni, who had also lost his way at sea and had come to an unknown land. The voyage from Iceland was shorter, and judging from the information provided by the account of his voyage, Bjarni must have reached the coast of North America considerably further north than the position of Leif's alleged landfall – probably the coast he sighted was that of Newfoundland.

Moreover, provisions and equipment must have constituted a formidable problem for Leif and his crew. Their ship was equipped only for a voyage to Greenland, and mainly loaded with goods for trading with the Greenlanders, and not for an extremely long voyage of several thousands of nautical miles. The shortage of food would probably have reached a critical point already by the time the difficult Atlantic crossing to America had been accomplished, and the prospect of having to spend the winter in the wilderness must have been a veritable Damocles' sword for Leif's crew of thirty men.

We know from the *Saga of Ólaf Tryggvason* that Leif sailed on from the land with vine trees (vines) to Greenland that same summer. But no source explains how he was able, after having crossed the Atlantic, to carry out this almost hopeless task in the course of one summer.

As Gathorne-Hardy (1921: 122, 123) has shown, the information to the effect that Leif sailed on that same summer is in conflict with the reliable observation of the sun given in Grœnlendinga Saga. This observation presupposes that the winter was spent in Vinland, for it was taken on the shortest day of the year. If this is correct, Leif and his crew must have started the winter with scant provisions, and they would probably not have survived the cold season.

On the other hand, even if we accept the information of the sources and assume that they set out the same year in the hope of finding Greenland, their chances of survival would, in my opinion, hardly have been any better.

Firstly, it is obvious that the ship and her sail must have required considerable repairs after the havoc wrought by the storms which raged in the Atlantic for a long time. Valuable time would thus be lost, and winter was approaching. Taking all the aspects involved into consideration, it seems unlikely that they would have been ready to sail again before the end of September.

As for the route to be followed, Leif had no choice at all, as he had no means of determining the longitude of his position. It would have been quite foolhardy to put out to sea and lose sight of the land, since he did not know in which direction he ought to sail. Only one possibility was open to him: to follow the coast northwards.

We must also consider the distance Leif had to cover in these dangerous, foreign waters. The following distances are those measured on navigational charts, not the actual distances sailed: if we cautiously assume that Leif came to the northernmost vine districts, those in Massachusetts, he would have to sail about 1,000 nautical miles from Boston to the northern point of Newfoundland. The distance from there to the northern point of Labrador, Cape Chidley, is approximately 800 nautical miles, while another 500 nautical miles would take him from Cape Chidley to the south coast of Baffin Island and east to the Davis Strait, and then across to western Greenland. Finally comes the journey south along the west coast of Greenland, to the Eastern Settlement, and that is another 700 nautical miles or so. Thus the total distance from Boston to the Eastern Settlement may be estimated at about 3,000 nautical miles.

However the route could not, of course, have been so direct for an open ship with a square sail, plying the ocean in varying weather and ice conditions. The first, southern part of the journey would not, perhaps, present such great problems, but when one comes to the Cabot Strait, the open stretch of sea between Nova Scotia and Newfoundland, what is one to do? From the north coast of Nova Scotia one can hardly see Newfoundland. In clear weather one might sometimes just be able to discern it vaguely from Cape North, but fog and overcast weather are common in these parts. In any case, it does not seem likely that Leif would have taken unnecessary chances by leaving the coast he had followed so far. But if he sailed along the north coast of Nova Scotia, he would soon discover that the coast turns south, and then towards the north-west, and here one entered the great Gulf of St. Lawrence. It seems very doubtful that Leif would have been able to find the Strait of Belle Isle, the narrow passage north.

But supposing that he did find this strait, he would now be confronted with the difficult waters along the extensive coast of Labrador. There are any number of islands and reefs here, icebergs and drift-ice are carried southwards by the strong Labrador current. Assuming that Leif did reach the northern point of Labrador, his next problem would be that of finding the south coast of Baffin Island, and the Davis Strait. And then the long journey southwards along the west coast of Greenland, to the Eastern Settlement, would still lie ahead of him.

Such a complicated and dangerous voyage under sail comprises a number of quite exceptional aspects. The enormous distance involved cannot have been covered in one leg. A ship rigged with a square sail can sail by the wind only to a limited extent; if the head wind grows too strong, one must lay by – the sagas contain a number of references to ships waiting for a favourable wind. Then there is fog, a frequent occurrence in the waters off Newfoundland and further north – at times it can form a veritable wall for days on end. And in autumn, storms may wreak havoc in the Labrador Sea.

This must have been a voyage into the Arctic, a long voyage with many interruptions. Leif would hardly have come very far north before some time in October or November. The days grew shorter, the light poorer, sailing was now possible only in day-time. And so late in the year there were many perils – slushy ice, newly formed ice which would cut into the ship like a saw, drift-ice and icebergs – and the danger of icing on the ship was not the least of all the hazards. Sailing at dusk or dawn under such conditions would be equivalent to risking one's life.

This, then, is the long, dangerous voyage Leif is said to have undertaken after he had crossed the Atlantic in a storm, landing in a region where vines grow, south of 45° N. The total distance, measured on a chart, amounts to almost 6,000 nautical miles, as we saw above, but the actual distance sailed would certainly be much greater.

In my opinion the above shows not only that some of the most important elements of Eirik's Saga's account of Leif's voyage to Norway are of a legendary nature; the return journey, when he crossed the Atlantic to a land where vines and self-sown wheat grew, sailing from there north to Greenland, seems incredible. As far as I can see, this alone is reason good enough for rejecting this account of Leif's Norwegian voyage as being historical. Jón Jóhannesson, as we saw, arrived at the same conclusion, adducing more factors to support his view; it is, however, of interest that the material which is here submitted gives a new and different argument for rejecting the authenticity of Leif's voyage to Norway.

This matter has a wider perspective, as shown above. The long, elaborate account of Karlsefni's Vinland voyage given in Eirik's Saga is entirely dependent on Leif's voyage from Norway, as a result of which he discovered Vinland. If I am right in saying that this latter voyage cannot have taken place, then the foundation for the whole story in Eirik's Saga disappears.

Although the author says extremely little about the actual journey which – if it took place – must have been a unique achievement, he is, strangely enough, not at a loss to give a detailed description of Leif's return home and of his work on behalf of the Church. Soon we find him preaching the Catholic faith in the far-flung settlements of Greenland; the author certainly does not give Leif much time to rest after his arduous voyage. We are given a pious account of the splendid work he did in preaching the true faith to all the people, and the author makes it very clear that Leif was carrying out the mission with which Olaf Tryggvason had entrusted him.

The verbose, edifying contemplations which occur in Eirik's Saga are more than merely suspect; they are revealing, in that they run counter to the spirit of the Viking Age, when men's mind were still in the sway of heathendom. Here the clerical author of Eirik's Saga brings to a climax the element which presumably was responsible for his fictitious account of Leif's voyage to Norway – the introduction of Christianity by King Olaf, a motif designed to enhance the prestige of the Church.

Eirik's Saga continues by reporting that Eirik was not in favour of the new faith, whereas his wife Thjodhild was baptized and had a church built, not over near the farm (Brattahlið). The ruins of this small church and its grave-yard have, as we saw above, been found and excavated. This is the only element of the account concerning Leif's voyage to Norway which is certain to relate to historical fact. This information may derive from an old Icelandic church register, or may be traced back to one of the bishops of Greenland who visited Iceland. We know of four Greenland bishops who paid such visits: Olaf, Arnald, Jon and Helgi. It is also possible that the information may have come from a Greenlander who had moved to Iceland.

THORSTEIN'S ABORTIVE VINLAND VOYAGE
Eirik's Saga V and VI

There was much talk about voyaging to the land Leif had discovered, and Thorstein was the leader of an expedition which set out to find Vinland. They used Thorbjorn Vifilsson's ship, with a crew of twenty. They had little equipment with them, mostly weapons and provisions. Eirik, who had at first been unwilling, had agreed to take part in the expedition. The morning they set out, he hid a casket which held gold and silver, before he left his home. On the way down to the ship, he was thrown by his horse, broke some ribs and injured his shoulder. Then he sent word to his wife, asking her to retrieve the treasure, for he looked upon his fall as a punishment for having hidden it. Then they sailed out of Eiriksfjord, and their expectations were great, but they were in difficulty at sea for a long time, and lost their way. They sighted Iceland, and they also saw birds near Ireland. It was not until the beginning of winter that they found their way back to Eiriksfjord, exhausted and worn out.

The purpose of this voyage was that of finding the land of vines which Leif was said to have discovered far in the south. The name Vinland is, strange to say, not mentioned even yet. Grœnlendinga Saga cites a different purpose for this voyage: Thorstein wanted to bring home the body of his brother Thorvald. But the author of Eirik's Saga could not make use of this version, since Thorvald, according to Grœnlendinga Saga, had journeyed to a Vinland discovered by Leif, but not on a journey from Norway. The same method is used also later in Eirik's Saga, where Thorvald dies under mysterious circumstances, quite different from those described in Grœnlendinga Saga.

A similar method must have been employed also when the author describes Eirik's fall from his horse. In Grœnlendinga Saga this episode occurs in direct connection with Leif's Vinland voyage, which started out from Greenland. Here it is particularly clear that the text was incompatible with the version according to which Leif was said to have discovered the new land when on his way home from Norway. The author therefore moved this episode to the 'neutral' chapter dealing with Thorstein's abortive Vinland voyage. Jóhannesson (1962: 64) calls attention to this example of how Eirik's Saga makes use of Grœnlendinga Saga and discusses the point in some detail. He rightly maintains that this is a typical example illustrating the author's methods.

A similar view is borne out by Sven B.F. Jansson (1945: 131-2), who shows that Grœnlendinga Saga expresses the ancient way of thinking; implying that it is not the injury but the actual fall, a bad omen, that led Eirik to desist from the voyage.

Eirik's Saga moreover adds details and imaginative embellishments which do not occur in Grœnlendinga Saga to this episode. The statement about Eirik having concealed a casket filled with gold and silver shows that the author was quite unfamiliar with conditions in Greenland at the time of the Vinland voyages, and also later. The economy of Greenland was based on barter, and not a single coin has been found during the many excavations of Norse houses on the island. The motif of the concealed treasure is also known from several other sources (Jansson 1945: 132, n. 19). It is, moreover, worth noting that Eirik injured only his foot in Grœnlendinga Saga; in Eirik's Saga, on the other hand, he breaks several ribs and injures his shoulder.

These imaginative additions, and the description of injuries quite different from those resulting from Eirik's fall from his horse in Grœnlendinga Saga, presumably serve the same purpose as the transfer of the episode from the chapter about Leif to the neutral chapter dealing with Thorstein. By making a number of changes, the author of Eirik's Saga evidently wanted to conceal as thoroughly as possible the fact that this episode was connected with the Grœnlendinga Saga version of Leif's voyage to Vinland.

There is yet another aspect lending weight to the view that the episode of Eirik's fall from his horse, as it appears in Eirik's Saga's chapter about Thorstein, is fiction. According to Grœnlendinga Saga, Eirik died the winter after Leif had returned from his Vinland voyage. Eirik was probably dead when Thorstein, some years later, set out on his unsuccessful voyage. There is little reason to doubt the authenticity of Grœnlendinga Saga's version of Eirik's death (*see p. 47*).

In Grœnlendinga Saga we learned that Gudrid took part in Thorstein's expedition, but Eirik's Saga contains no such information. There Thorstein sets out to find the new land Leif was said to have discovered on his way home from Norway, the land with vines, far to the south. A northerly route to Vinland, such as that described in Grœnlendinga Saga, was out of the question in this context; a south-westerly route, a long voyage to Leif's land of grapes, was called for.

In connection with Thorstein's straying about on the ocean, the saga has the following statement: *Rak pá skip þeirra um haf innan* – their ship was driven all about the inner ocean. This shows that the author was acquainted with the cosmography current in southern Europe, according to which the earth was conceived as a round disc surrounded by an outer ocean, and with an inner ocean within the circular limits of the earth. From this we may in turn conclude that the author was a man of learning, and that the description cannot represent any original tradition concerning the Vinland voyages. At the time when these voyages took place, the Norse conception of the world was based on experience and on mythology; the imaginative cosmology of southern Europe is not likely to have gained ground in Iceland until Christianity had been established for a considerable time.

Thorstein saw birds from Ireland, and this points to a southerly route. We cannot but wonder how, in the author's view, Thorstein should have had any chance of finding Leif's Vinland, an unknown region far south on the far-flung coast of North America. The saga gives not a single item of geographical information in connection with the discovery, nor any kind of information about routes or times of sailing. Had this been genuine tradition, we would sure-ly have been entitled to expect that at least some reminiscence of such information had been pre-served.

It is obvious that the talented author of Eirik's Saga was aware of this weakness in the narrative, and here he was confronted with a problem requiring solution. He probably thought the remedy of this weakness, which he undertook in the brief account of Thorstein's abortive voyage, fairly unimportant, but in the principal narrative, that of Karlsefni's Vinland voyage, he had no way of avoiding a description of the route. There he chose to employ the route assigned to Leif in Grœnlendinga Saga, and to give Karlsefni the credit for Leif's discovery.

THE DEATH
OF THORSTEIN EIRIKSSON

Thorstein asked for Gudrid's hand in marriage, and a magnificent wedding was held at Brat-tahlið. Then the newly married couple went to Lysufjord in the Western Settlement, where Thorstein owned a share in a farm. That winter a sickness befell the people, and many died, and we are told about dreadful things that happened, and about ghosts. Thorstein Eiriksson is among those who died, but he rises from the dead and talks with Gudrid. His communication is of a highly religious character, and finally he predicts a brilliant future for her, and admonishes her not to marry a Greenlander. He asks her to give their

money to the Church or to the poor. After having spoken these words, he dies for the second time. Next comes a description of tempo-rary burials in unconsecrated ground, a stake was driven into the ground above the breast of the dead, and when a priest came that way, the stake was pulled up and holy water poured into the hole. Finally, Thorstein's body is taken to the church at Eiriksfjord: Gudrid also goes there, and lived with Eirik the Red at Brattahlið.

Thorstein and Gudrid were married after his voyage, and their wedding is said to have been magnificent. According to Grœnlendinga Saga, they were married before he set out for Vinland, and there the wedding is merely mentioned, briefly and prosaically.

As we saw in connection with Grœnlendinga Saga's chapter on Thorstein, there is reason to believe that the pestilence at the Western Settle-ment is a historical event, and that it had been transmitted from the Eastern Settlement (*see p. 52*). The description of the sickness given in the two sagas, the superstition attaching to it, etc., have a number of features in common, but they also deviate on important points. Both sagas cite gro-tesque instances of superstition; the account given in Eirik's Saga is the more elaborate, and it contains unhistorical elements which are not found in Grœnlendinga Saga.

The account of Thorstein's death in Eirik's Saga contains a number of edifying reflections, piously worded, and piled high as though the author simply could not get enough. In various ways we are told about the will of God, about His mercy, His help, and about salvation. There is no reason to doubt the genuine piety of the author – but we must simply note that this verbose communica-tion about Christianity can hardly agree with the spirit of the Viking Age. Particularly revealing would seem to be the passage in Eirik's Saga where Thorstein, on his death-bed, asks Gudrid to give their money to the Church.

Moreover, an element of cultural history makes its appearance, without much motivation: a detailed description of burial in unconsecrated ground. A stake was set up from the breast of the dead, and when a priest came that way, the stake was withdrawn and holy water was poured into the hole. This procedure is also described in article 23 of the Norwegian Gulathing Law. It seems reasonable to assume that this element was added by the erudite author; clearly he knew a great deal about folklore, a subject in which he must have been very interested, as appears quite clearly from the highly adorned chapter dealing with the sibyl's prophecy about Gudrid's splendid future. Finally we read that Gudrid settled at Brattahlið, where Eirik the Red received her well, and arranged everything in the best possible way for her. But we have already seen that Eirik must have been dead by that time.

THORFINN KARLSEFNI SAILS TO GREENLAND
Eirik's Saga VII

Thorfinn Karlsefni is introduced as a man of high birth from northern Iceland, a wealthy merchant. He sailed to Greenland together with Snorri Thorbrandsson, and that same summer Bjarni Grimolfsson and Thorhall Gamlason also sailed to Greenland with another ship. Each of the two ships had a crew of forty. When they came to Brattahlið, they started trading, and Eirik was invited to help himself to anything he might want.

Eirik did not want to appear less generous, and invited both the crews to be his guests that winter. But when Yule was approaching, Eirik became depressed, and when Karlsefni asked him what was wrong, he replied that he was troubled for he was unable to offer his guests as generous a Yule as he wished. Then Karlsefni invited him to help himself to flour, corn and other goods from the ship, and a choice and costly Yule feast was prepared, the best that had ever been held in Greenland.

Later Karlsefni asked for Gudrid's hand in marriage. Eirik agreed immediately, and said that what destiny had ordained would be fulfilled by this marriage. Then the wedding feast was held, and there was great and merry entertainment at Brattahlið all winter long.

The statement that Thorfinn Karlsefni met Eirik the Red at Brattahlið can hardly be correct. There are several factors indicating that Eirik had died quite some years earlier. According to Grœnlendinga Saga, he died the year when Leif Eiriksson returned to Greenland after his Vinland voyage. And the time of his death is confirmed in the next account, that dealing with Thorvald's Vinland voyage. These items of information form a natural part of a simple, straightforward text, and they give every appearance of being reliable. Moreover, Gathorne-Hardy, basing his results on an investigation of the gene-alogy of the descendants of Thorfinn Karlsefni's son Snorri who, according to Grœnlendinga Saga, was born in Vinland, arrived at the conclusion that Karlsefni would have been about 70 years of age at the time in question, and thus hardly fit to undertake so strenuous an expedition as a Greenland voyage. If the above is correct, the story of Karlsefni's stay at Brattahlið must obviously be fiction. The story about the Yule feast and Karlsefni's generosity on this occasion would also seem to be a literary product. Surely a great chieftain like Eirik would not sit around and be miserable because he was unable to offer his guests a Yule feast worthy of his position, and even make excuses for his poverty. He would undoubtedly have been able to serve his guests choice dishes of game and fish. And if he wanted to add more variety to the menu, he would certainly have been able to procure anything he wanted from Karlsefni's cargo, in exchange for such valuable commodities as walrus ivory, furs, white falcons or other arctic products. The version presented by the author here leaves us with the impression that Karlsefni, the generous Icelander, outshone the poor, depressed Greenlander Eirik the Red. The marriage between Karlsefni and Gudrid is given romantic treatment, whereas it is only tersely mentioned in Grœnlendinga Saga. Eirik's saga emphasizes that this marriage was worthy of Gudrid, and that her destiny was thereby fulfilled – a phrase which refers to the sybil's prophecy at Herjolfsnes. The description of the wedding is equally romantic in character, making it clear that this passage must also be a literary product.

One cannot but wonder why Leif Eiriksson's name is not mentioned at all in connection with Karlsefni's stay at the farm where Leif also lived. As Vinland was the goal of the long and hazardous expedition that Karlsefni was going to carry through, it must have been imperative for him to get as much information as possible from Leif, with regard to the route, ice conditions, currents etc. It would also seem natural if Karlsefni had asked Leif to join his expedition. But Leif's name is eliminated completely. One would also have thought that the name Leif Eiriksson could not possibly have been avoided during the long account of Karlsefni's search for the Vinland Leif had discovered – but again there is no mention of him, apart from an entirely legendary story about two Scottish runners whom King Olaf Tryggvason is said to have given to Leif.

This disregard of Leif the Greenlander seems to be conducted so systematically that it can hardly have been due to coincidence. The explanation is likely to be the following: from the point of view of the author of Eirik's Saga, the Icelander Karlsefni and his wife Gudrid constitute the principal motif of the story. Obviously the most important part of the saga was, to him, the long account of Karlsefni's Vinland voyage, in which he appears as the great discoverer. The story about Leif's voyage to Norway, which led

to the discovery of a land with grapes (only a couple of lines are accorded to this) and to the conversion of Greenland to Christianity, was not only an essential precondition for Karlsefni's discovery, but also a means of enhancing the prestige of the Church. Once this had been achieved, it seems that the Greenlander Leif had served the author's purpose, and thus he could be dismissed for the benefit of an apparently independent description of the achievements of the author's compatriot, Thorfinn Karlsefni. Probably the reason for this is a claim for priority which appears still more clearly in later passages, for instance where the author makes use of Grœnlendinga Saga in such a way that Karlsefni is said to have followed Leif's route and discovered the lands which Leif had discovered.

KARLSEFNI'S VINLAND VOYAGE
Eirik's Saga VIII

In the course of the winter there was much talk about setting out to find Vinland, which was said to be a promising land. Karlsefni and Snorri Thorbrandsson fitted out their ship for going to Vinland, and Bjarni Grimolfsson and Thorhall Gamlason prepared theirs. Yet a third ship set out with them, that which Thorbjorn Vifilsson had sailed from Iceland. The crew of that ship consisted mainly of Greenlanders, including Thorvard, Eirik's son-in-law, and a man called Thorhall, a hunter of much experience who had served Eirik. He is described in a strange way, in great detail, as being swarthy and taciturn, evil and quarrelsome, and a heathen. One hundred and sixty people sailed on these three ships.

This is the beginning of the account of Karlsefni's voyage, which is said to have been intended to find and settle the land with vines which Leif had discovered, ostensibly on his journey home from Norway. Before examining the texts more closely, we would again point out that if Leif's voyage from Norway is unhistorical, as maintained above, then the account of Karlsefni's Vinland voyage is without foundation.

Here we have the saga's first mention of Vinland, a very vague mention without any details. We have already seen how strange it is that the name Vinland is not mentioned in connection with Leif's discovery of that land in Eirik's Saga. It seems to be a common feature of sagas that a discoverer of a land names his discovery. It is, in fact, a prerogative which a discoverer would hardly be likely to renounce, a prerogative normally respected by narrators throughout the ages.

Whereas Grœnlendinga Saga contains instructive advance information concerning Karlsefni's expedition, Eirik's Saga has only some obscure elements, including suspect ones. The author appears to have attached a great deal of importance to the lengthy description of a subordinate member of the crew of the Greenland ship, Thorhall the Hunter.

This swarthy, wicked pagan is described at such great length that he appears as one of the main characters. However, in all probability he is as fictitious a character as similar baroque personages in other sagas.

The total number of men on board the three ships is stated to have been 160, in other words rather more than fifty people on each ship. This figure seems too high for an expedition intending to settle in a new land, for they would also have to take along a heavy, voluminous cargo of provisions, equipment, cattle, horses and sheep. We saw above that the normal size of a crew sailing the north-western waters seems to have been from twenty to forty.

With its three ships and 160 participants Karlsefni's expedition is far more impressive than Leif's, a point worth noting. According to Grœnlendinga Saga, Leif had sailed with one ship and thirty-five men.

THE VOYAGE TO STRAUMSFJORD

The expedition sailed away for the Western Settlement and then for *Bjarneyjar* (Bear Isles). From Bjarneyjar they sailed with a north wind, were at sea for two days and nights, and then found unknown land. There they found many flat stones, so big that a pair of men could easily clap sole to sole on them. There were many arctic foxes there.

They gave the land a name, calling it *Helluland* (Flatstone Land). Then they sailed with a north wind for two days (*dœgr*), when land lay ahead of them, with a great forest and many wild animals, and they called it *Markland* (Wood Land). On an island they felled a bear.

After they had sailed on for two days and nights with the land to starboard, they came to a cape and then to an open, harbourless coast, with long beaches and sands. They put ashore, and found the keel of a ship, and they called the place *Kjalarnes* (Keelness). Likewise they gave a name to the long beaches, calling them *Furðustrandir* (Marvelstrands).

Then the land was indented by bays, and they headed their ships into one of these. Two Scottish runners, Haki and Hekja, whom Olaf Tryggvason was said to have given to Leif, and whom Leif and Eirik had provided to accompany Karlsefni, wore a garment which was called *bjafall*. They were sent southwards, to spy out the quality of the land. After three days they returned with grapes and ears of self-sown wheat in their hands. They seemed to have found a rich land.

Then the expedition sailed on, and at the mouth of a fjord they came to an island which they called *Straumsey*. There were so many birds there that a man could hardly set his foot down between the eggs. They sailed up the fjord, which they called *Straumsfjord*.

The purpose of this expedition was to find the land of vines Leif had seen far south-west of Greenland, along the extensive coast of North America. This discovery is merely mentioned in a couple of lines, without the slightest geographical or maritime information. It seems almost incredible that 160 people, including women, should embark on such an adventure, setting out to sea with a view to emigrating to a distant, unknown land, which they could hardly have much hope of finding, and whose nature was uncertain. Grœnlendinga Saga's account of Karlsefni's Vinland voyage is far more credible on a point of paramount importance: there the attempted emigration does not take place immediately after Leif's discovery, but after Thorvald's expedition had *explored* the land, assuring themselves of the possibilities it offered, and gaining far more knowledge of the route.

According to Eirik's Saga, Karlsefni had to follow a south-westerly course; there is not the slightest indication of a northern course. We also saw above that it must have been impossible for Leif, after having been blown across the Atlantic to a land in the far south where vines grew, to follow the coasts into arctic regions and finally sail south along the west coast of Greenland to the Eastern Settlement.

But – again according to Eirik's Saga – Karlsefni sailed not southwards, but in the *opposite direction*. He sailed north along the west coast of Greenland to the Western Settlement, and then to Helluland (Baffin Island). This is very strange. And, in fact, for those scholars who maintain that Eirik's Saga is the more reliable of the two Vinland sagas, the problem of Karlsefni's northerly route has proved insoluble. Reeves (1890: 172 ff.) states: 'This passage is one of the most obscure in the saga ... it is not apparent why Karlsefni should have first directed the course to the north-west, when his destination lay to the south-west.'

Here the author of Eirik's Saga ignores his own preceding text, and lets Karlsefni sail north instead of south; in other words, he assigns to Karlsefni the route which Leif had followed according to Grœnlendinga Saga. There can be only one explanation: the author must have made use of Grœnlendinga Saga, here as elsewhere. He 'borrowed' the Vinland route of that saga, a fact borne out by a number of elements in the subsequent account of Karlsefni's voyage. If Eirik's Saga's northerly route is a literary construction, then the entire basis of the account of Karlsefni's Vinland voyage fails.

Eirik's Saga not only tells us that Karlsefni 'borrowed' the route which Leif had taken according to Grœnlendinga Saga – it also gives Karlsefni the credit for having discovered the very land which Leif had discovered. He even gives this land the same name which Leif had given it – *Helluland*.

The description of Helluland is somewhat different from that given in Grœnlendinga Saga; it seems likely that the author of Eirik's Saga here employed as camouflage the same method as the one he used in the elaborate account of Eirik's fall from his horse, an episode which must also be a loan from Grœnlendinga Saga.

Karlsefni is also given the credit for having discovered Markland, which, according to Grœnlendinga Saga, Leif had discovered and given this name. Karlsefni continues to sail along a route which he cannot have sailed, and there can hardly be any doubt as to the author having employed Grœnlendinga Saga also here, in favour of his own compatriot.

Next we learn that Karlsefni found a keel on a cape, which was then called Kjalarnes (Keelness). This is a parallel to a passage in Grœnlendinga Saga's account of Thorvald's voyage. After he had repaired his ship, Thorvald had raised the old keel on a cape and called it Kjalarnes. This event took place during an exploratory voyage undertaken by Thorvald, when he sailed from *Leifsbúðir* in Vinland to the north-eastern parts of the country. Thus these two accounts cannot possibly refer to the same cape. Grœnlendinga Saga gives a down-to-earth explanation while Eirik's Saga gives no explanation at all of the remarkable fact that the keel of a ship was found on a cape on a strange and distant coast. In any case, it is highly improbable that a ship's keel should have drifted to a cape in Labrador, about a thousand years ago.

Thus Eirik's Saga has identically the same, most unusual element as Grœnlendinga Saga – a keel on a cape which is then called Kjalarnes. This can hardly be a matter of coincidence. I have no hesitation in maintaining that we here have yet another example of the author's use of Grœnlendinga Saga. Again we meet this method – an element which in Grœnlendinga Saga was connected with Leif's discovery of Vinland, and unrelated to his Norway voyage, is moved to a 'neutral' place in the text.

Further, we read that Karlsefni came to a coast with long beaches and sands – *par var œrœfi ok strandir langar ok sandar*. Grœnlendinga Saga has a similar description of a corresponding region, there connected with Leif's Vinland voyage. The voyagers went ashore in a boat and found a flat land 'covered with forest, with extensive white sands wherever they went, and shelving gently to the sea' – *sandar hvitir víða par sem pier fóru, ok ósæbratt*. These features from similar regions, shared by the two sagas, indicate that the author of Eirik's Saga made use of Grœnlendinga Saga also here. The only new item of any importance in Eirik's Saga is the naming of the long beaches, they are called Furðustrandir, i.e. Marvelstrands, 'because sailing past them took so long'.

A factor of particular importance to the historical appraisal of Markland, Kjalarnes and the long beaches is the following: it is clear that, up to this Point, the author made systematic use of the Vinland route and, with some changes which would serve as camouflage, of the descriptions given in Grœnlendinga Saga, in connection with the various localities, and that he assigns to Karlsefni the honour of having made Leif's discoveries. He probably had Grœnlendinga Saga before him as a model, and thus it is hardly surprising that he continues to borrow from that saga for his description of Markland – on the contrary, it would have been surprising if he had not done so. But then, when Karlsefni has sailed from Markland, this is precisely what happens – the author of Eirik's Saga stops using Grœnlendinga Saga as his model. The account dealing with the remainder of the voyage is entirely new: first we are given a diffuse piece of information about some fjords, and a fable about two Scottish runners who return with bunches of grapes and ears of wheat in northerly regions, and then we are presented with Straumsfjord, where Karlsefni is said to have made his headquarters.

There can only be one explanation why the author of Eirik's Saga should have departed from the essential description of Grœnlendinga Saga precisely at that final phase of the Vinland voyage. In his account of the voyage from the Eastern Settlement and as far as Markland, the author of Eirik's Saga could transfer material from Grœnlendinga Saga – provided he made certain changes and additions, without much risk of being discovered. But when he reached the final stage, Leif's voyage to Vinland, the description of the land where Leifsbúðir were built, and the events which took place in Vinland, matters were entirely different. This material was so obviously incompatible with the version according to which Leif was alleged to have discovered Vinland when on his way home from Norway, that it had to be discarded. The author, as we have seen, chose to give Karlsefni a new route, and a new headquarters, and he does not use the name Vinland but invents the name Straumsfjord.

The expedition can hardly have sailed very far, according to the account, when the fable about two Scottish runners, Haki and Hekja, comes into the story. They run southwards for a day and a half, and return with grapes and ears of self-sown wheat in their hands.

This interpolation is highly instructive with regard to the literary methods employed by the author. Karlsefni's task was to find the land with vines and self-sown wheat which Leif is said to have discovered. The present section prepares the way for his ostensible discovery of the wonderful Hóp, where these blessings are later found. But the author is unaware of the fact that he is seriously undermining the credibility of his own, subsequent account. Firstly, the whole description indicates that Karlsefni's position must be far north of the region where wild grapes grow. If we were to take the story of the two Scottish runners seriously, they could not possibly have reached a land of grapes by running south for a day and a half, through forests and shrubby undergrowth in a rugged wilderness. The next port of call, Straumsfjord, must lie fairly far north; the account makes it quite clear that there are no grapes there, even though the expedition must by now have been in a more southerly position than the ostensible land of grapes and wild wheat, which the two Scottish runners are said to have reached. There is no logic of any kind in this. The author has overplayed his cards.

Then Karlsefni came to an island which he called Straumsey. It lay at the mouth of a fjord. There were so many eggs that one could hardly set a foot down between them. This cannot be correct. Because of the ice conditions the expedition must have started fairly late in the year, and by the time they reached these parts, the eggs must have been hatched.

STRAUMSFJORD, KARLSEFNI'S HEADQUARTERS

The saga continues: They held on into the fjord, and called it Straumsfjord, and here they carried their goods off the ships and made their preparations. They had brought all sorts of livestock with them, and looked around at what the land had to offer. There were mountains there, and tall grass and the prospect round was beautiful. They spent the winter at Straumsfjord, and a hard winter it proved, with no provisions made for it; they were in a bad way for food, and the hunting and fishing failed. Then they went out to the island, and their stock did well there, but there was little for them to eat. So now they prayed to God, that He should send them something to eat. Then it happened that Thorhall the Hunter disappeared. Men set off to look for him, and Karlsefni and Bjarni found him on the peak of a crag, staring up at the sky, with both eyes and mouth and nostrils agape, scratching and pinching himself, and reciting something incomprehensible. A little later a whale drifted in, but they had no notion of what kind of whale it was. Karlsefni had a wide knowledge and experience of whales, but for all that did not recognize this one. They ate of it and were all taken ill of it, at which Thorhall came forward and said, 'Was it not the case, that Red Beard (Thor) proved a better friend than your Christ? This is what I get for the poem I made about Thor my patron.' But the moment men heard this, no one would make use of the food; they threw it over the cliff and committed their cause to the mercy of God. Then all went well, the weather improved and they were enabled to row out fishing and there was no shortage of provisions.

The accounts dealing with Karlsefni's headquarters, Straumsfjord, must not in any way call to mind Leifsbúðir in Vinland. This the author has achieved partly by moving certain elements of Grænlendinga Saga, partly by changing others. Thus the detailed description given in Grænlendinga Saga of the land around Leifsbúðir is transferred almost identically to that of *Hóp*, the next place to which Karlsefni is said to have come. Both passages mention the shallow waters; there is a river flowing out of a lake, and the ship could be brought up this river only at high tide. We read about houses being built by the lake. Even the climate seems to have been transferred to Hóp. In both sagas we are told that the cattle might graze out in the open during the winter. These identical and detailed elements can hardly be the result of coincidence: if we compare these passages with the author's earlier systematic use of Grœnlendinga Saga, according to the method that nothing must conflict with Leif having discovered Vinland on his way home from Norway, and bear in mind other very suspicious aspects of the description of Karlsefni's headquarters, there can hardly be any doubt about Straumsfjord having been substituted for Leifsbúðir in Vinland.

Now the question is this: what can we conclude from Eirik's Saga's account of the expedition to Straumsfjord? Establishing a headquarters is of great importance for any expedition in a distant, unknown land. Matters concerned with the building of houses will be remembered by the participants, and at least some information about such a 'home' in the wilderness would normally go down in tradition. Grœnlendinga Saga has factual information to the effect that Leif first built booths, and later 'large houses'. But Eirik's Saga has only this to say about the establishment of a headquarters for 160 people: they made their preparations – *ok bjǫggusk þar um*. Surely this is surprisingly little, seeing that the subject was of great importance.

At this point we have the first mention of the livestock of all sorts which they had brought along – *alls konar fénað*. Jóhannesson (1962: 65) shows that Eirik's Saga's account of the livestock is word for word the same as that of Grœnlendinga Saga, and he adds: 'It would be dangerous to assert that this is pure coincidence.'

About the winter they spent at Straumsfjord, Eirik's Saga states that the people experienced great want, for they had not made any preparations for the winter. They paid no heed, so we are told, to anything except exploring this beautiful land. If this should be in accordance with actual fact, then Karlsefni must have been the worst expedition leader ever, for the first task of a leader of an expedition in a strange and unknown land will always be that of making provisions for the winter by hunting and fishing. Next follows the description of their desperate plight, when the expedition barely managed to survive by moving out to the island.

Above I pointed to the untrustworthy impression of the strange, verbose description of Thorhall the Hunter at the beginning of this chapter; we must also consider the following in this connection – he disappears, and is found in a most peculiar state of mind, he is staring up at the sky with open mouth and nostrils, he scratches and pinches himself, and mumbles something. The similarity between Tyrkir's behaviour in Grœnlendinga Saga and Thorhall's in the present context is so striking that it cannot be a matter of coincidence. The author must have had Tyrkir in mind when writing this passage.

Moreover, this chapter also contains a number of other improbable features connected with Thorhall, and we must infer that he is an unhistorical character.

The statement to the effect that no one knew what kind of whale it was that came in also gives grounds for scepticism, for the Norsemen were whalers. But the author may, by stating that they did not know what sort of whale this was, have intended to endow it with a supernatural element.

Thorhall the heathen now becomes the most important character, the red-bearded god Thor enters the story, and the account acquires the nature of a contest between heathendom and Christianity. Christ is victorious, and the people commit themselves to His mercy. This reads like a verse of the Bible, and clearly it is entirely foreign in spirit to the Viking Age.

Grœnlendinga Saga merely states that a large rorqual washed ashore, providing the people with plenty of food. Just as he had taken Grœnlendinga Saga's Tyrkir as his model for Thorhall, so the author of Eirik's Saga probably borrowed the whale as a motif for the supernatural account above. In both cases the subject matter is greatly extended and embellished, and in its new form one would hardly suspect that it had derived from Grœnlendinga Saga.

Altogether Eirik's Saga's description of the ostensible headquarters at Straumsfjord includes a number of salient points which are improbable, and several of these would seem to show that the author made use of Grœnlendinga Saga. This fact adds weight to my previous argumentation showing that Karlsefni's headquarters at Straumsfjord is the author's invention, a substitute for Grœnlendinga Saga's Leifsbúðir in Vinland.

THORHALL SAILS AWAY
TO THE NORTH
IN SEARCH OF VINLAND
Eirik's Saga IX

Now they talked over their expedition and made plans. Thorhall the Hunter wished to proceed north by way of Furðustrandir and Kjalarnes, and so look for Vinland. His crew consisted of no more than nine men. Karlsefni wished to travel south along the coast, and explore the land there together with the other members of the expedition.

Thorhall now made ready for sailing, and one day, when he was carrying water to his ship, he took a drink and recited a lay. In this he declared that he had been promised the choicest of drink, and cursed the fact that he now had to toil and carry water, while not a drop of wine had passed his lips. When he put to sea, he chanted another high-sounding lay to the effect that he was now sailing back to his own Greenlanders, while those who remained and who thought that this new land was so wonderful could go on boiling whale at Furðustrandir.

The prose text which follows this lay states that Thorhall sailed north past Furðustrandir and Kjalarnes, intending to bear to westward, but he met with a storm and was shipwrecked off Ireland where he and his crew were badly beaten and enslaved. Thorhall lost his life there.

It seems most peculiar that Thorhall, who was a subordinate member of the expedition, suddenly appears in a position of authority. The prose text gives the impression that it was he who decided that the ship was to leave the expedition. The ship in question is presumably that belonging to the Greenlanders.

Why ever would Karlsefni and the others allow Thorhall to leave the expedition with only nine men on board the ship? As a result, those who remained behind would be in a very perilous situation. If the expedition consisted of 160 men and some women on three ships, as the saga states, the remaining 151 would have to sail on two ships only, once Thorhall had left with one ship. This means that seventy-five people would have to sail on each ship, and so great a number is likely to have constituted a serious overload in the perilous waters in which they must sail. Moreover, so numerous a crew would take up much of the space required for cargo.

Furthermore, the statement about Thorhall wishing to look for Vinland in the north does not seem to make sense. It is quite clear that Straumsfjord was a fairly northerly area, where the expedition encountered great difficulties, and where no vines grew. How, then, could one expect to find Vinland by proceeding further north? The account becomes no less incomprehensible when we read that Thorhall wanted to sail so far north that he would go by way of Furðustrandir and Kjalarnes, places which the expedition had passed when they were on their way out, sailing southwards, and which they had found too unfavourable for settlement! As Furðustrandir are probably the long, striking beaches near Cape Porcupine in Labrador, one must bear in mind that there is so little grass in Labrador that the land can by no means be said to be favourable for stock-keeping. It is quite out of the question that anyone should expect to find grapes at this latitude.

Thorhall's search for Vinland in the north is fiction. The author may possibly have been thinking of the fantastic story of Haki and Hekja, who were said to have found grapes and wild wheat when they ran from a fjord north of Straumsfjord.

The verses are constructed with great care, with kennings, internal rhyme, etc.; their structure is grandiosely conceived, with figures such as warriors, helmets, swords, blood etc. Obviously the author was a professional poet who mastered the technically difficult art of Norse poetry. A surprising aspect of these verses is the fact that they diverge from the prose text on several important points, as we show below:

PROSE TEXT

1. Thorhall leaves the expedition while they are at Straumsfjord, and with nine men he sails north in order to find Vinland.
2. The remaining members of the expedition stay at Straumsfjord.
3. Karlsefni's expedition had fallen ill after eating of the whale Thor had poisoned. This happened at Straumsfjord.

VERSE

1. Thorhall declares in his lay that he is leaving the new land in order to sail home to Greenland.
2. The remaining members of the expedition are at Furðustrandir.
3. Those who remained behind boiled whale meat at Furðustrandir.

These verses have been interpreted in various ways in the course of time. Discrepancies between prose text and verses are not uncommon. Such discrepancies do not justify the conclusion that the verse is authentic and historical. The fact that Thorhall is undoubtedly an unhistorical figure is of importance in this matter. The assertion that the version given in the verses with regard to this fictitious personage is authentic requires a burden of proof, a requirement no one seems to have fulfilled. The verses' references to a land of vines and grapes – a leitmotif in the Vinland sagas – and to Thorhall's patently absurd voyage north to find Vinland lead to the conclusion that these verses are a later literary composition. It can hardly be regarded as being over confident to reach this conclusion.

The final part of this chapter corresponds well with the earlier fanciful account of Thorhall, who defied God and the Church. We have seen that he sailed far north expecting to find grapes in regions where no grapes could possibly grow. It is no less incredible that he then sailed westwards, only to be tossed by a storm across the Atlantic to Ireland.

Thorhall's fate fits in well with the rest – in Ireland he is beaten, enslaved, and dies. And thus the author concludes his moralizing Christian account about this man: the wicked pagan has received his punishment – Christianity emerges victorious.

KARLSEFNI'S EXPEDITION
SAILS SOUTH TO HÓP
Eirik's Saga X

Karlsefni sailed south along the land with Snorri and Bjarni and the rest of their company. They sailed for a long time and came to a place which they called *Hóp*. Here a river ran from a lake down to the sea, and there were extensive shallows off the estuary so that one could get up the river and into the lake only at high tide. There they found self-sown fields of wheat in the low-lying land, and vines where it was hilly. There was a vast number of animals of all kinds in the forests, and every river was full of fish. They dug pits by the shore, and at low tide there was halibut in these pits. They had their cattle with them.

When two weeks had passed, they saw nine skin-boats on the water, on board which staves were being swung. Their motion was sunwise, and they sounded just like flails threshing. Snorri thought that this might be a token of peace, and said that they should meet these people with white shields. They did so. The natives came ashore, looked around for a while, greatly puzzled, and then they returned to their boats and disappeared. They were small, ill-favoured men, with ugly hair, big eyes and broad cheekbones. Karlsefni and his men built houses, some near the lake, others a little away from it. They spent the winter there. No snow fell, and the cattle grazed out in the open.

This description of Hóp is, as we have already seen, almost identical with that of Leifsbúðir given in Grœnlendinga Saga: the shallow waters, a river flowing from a lake into the sea, where ships could enter only at high tide, houses built near the lake, a winter so mild that the Norsemen's cattle could graze out in the open. The fact that the two accounts share these significant features can hardly be due to coincidence; we have already seen that it is most likely that the author here transferred Grœnlendinga Saga's description of Leif's Vinland to Hóp, which becomes Karlsefni's Vinland.

Next comes an effusive description, almost like a fairytale, of all the blessings found at Hóp. This land had everything the Norsemen might wish for – vines, fields of self-sown wheat, and large quantities of game and fish. Nansen (1911, I: 345-6) seems to be right when he maintains that this description must have been inspired by Isidore's Fortunate Isles, *Insulae Fortunatae*, where all good things are to be found, including self-sown fields of corn on the plains and wild grapevines on the hills.

One would have expected the author of Eirik's Saga to have made mention not only of vines, but also of grapes, obviously the most interesting part of the plant. The reason for this omission is probably the fact that only vines – *vinviðr* – are mentioned in connection with Leif's discovery of Vinland. The author of Eirik's Saga may have used the identical word in order to emphasize that Karlsefni had come to Leif's Vinland.

The statement about trenches being dug by the shore, about fish being caught in this way at low tide, is interesting. It refers here to an unhistorical 'fortunate land', but it may derive from a source different from that of the rest of the text. This is an ancient Norse method of fishing, employed in northern Norway, but the saga is on the wrong track when specifying halibut, a deep-water fish – this method was employed when catching flounder.

It is of interest to note that immediately off the Norse settlement at L'Anse aux Meadows there are such great quantities of small flounder that they can at times, in shallow water, be seen lying packed close like tiles on a roof. We made use of the method described in the saga, dug trenches by the shore when the tide was low, and at the next low tide there were flounders in them.

The description of the meeting with the natives is remarkable in several respects. The magic number nine is employed; moreover, it seems most unlike either Eskimos or Indians to engage in this mysterious swinging of staves, at their first meeting with Europeans. In any case, how could the people who saw the boats from land be sure that all the staves were being swung sunwise, when the position of these native boats would be constantly changing? Why ever should Karlsefni's men interpret this swinging of staves, accompanied by the sound of threshing, as a token of peace? And how on earth could the natives know that the white shields held out by Karlsefni were intended as a token of peace?

This latter element is, in any case, anachronistic, for the use of white, and of white shields, as a token of peace is connected with Christianity (Falk 1914: 128ff.). In Karlsefni's day Christianity had only just reached Iceland and Greenland. Moreover, the idea of Norse seafarers on a voyage to a far distant wilderness taking along not only many white shields but also, as appears from a later passage of the saga, red shields, seems absurd.

TRADE AND BATTLE
WITH THE NATIVES AT HÓP
Eirik's Saga XI

The expedition spent the winter at Hóp, and then, in the spring, they met the Skrælings for the second time. On this occasion so many skin-boats appeared that the bay looked as though it were sown with coals, and staves were being swung on every boat. Karlsefni and his men raised their shields, and they began trading together. Above all, the natives wanted to barter red cloth in exchange for fur. They also wanted to buy swords and spears, but this Karlsefni would not allow. Then a bull ran out of the forest bellowing loudly; the Skrælings were terrified, ran to their boats and disappeared.

Here we again have the same peculiar tokens of peace – the waving of staves, probably sunwise as on the earlier occasion, and the raising of shields which must presumably again have been white. There is certainly an element of truth in that primitive people are often fond of highly coloured objects, and it seems not unlikely that they would be interested in acquiring red cloth – but the author's knowledge of this need not derive from America. For hundred of years the Norsemen had traded with the Lapps of northern Norway and with the Beormas living by the White Sea. At the time the saga was written, there was probably also trade between the Greenlanders and the Eskimos, and it would be strange if knowledge of this had not reached Iceland.

We saw above that almost the entire description of the landscape and of the climate contained in Grœnlendinga Saga's account of Leifs-búðir in Vinland was transferred to Eirik's Saga's Hóp. The present chapter also contains examples of the same practice.

According to both sagas Karlsefni traded with the Skrælings at their second meeting. In both, Karlsefni forbids his men to give the Skrælings weapons in exchange for their goods, and in both we have the extraordinary episode of the bellowing bull frightening the Skrælings, who then run away in a panic. These extraordinary, parallel elements connected with entirely different regions and events can hardly be due to coincidence – it seems that the author of Eirik's Saga must have employed Grœnlendinga Saga also for these accounts dealing with Hóp.

THE FIGHT WITH THE
SKRÆLINGS

The saga continues: After three weeks a great number of skin-boats again appeared, like a current streaming towards the camp. This time all the staves were swung anti-sunwise, the

Skrælings yelled, and Karlsefni's men raised red shields. The Skrælings ran from their boats, and a violent battle ensued. A shower of missiles flew through the air, and they sent a big, blue, ball-shaped object flying from poles. It made a hideous noise as it fell among Karlsefni's men, who were so frightened that they fled to some cliffs, from where they continued to fight.

Then Freydis appeared, deriding them for their cowardice. She incited them to continue fighting, and herself took the sword belonging to Thorbrand Snorrason, who had been slain. When the Skrælings made a rush at her, she pulled out her breast from under her shift and slapped the sword on it, at which the Skrælings took fright, ran off to their boats and disappeared. During the battle one of the Skrælings found an axe lying beside a dead Norseman, he tried it on a stone, and it broke. Then he thought it useless and threw it away. Two of Karlsefni's company had fallen, and four Skrælings.

This is the third meeting with the Skrælings, and it is suspicious that Grœnlendinga Saga also has accounts of precisely three such meetings in connection with Karlsefni's Vinland voyage, but in an entirely different region. There they take place at Leifsbúðir in Vinland, where Leif had come during his voyage of discovery which started out from Greenland. Further, according to both the sagas there was no fighting during the first two meetings; the battle took place at the third. Again an adaptation from Grœnlendinga Saga seems probable, a loan transferred to a 'neutral' place, and thus compatible with Leif's discovery of Vinland during his voyage from Norway.

The methods of fighting employed by the Skrælings are most peculiar, and not at all in keeping with what we know about primitive peoples. Again we have this strange swinging of staves, but this time they are swung anti-sunwise, obviously with a view to indicating combat. The au-

thor apparently expects Karlsefni's men to be sufficiently shrewd to understand this. Again the Norsemen raise their shields, red ones this time, an element suggesting the age of chivalry.

The description of the natives steering their boats out into the open, so that the enemy on land could see them and prepare for battle, is not at all in accordance with the behaviour normally associated with native peoples. Karlsefni and his company were then at an advantage in many respects – they could, for instance, attack the Skræling boats as they reached the shore more or less scattered.

There is another important aspect to this matter: Eirik's Saga gives no motive at all for the Skrælings' sudden attack, shortly after they had peacefully traded with Karlsefni's men. Repeated experience has shown that if white men conducted themselves peaceably when meeting primitive Indians or Eskimos, they were as a rule also received in a friendly way, especially when there was a chance of trading. To primitive people the chance of acquiring cloth, fragments of iron, needles, nails, etc., must have seemed wonderful, almost incredible. Once peaceful trading had been established, fighting would be most unlikely to ensue shortly afterwards, unless the natives had reason to feel affronted. But there is no indication of any such affrontery.

It is typical that Grœnlendinga Saga, unlike Eirik's Saga, does give a motive for the battle. There a Skræling, who had tried to steal weapons during the second encounter between the Norsemen and the natives, was killed. During the third meeting the Skrælings attacked, for the killing had to be avenged.

The battle is vividly described in Eirik's Saga. We hear that the natives had war-slings – valsŋngur – and that there was a shower of missiles. There is also mention of a most peculiar weapon, a large, ball-shaped object which was sent flying from a pole, and which made a hideous noise as it landed. Several scholars have tried to associate this with a weapon used by the Algonquin Indians, described by H.R. Schoolcraft (1851, 1: 85). This consisted of a large stone sewn into a cover of leather and painted with various symbols, and it was attached to a pole. The name of this weapon may be 'balista'.

It seems difficult to believe that such weapons would have been practical in a guerilla encounter, the method of fighting which was typical of Indians as well as Eskimos. But Schoolcraft maintains that a weapon of this kind could be used for sinking boats and canoes, and this, I believe, is where it may have been of greatest importance. It seems very doubtful, however, whether this Algonquin weapon really was similar to that described in the saga. How are we to explain the hideous noise it made as it landed, a noise so frightening that Karlsefni's men, who were no cowards, ran away?

Freydis, the Greenlander, daughter of Eirik the Red, suddenly appears on the scene now, although there is not one single mention of her earlier in the saga. Her appearance is highly dramatic, she seizes a dead man's sword and slaps her bare breast with it; the Skrælings are so terrified that they flee. Now Freydis is given the role of the heroine who saves her people. This is in marked contrast to Grœnlendinga Saga's Freydis, who slights an Icelandic crew and has all its members killed.

It seems probable that Freydis represents a loan from Grœnlendinga Saga, rather like Thorvald later in the saga. The Icelandic author of Eirik's Saga would, however, be most unlikely to transfer any elements referring to the grotesque account given in Grœnlendinga Saga, according to which Freydis humiliated a large number of Icelanders, finally killing them. On the contrary, the author chose to show her as a splendid heroine, possibly an attempt at obliterating the impression given by the account in Grœnlendinga Saga, where the wicked Freydis reduces the Icelanders to such sorry wretches.

One of the fallen men is said to have been the Icelander Thorbrand Snorrason. This may be identical with an item contained in Eyrbyggja Saga (ch. 48), where we read that he went to Vinland together with Karlsefni, and lost his life fighting the Skrælings. The erudite author of Eirik's Saga may well have been familiar with Eyrbyggja Saga, deriving the information about Thorbrand's death from that source.

The next element has a clear parallel in Grœnlendinga Saga's account of the battle between Karlsefni and the Skrælings. Eirik's Saga states that a Skræling found an axe lying beside a dead man, cut at a stone with it, and when it broke, he threw it away, considering it useless. According to Grœnlendinga Saga a Skræling found an axe, killed one of his comrades with it, and then another Skræling threw it into a lake. Neither of these two versions makes any sense, a fact of which the author of Hauksbók was aware, for he tried to 'improve' the text. In Hauksbók we read that one Skræling after another cut at a tree with the axe, and that they thought it an excellent tool. Then they tried it on a stone, whereupon it broke and was thrown away. And all this is supposed to have taken place during the battle! The 'improvement' does not make for any better sense.

Thus the versions given in the two sagas have important and highly unusual features in common: a Skræling finds an axe during the battle, he uses it and then throws it away. The fact that so extraordinary a piece of information is presented in a similar way in the two sagas in connection with the account of the battle with the Skrælings, a battle which in both cases took place during the third meeting between the Norsemen and the natives in two different regions, cannot be due to coincidence. The author of Eirik's Saga must presumably have made use of Grœnlendinga Saga also here, modifying the account to some extent, as he did also in other passages.

The battle is described as being fierce and bitter. One would think that quite a number of men would be killed in a clash between about a hundred and fifty Norsemen and a large number of natives, but the saga has it that only two Norsemen and four Skrælings lost their lives. This does not correspond with the impression given by the grandiose description of the battle.

KARLSEFNI RETURNS TO STRAUMSFJORD

It now seemed plain to Karlsefni and his men that though the quality of the land was admirable, there would always be fear and strife dogging them there on account of those who already inhabited it. So they made ready to leave, setting their hearts on their own country, and sailed north along the coast to Straumsfjord. On the way they found and killed five fur-clad Skrælings asleep near the sea, who had with them wooden containers in which there was animal marrow mixed with blood. They saw a great number of animals, and on the cape there was like a cake of dung from them. At last they came to Straumsfjord, where they found everything they needed.

The account of this journey includes a few interesting elements which may be authentic, a surprising aspect in an account which must otherwise be assumed to be fiction. We read that five Skrælings were slain, and that containers with a mixture of marrow and blood were found together with them. Having spent several years living together with Indians and Eskimos in northern Canada and Alaska, I know what great store these natives set by marrow. They often eat it raw, considering it to be the greatest of delicacies. From a nutritional point of view it is, of course, of great value. All hunting peoples living in northern regions share this partiality for marrow, as is also shown by the great quantities of split marrow-bones found on ancient settlement sites. When many caribou were killed, the marrow had to be stored, and in my experience it was stored in containers made from the animals' guts or stomachs, and some blood would as a rule adhere to the marrow. The mention of wooden containers for this purpose may indicate one particular Indian tribe, the Beothuk Indians of Newfoundland, who made extensive use of birch bark for many purposes, not least for making various types of containers, some of them very large (Howley 1915: 69, 84, 87).

Further we hear that the expedition saw many animals, and that on a cape there were so many of their excrements as to resemble a large cake. This may suggest Newfoundland. In the past there must have been a wealth of caribou here, a vital commodity for the Beothuk Indians. Large accumulations of excrements must have been a characteristic feature of the places where these animals gathered. In any case, no other kinds of animals of this coast would leave behind such large quantities of dung in confined areas that it would be worth mentioning in the saga. Moreover, the natural pattern of migration of the caribou indicates that the animals would be in areas near the coast in summer. Interesting in this connection is John Day's famous letter, almost certainly addressed to Christopher Columbus, in which he deals with Cabot's discovery of a land which must presumably be Newfoundland – he, too, mentions that 'dung of animals' was found there.

We have demonstrated a number of fundamental elements of a highly suspect nature in the above part of the chapter, and there can hardly be any doubt about Hóp being fictitious. The mere fact of the description of this region being a loan from Grœnlendinga Saga's description of Vinland seems to be almost decisive. Yet at this point the author surprises us by presenting the apparently authentic elements described above. The explanation of this would seem to be that even though most of Eirik's Saga appears to be fiction, it does contain certain elements of a reliable nature. Such elements may derive from unknown sources related to Grœnlendinga Saga. In the present case, the above elements, which bear the mark of authenticity, may be connected with the curious piece of information which follows:

'It is some men's report that Bjarni and Freydis had remained behind there (in Straumsfjord), and a hundred men with them, and proceeded no farther, while Karlsefni and Snorri had travelled south with forty men, yet spent no longer at Hóp than a bare two months, and got back again that same summer.'

We thus have two versions and, as we saw above, the main version must be fictitious. The version quoted here differs radically from the other, and is incompatible with it in every respect. It must have been practically impossible to sail from Straumfjord in the north, where there were neither grapes nor vines, south to the land of grapes – Massachusetts, New York, Virginia etc. – stay there for two months and then sail back to the headquarters in the north, all in one summer. On the other hand – a fairly short expedition of this kind is exactly what we would expect of people who had settled in a wilderness; they would wish to explore the nature of the land, and hunt at the same time. The account of the brief voyage with a limited number of people seems reasonable and may be genuine.

Most of the principal elements of the main version are incompatible with this account of a short voyage: only some members of the expedition left for the south, the winter was spent at Hóp, their cattle grazed in the open during the winter, the fight with the natives the second year, the story about Freydis who did not participate in the voyage, etc.

Even though this version about Karlsefni's short voyage from Straumsfjord implies that the main account about Hóp is left without any founda-tion, the author nevertheless felt obliged to mention it. This seems to indicate a tradition so strong that it could not be ignored.

KARLSEFNI SAILS NORTH IN SEARCH OF THORHALL

The chapter continues: After the expedition had come to Straumsfjord, Karlsefni set off with one ship to look for Thorhall the Hunter, while the rest of their party stayed behind. He sailed north past Kjalarnes, and then bore away west, with the land on their port side. There was nothing but a wilderness of forest-land. And when they had been on their travels for a long time, there was a river flowing down off the land from east to west. They put into this river-mouth and lay at anchor off the southern bank.

As we saw above, Thorhall must be a fictitious character. His ostensible search for Vinland north of the quite northerly Straumsfjord, Furðustrandir, and Kjalarnes, where no grapes grew, as Karlsefni's expedition must have known from the outward trip is, as we have already seen, devoid of any meaning. Karlsefni's voyage in search of Thorhall makes no more sense than that undertaken by Thorhall. This is corroborated also in another way: we would be grossly underestimating Karlsefni's ability as a sailor and a leader if we were to assume that he would engage in as hopeless a task as searching for Thorhall's ship along North America's enormous, quite unknown stretches of coast, where there is a multitude of islands and fjords, a whole year after Thorhall had left! Thorhall could easily have left the coast and sailed back to Greenland, as the verse he had recited indicated. Moreover, he is said to have come to Ireland. In any case – why should Karlsefni search for him?

Further, Karlsefni had just returned to Straumsfjord from the south, from Hóp, where there were said to be grape-vines; in that case he must

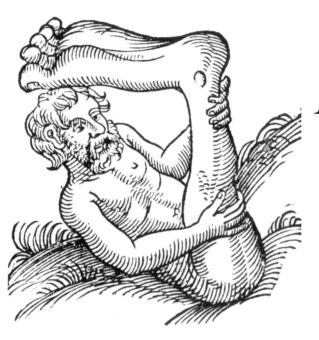

Fig. 27. A uniped (einfœtingr). From Olaus Magnus.

As we saw in the previous chapter, Karlsefni is said to have sailed from Hóp to Straumsfjord, and from there northwards, with one ship, in order to search for Thorhall. North of Kjalarnes he bore westwards, and cast anchor in the mouth of a river. The saga continues:

One morning they caught sight of a uniped – *einfœtingr* – which hopped down to the river-bank off which they were lying. Thorvald the son of Eirik the Red was sitting by the rudder, and the uniped shot an arrow into his guts. 'There is fat round my belly!' he said. 'We have won a fine and fruitful country, but will hardly be allowed to enjoy it.' Thorvald died of his wound a little later. The uniped skipped away and back north, and Karlsefni and his men gave chase. Then one of the men sang a ditty. Then they moved away and back north, believing they saw *Einfœtingaland* (Uniped Land). They were unwilling to imperil their company any longer. They intended to explore all the mountains, those which were at Hóp and those they had now discovered. They went back and spent that third winter in Straumsfjord. There was bitter quarrelling on account of the women. Karlsefni's son Snorri was born the first autumn, and was three years old when they left.

The story of the uniped and of Uniped Land is related to the classical European legend of the uniped, known also in Iceland, and thus it forms yet another example illustrating the author's familiarity with matter derived from foreign literature. The uniped occurs, for instance, in Isidore's widely read works, which were written during the seventh century. Adam of Bremen (*c.* 1075) has the following:

have sailed a very considerable distance from Massachusetts, Rhode Island, New York or Virginia. He would hardly set off on another perilous voyage to the far north very soon after such a strenuous voyage, with the obscure intention of looking for Thorhall.

Nor does such a voyage agree with the saga's text concerning Hóp, which states clearly that the Skrælings were considered to be such a menace that Karlsefni and his men wanted to return to Greenland.

Karlsefni's ostensible northerly voyage compelled the expedition to spend yet a third winter in Vinland; Grœnlendinga Saga, on the other hand, speaks of two winters spent in the new land.

Thus there are a number of points which indicate that the saga's account of Karlsefni's northerly voyage must be unhistorical.

'There are those whom Solinus calls "Ymanto-podes" (one-footed men), who hop upon one leg, and those who delight in human flesh for food, and just as one avoids them, so one is rightly silent about them...' (B. IV, ch. XXV).

The story of Thorvald's death as the result of an arrow shot by a uniped is fictitious. It is quite evident that we here have a loan from an account in *Ólafs Saga helga* (The Saga of St. Olaf), that dealing with Thormod Kolbrunarskald's death. Thorvald, so Eirik's Saga has it, pulled the arrow out of his wound and announced dramatically that the good land had put fat around his guts, but that he would hardly live to enjoy the land. Apart from this, the passage about Thorvald seems to be another modified loan from Grœnlendinga Saga. All elements in that saga in any way suggestive of Leifsbúðir, and indicative of a different discovery of Vinland from that described in Eirik's Saga, have been eliminated. But one well-defined feature is preserved: in both sagas Thorvald is killed by an arrow shot by a native of the new land, but in Eirik's Saga the arrow was shot by a legendary uniped and not by a Skræling, for a reference to one of these natives in this context might be too reminiscent of the version given in Grœnlendinga Saga.

The verse included in the account dealing with the uniped may well be ancient, but it is hardly likely to form part of the original saga, for in that case it would seem incredible that as important an event as Thorvald's death should not be mentioned in the text.

Next we hear, suddenly and without any motive, that the expedition intended to explore all the mountains which had been discovered now, as well as those at Hóp; this is not only curious, it is also in conflict with the remainder of the text, which states quite explicitly that once they had seen the so-called Uniped Land, Karlsefni and his men did not wish to expose their company to any further peril and, so we are told,

they wanted to return to Straumsfjord. As in other legends about unipeds, they are here described as being dangerous creatures. It is no less incomprehensible that these planned voyages of discovery are also said to include the mountains at Hóp, far south of Straumsfjord, the region with vines which the expedition had left because of the danger represented by the Skrælings. They had then intended to return to Greenland. And, in fact, the rest of the saga does not mention these planned explorations with one single word.

The author of *Hauksbók* must obviously have realized that the above text is quite meaningless, and he therefore attempted to improve it. His version runs as follows:

'They concluded that those mountains which were at Hóp and those they had now discovered were one and the same range, that they therefore stood directly opposite each other and extended the same distance on both sides of Straumsfjord.'

But this variant is no more logical than the text of *Skálholtsbók*. Hóp was said to lie in the land of grape-vines, i.e. Massachusetts, New York, Virginia, etc. From here, then, Karlsefni is assumed to have sailed first a long time to the fairly northerly Straumsfjord, and then still further north, past Furðustrandir and Kjalarnes to regions which must correspond to parts of Labrador. Obviously, then, in an unknown region one cannot speak of the same range of mountains in this northerly Uniped Land and Hóp in the land of grape-vines, perhaps more than a thousand nautical miles to the south.

The expedition returned to Straumsfjord, and spent their third winter there. According to Grœnlendinga Saga, Karlsefni spent two winters in the new land, at Leifsbúðir, and we have reason to believe that this is correct. But as the author of Eirik's Saga wanted to include the fantastic version according to which Karlsefni also came to Uniped Land, he had to let the expedition spend a third winter at Straumsfjord, for the voyage from Hóp to Straumsfjord and on to the far north was so long that Karlsefni could not possibly have returned to Straumsfjord in time to risk sailing back to Greenland that same year. According to Eirik's Saga, Karlsefni's son was three years old when the expedition returned to Greenland. Grœnlendinga Saga, on the other hand, states that he was born during the second – and last – winter spent in the new land, and was about one year old when the expedition returned to Greenland. This version is preferable.

Up to this point of Eirik's Saga only one woman, Freydis, has appeared on the scene; she enters the story for no apparent reason, and is accorded a dramatic description which must be a literary product. It is not until now, towards the end of the saga, that there is quite an incidental intimation of the presence of women; yet they are mentioned as though the reader, as in Grœnlendinga Saga, had been aware of them all along. This seems strange.

The saga states that there was bitter quarrelling among the men on account of the women, and this may well be an authentic element, although it must in any case refer to a different text, not to the present, unhistorical account. Perhaps it derives from a source related to Grœnlendinga Saga.

KARLSEFNI
RETURNS TO GREENLAND

The chapter continues: On the way back to Greenland they got a south wind and reached Markland (Labrador), where they found five Skrælings, one of them a grown man with a beard, two women, and two children. Karlsefni captured the boys but the others escaped and sank down into the ground. These boys they kept with them, taught them their language, and they were baptized. They gave their mother's name as Vætilldi, that of their father as Uvægi. They said that kings ruled over Skrælingaland,

one of whom was called Avalldamon and the other Valldidida. There were no houses there, the people lodged in caves or holes. A country lay on the other side, they said, opposite their own land, where men walked about in white clothes and whooped loudly, and carried poles and went about with flags. They concluded that this must be *Hvitramannaland* (the White Men's Land). And now they came to Greenland and spent the winter with Eirik the Red.

This story has some extraordinary features: one of the Skrælings is said to have been bearded, a rare phenomenon among Indians and Eskimos. They were chased, but sank down into the ground. All in all, they appear like legendary beings. The two Skræling boys who were captured told the Norsemen that their land was ruled over by two kings, Avalldamon and Valldidida; this is quite out of keeping with the social order obtaining among the Indians and Eskimos of this northerly part of North America. The natives of these parts were nomadic hunters, who roamed about large districts in groups, and their social order was adapted to their hard struggle for existence, according to a system without a nominal leader. A particularly skilled and experienced hunter might, however, acquire a special position. The saga misleadingly transfers the European concept of kings and rulers to these primitive peoples, which shows how far the author was removed from the original background of the Vinland voyages.

The two names which the captured boys give as those of their parents, Vætilldi and Uvægi must, according to Thalbitzer (1905: 185-209 and 1913: 87-95), undoubtedly be corrupted Eskimo words. This definite conclusion has been accepted by most scholars, and is generally held to be a historical element illustrating the reliability of Eirik's Saga, but to the best of my knowledge, Thalbitzer's statement has never been subjected to any critical study by experts in Eskimo languages. I have put this problem to Professor

Knut Bergsland, who has the most intimate knowledge of the Eskimo languages of Greenland and North America. He kindly prepared a detailed statement on the subject, and made it clear that Thalbitzer's conclusion to the effect that the above words are of Eskimo origin, is based on untenable arguments, and that his account has no claim to any scientific interest.

We are told that the two boys whom the expedition had captured learned the Norse language and were baptized, another point definitely inviting our scepticism. Particularly revealing is the renewed stress on the importance of Christianity – this must be viewed in relation to the unhistorical account of Christianity earlier in this saga, which purports to deal with conditions as they were during the Viking Age.

Another highly suspect element is the Skræling boys' story about a White Men's Land – Hvitramannaland – said to lie opposite their own land which, according to the saga, is Markland (Labrador). There men walked about in white clothes, carried poles and flags, and whooped loudly. Gustav Storm (1888a: 63ff.) is probably right when he identifies this land with the legendary 'Ireland the Great', and maintains the procession must be one of Christians wearing white clothes, carrying banners and singing hymns. Altogether, it seems absurd that all this should have happened in a land opposite a part of Labrador or Newfoundland.

The reason why the author of Eirik's Saga locates Hvitramannaland in North America is probably that he was familiar with, and made use of, the following legendary text from the *Book of the Settlements*, which has an account of a similar Hvitramannaland. The passage deals with Ari Másson, who lived around 980: 'He was driven off course to Hvitramannaland, which some call Ireland the Great. It lies west in the ocean, near Vinland the Good. It is reckoned six days' and nights' sail west from Ireland. Axi failed to get away again and was baptized there.'

THE DEATH OF BJARNI GRIMOLFSSON
Eirik's Saga XIII

On the return voyage, Bjarni Grimolfsson's ship was carried into the Greenland Sea, and came into wormy waters, and before they knew it the ship grew worm-eaten under them. They had a ship's boat, which was coated with melted blubber, and thus it could not be eaten by worms, but it held no more than half the ship's company. Then Bjarni proposed that they go into the boat, but go by lot, and not by rank. And the way the lot fell out, it fell to Bjarni to go into the boat. A young Icelander who had been Bjarni's shipmate, and who had to stay behind on the sinking ship, reminded Bjarni of a promise he had made his father as they left Iceland, and proposed that they change places. Bjarni agreed to this, and went aboard the ship again, and it was said that all those who were on board perished in the wormy sea. Those who were in the boat were saved and reached land.

This romantic story of self-sacrifice agrees badly with the ideas of the Viking Age. It contains such important suspect features that it seems not unreasonable to describe also this account as being unhistorical. First, no part of the cold Greenland Sea can be described as being a wormy sea, as Norse seafarers would know. The author of *Hauksbók* was clearly aware of this, and therefore he tried to 'improve' the text by substituting the Irish Sea for the Greenland Sea, but this does not make any better sense. In any case, it really seems too fantastic to imagine a swarm of worms attacking a ship during a single voyage in northern waters, riddling it so badly that it was bound to sink! We learn that the ship's boat was impregnated with seal-blubber, and thus immune to worms – why, then, had not the ship been prepared in a similar way, as was ancient practice? When Norse sailors, experts in maritime matters, were preparing for the long and difficult crossing back to Greenland, they would surely as a matter of course put their ship in first-class repair in all respects, a process which includes the thorough preparation of the bottom of the ship.

Thus this account can hardly be historical, but it is also obvious that the author was not familiar with maritime matters. The touching description of the self-sacrificing captain must, however, have fascinated any audience.

KARLSEFNI'S RETURN
TO ICELAND
Eirik's Saga XIV

Two summers later Karlsefni returned to Iceland, and Snorri with him, and went home to his place at Reynisnes. His mother considered he had made a poor marriage, and did not stay in the same house with them that first winter. But once she found Gudrid to be so remarkable a woman, she returned home, and they lived happily together.

The chapter ends by enumerating some of Karlsefni's and Gudrid's descendants: Hallfrid, the daughter of Snorri, Karlsefni's son, who was the mother of Bishop Thorlak Runolfsson (1118-33), their second son Thorbjorn, whose daughter Thorunn was the mother of Bishop Bjorn Gilsson (1147-62). Karlsefni's son Snorri had a son by the name of Thorgeir, the father of Yngvild, mother of Bishop Brand the first (1163-1202).

It is probably correct that Karlsefni's home was at Reynisnes. It seems very strange, however, that the long account of the Vinland voyage does not mention Gudrid even once, although she had been accorded a detailed and laudatory description in the first part of the saga. Now she appears at this late stage, after the expedition was over.

Karlsefni's mother's attitude is difficult to understand – she refused to live together with Gudrid during their first winter in Iceland, considering as she apparently, did that Karlsefni had married beneath himself; yet it was her own son and his wife who had returned home after many years abroad. They had been in a distant, unknown land, where they accomplished a great feat, a feat which must have been renowned all over Iceland.

In the genealogy appended to the saga Bishop Brand Sæmundarson is described as Bishop Brand the first, thus differentiating between him and his grandson Bishop Brand Jonsson (1263-64). In other words, the author knew of the latter, and thus the saga may well have been written after 1264.

SUMMARY
Eirik's Saga

It is clear that the author of Eirik's Saga was a learned man, probably a cleric. He seems not only to have possessed an extensive knowledge of Icelandic literature, but he was also familiar with ideas deriving from the literature of Europe.

The saga's heroes are Thorfinn Karlsefni and his wife Gudrid, who are frequently accorded great prominence. The Greenlander Leif is mentioned merely in so far as he served as a necessary precondition for Karlsefni's Vinland voyage (Leif's discovery of Vinland), and to promote the prestige of the Church. Once these aspects were fulfilled, Leif had served the author's purpose, and is completely eliminated from the saga. He is not even mentioned in connection with Karlsefni's stay at Brattahlið before he set out on his expedition, in spite of the fact that conferences with Leif regarding his discovery would have been essential.

According to Eirik's Saga, Leif had quite incidentally discovered a land with vines on his way back to Greenland from Norway, where King Olaf Tryggvason had commissioned him to christen Greenland. This version differs greatly from that of Grœnlendinga Saga, in which Leif discovers Vinland as the result of a planned expedition starting from Greenland. He takes the route which Bjarni, who had been lost at sea, had followed, but in the opposite direction, and thus he had a sound foundation for his voyage.

Three distinct elements of Eirik's Saga appear to be decisive for an evaluation of the historicity of this saga: firstly – it seems unlikely that Leif should have been able to carry through this extraordinarily long and perilous voyage to a land of vines far south in North America, and back to the colony in Greenland. Secondly – it is obvious that Thorfinn Karlsefni ought to have sailed towards the south-west during his Vinland voyage if he was to find Leif's land with vine-trees, but instead he sailed north along the west coast of Greenland – in other words, he followed Leif's route from Grœnlendinga Saga. And thirdly – it is quite clear that in his description of Karlsefni's Vinland voyage the author of Eirik's Saga made systematic use of Grœnlendinga Saga, in such a way that nothing must conflict with the assertion that Leif had discovered Vinland during a voyage home from Norway. In his use of Grœnlendinga Saga he even goes to the length of according to Karlsefni the honour of having discovered and named Helluland and Markland, regions which, according to Grœnlendinga Saga, Leif had discovered and named. But the next place-name which occurs in Grœnlendinga Saga, Vinland, refers to a region quite different from that which bears the same name in Eirik's Saga, and thus the author of the latter saga could not, of course, use it here. Instead he invented a substitute, which he named Straumsfjord, and this is to be Karlsefni's headquarters. But even so, he still needs a Vinland, and for this he invents Hóp. There are vines, fields of wild wheat and all kinds of other good things here – a promised land. Here again he makes use of Grœnlendinga Saga, the description of Hóp is almost identical with Grœnlendinga Saga's

description of Vinland.

Eirik's Saga contains many other elements of such a character that they must be termed literary constructions. This applies not only to lesser features, but also to rather long sections, such as Thorhall's absurd voyage north, in order to find Vinland, and Karlsefni's subsequent expedition to search for Thorhall, which took him to Uniped Land.

By no means least important is the fact that Eirik's Saga is permeated with Christian reflections, sometimes almost in the form of biblical texts. This practice is most misleading in a text which aims at describing Viking Age Norsemen. Grœnlendinga Saga is far more sober on this point, simply pointing out that Christianity was in its infancy at that time.

The detailed examination of Eirik's Saga given above shows that it is a conglomerate of a number of different sources, combined into a fascinating story about Karlsefni and his great achievement, with all outward appearances of being a historical saga. The various elements are so skillfully combined that it has for many years been held that Eirik's Saga, and not Grœnlendinga Saga, is the authentic saga about Vinland. We are reminded of *Njáls saga*, whose author also employed a great number of sources; this saga, too, gives the impression of being a historical saga, although it is in fact a literary masterpiece. The author of Eirik's Saga was a man of great literary talent, and in my opinion, his saga ranks with some of the finest of the Icelandic sagas from the point of view of literary merit. Although Eirik's Saga is largely unhistorical, it may include, as we have shown, a few authentic elements, which derive from unknown, earlier sources. One of these is probably the mention of Bjarney, i.e. Disko, as the starting-point for the crossing to Helluland (Baffin Island), another the information about Thjodhild's church.

Fig. 28. A whale breaches in lonely splendour over the iceberg-studded waters near Labrador's coast. Photo by Xabi Otero.

The earliest mention of Vinland occurs in Adam of Bremen's Gesta *Hammaburgensis ecclesiae pontificum* (The History of the Archbishopric of Hamburg), which is thought to have been completed in about 1075.

This archbishopric embraced the entire North at that time. In the fourth book of his work, *Descriptio insularum aquilonis*, Adam gives a geographical-ethnological description of the northern countries, including Denmark, Sweden, the Baltic countries, Norway, Orkney, Iceland, Greenland and Vinland.

We know little about Adam, except for the fact that he probably came from southern Germany, and moved to Bremen in about 1066. He was canon in that city, where he also held the important position of teacher at the cathedral school. He was a learned man, well qualified for his authorship. It seems clear that he was familiar with a great many classical and other works, which he employed in his writing: Pliny, Macrobius, Solinus, Bede, Orosius, Isidore and others. Moreover, his sources also included annals, lives of the saints, papal edicts, etc.

The fourth book of Adam's work is one of the most valuable sources for the study of the earliest history of the North. But it bears the mark of the age during which it was written, and it is largely based not on the author's own experience, but on literary and oral sources. There are a number of elements of superstition, there are misconceptions and distortions, and one cannot help being struck by the fantastic legends cited from various sources. We must here bear in mind that in the early Middle Ages many accounts dealing with fantastic or supernatural matters were taken to be reality.

Adam was aware of the fact that the earth was a sphere, but his knowledge in this respect seems to have been theoretical. In accordance with the cosmography current in the Middle Ages, he conceived the earth as a round disc surrounded by an outer ocean. He seems eager to stress the

ADAM OF BREMEN

About
the discovery of Vinland and
conflicting evidence

Fig. 29. The old municipal seal of the Hanse town of Hamburg.

merits of the archbishopric, with the result that facts may become distorted. A typical example of this is his deprecating discussion of Olaf Tryggvason and Harald Hardrade, probably because they followed the English church.

Further we read that in 1053, the Pope had granted ecclesiastical authority of the entire North to Archbishop Adalbert of Hamburg, and to his successors. Adalbert, so we learn, was sought out by people from all over the world, especially from the North, including those from the most distant parts of that region, Iceland and Greenland. They asked Archbishop Adalbert to send them preachers, and their request was granted. Adam also states that Adalbert, through the Icelandic Bishop Isleif, sent letters to the Icelanders and the Greenlanders. These elements do not give a reliable impression, not least when seen in the light of the absurd conception of Greenlanders which Adam expresses in other passages. Here we are probably confronted with an example of his overstatements designed to enhance the position of authority of the archbishopric of Hamburg.

As a historian and geographer, Adam occupies a prominent place among medieval authors, but the weaknesses of his work compel us to appraise the information contained in his books extremely critically.

The fourth book of Adam's work (ch. XXXIX) contains the earliest known source concerning Vinland; the fact that it is quite unconnected with Icelandic literature makes it especially interesting. Moreover, Karlsefni's voyage presumably took place in about 1020, and Adam's book appeared only about fifty years later. Adam gives the Danish king, Svein Estridsson, as his source here, as he does also on several other occasions. It is likely that he, like many authors in the Middle Ages, wanted to make his account appear more convincing by citing a king.

However, it seems much more likely that the information concerning Vinland should have come from Isleif Gizurarson, the first Bishop of Iceland (1005-80). As a young man, Isleif was sent to Germany, where he studied theology, and he was ordained in a monastic school in Westphalia.

In 1055 he went abroad again, this time in order to be consecrated as Bishop of Iceland. First he visited the Emperor Henry III, and then he travelled to Rome, and then to Bremen, to Archbishop Adalbert. He was consecrated here in 1056.

Adam mentions Isleif twice, once in connection with a description of conditions in Iceland, and once in a passage dealing with his long stay with the archbishop, during which great honours were bestowed on him.

It seems natural that Isleif, during so lengthy a stay, should have spoken about the sensational fact that, in his own day, voyagers had discovered vast, unknown regions west of Greenland, which were called Vinland.

In translation, Adam's account runs as follows:

'Moreover, he mentioned yet an island, which many had found in that part of the ocean: it is called Wineland, because vines grow wild there, which yield the most excellent wine. That there also is an abundance of unsown wheat there we have learned, not from fabulous fancy but from trustworthy information from the Danes. Beyond (post) this island, no habitable land is found in this ocean, but all that is beyond is full of intolerable ice and immense mist.'

It will be seen that Adam states that *many* had discovered an island which was called Vinland in the great ocean. This is in agreement with Grœnlendinga Saga, which describes the voyages of Leif, Thorvald, Karlsefni and Freydis, who all sailed to Vinland independently of each other, and who all had considerable crews. It also accords well with the Norse house-sites excavated at

L'Anse aux Meadows, which could probably accommodate almost a hundred people.

The account continues with the discovery of grapes that produced the most excellent wine and of an abundance of self-sown wheat.

As for Adam's final communication to the effect that there is no habitable land beyond Vinland in this ocean, but that all that is beyond is full of intolerable ice and immense fog, he plays havoc with all his own, preceding statements. It is, of course, quite absurd to imagine that a land where grapes grow should border on a polar sea.

Adam, who was from southern Germany, must have had some knowledge about the cultivation of grapes. It seems that he reacts against the absurdity of his own statements, for why else should he need to assert so strongly that this is not a fable, but hard fact? But the self-contradictory information about a Vinland facing an ocean with ice and fog seems to have been so essential an element of his source that he felt bound to include it.

It is of particular interest that Adam's description of ice and fog do not only presuppose a northern Vinland, he also emphasizes fatures which are typical to L' Anse aux Meadows where the Norse sites were discovered. Off the coast, masses of ice and huge icebergs are carried southwards by the Labrador stream. Once, during our excavations, one immense iceberg was stranded just near the coast. The gigantic formations of drifting ice in all kinds of shapes were impressive sights. It is likely that the recollection of such distinctive features would be recorded and retold.

Adam's source for the information of a northern Vinland with "intolerable ice and immense fog" was most probably Isleif from Iceland - who sought out Adam in order to be ordained as bishop.

VINLAND –
THE LAND OF MEADOWS

In 1888 Professor Sven Söderberg, the Swedish philologist, gave a lecture on the subject of the Vinland problems. This was not published until after his death, when it appeared in a newspaper, *Sydsvenska Dagbladet Snällposten* (30th October 1910).

In his opinion the name Vinland had no connection whatever with grapes or vines; he considered it to have been associated with grapes as a result of a false etymological derivation. Adam's conception of the name as meaning the Land of Wine was, according to Söderberg, responsible for the stories of vines and of an abundance of self-sown wheat in the new land, and of the production of the most excellent wine.

Söderberg emphasizes that stock-keeping was, apart from fishing and hunting, the most important livelihood of the Icelanders and the Greenlanders. If they were to settle in a new land, this land must offer good pasture for their cattle. Here it is very much to the point that, according to Ari the Learned, the name Greenland was intended to tempt new settlers, for this name implied that there was good pasture for cattle there.

The name Vinland, according to Söderberg, had a similar, descriptive meaning originally, the syllable *vin* (with a short *i*) being the Old Norse term for pastures, meadows. It is well known that in Norway this word is common in place-names, sometimes as a root-syllable, as in Vinje, Vinju, Vinnan, but more often as a suffix, as in Bjørgvin, Granvin, Bryn (*brúvin), Hegge (*hegg-vin), etc. Norway has approximately a thousand such place-names compounded with vin, and similar names occur also in Sweden, but not on the Faeroes, nor in Iceland. In Söderberg's view there are several reasons for this, including the fact that the different character of the Icelandic place-names is a result of the country's nature, which is different from that of Norway. The absence of *vin*-names in Iceland does not mean that the word had become obsolete at the time of the settlement of Iceland.

Söderberg further assumes that the word vin, in the sense of meadow, pasture land, was known and used in Norway early during the historical period; in support of this he cites *vinjartoddi*, a tribute paid to the king, and *vin-ey*, the island rich in grass, which occurs in the work of the poet Bragi the Old (ninth century) as the name of Zealand. One might add *vinjarspann*, a tribute paid to the king, another term in use during the historical period (Olsen 1928: 195, *Kult. Leks.* XX: Vin II cols. 77-87).

Söderberg considered that there were sufficient grounds for assuming that the term *vin* in the sense of meadow was current in Iceland around the year 1000, and that an Icelander might quite naturally use it in naming a place or a country. The fact that the sagas, as well as other Icelandic sources, mention vines, grapes and wine in connection with Vinland is, in Söderberg's opinion, a result of the authors being familiar with the work of Adam of Bremen, and having accepted his interpretation of the name Vinland.

We saw above that, in Söderberg's view, this incorrect interpretation by Adam is due to a false etymological derivation. The Icelandic term vin with a short *i* means meadow, while the similar term with a long *i* means wine. Adam can hardly have been aware of this difference. Moreover, having come from southern Germany, he was obviously familiar with grapes, and thus it was natural for him to associate the name Vinland with wine.

There are many other such false etymologies in Adam's work. He explains the name Greenland by stating that the people there had become blue-green from the ocean. *Sconia* or Scania is derived from Old High German *sconi* or *schön*. In addition to Söderberg's examples we might add that Adam explains Kvænland as the Land of the Women (Norw. *kvinne*; Old Norse *kvæn* = woman), *Hunner* (Huns) as dogs (Norw. *hunder*, Old Norse hundar = dogs), etc. No wonder then, that Vinland is also incorrectly interpreted. Distinguished scholars agree with Söderberg on several important points. Although it has been asserted that the term *vin* had ceased to be in use before the beginning of the historical period, Magnus Olsen shows convincingly that this can hardly be correct, stating: 'It is exceedingly risky to fix dates definitely where the word-material of an imperfectly known period of the language is concerned.' Like Söderberg, he cites compounds with *vin* known to have been in use during the historical period: *vinjartoddi, vinjarspann* and *vin-ey*.

Magnus Olsen further shows that there are a great number of place-names compounded with *vin* in Shetland. None of these are names of farms; they are all used to designate pasture land. As a rule vin occurs in the first syllable, as in Vinland, but there are also cases where *vin* is employed as a suffix.

The Norse colonization of Shetland dates back to about the year 800, possibly somewhat earlier. Most of the settlers probably came from south-western Norway. According to Magnus Olsen it would be strange if *vin*-names should have been obsolete in the Norwegian countryside at the time of this first emigration. He ends by stating:

'The fact that the Shetlands, who according to the available sources settled from Norway in the 9th century, can show a number of *vin*-names, seems to point to the word *vin* being still used for the formation of Norwegian place names – incontestably as a prefix and uncompounded, not improbably as a suffix.'

Magnus Olsen concludes: 'The theory of the time limit (*viz.* for the latest possible *vin*-formation) has been shaken' (1928: 195). With regard to Iceland he states, like Söderberg: Icelandic nature is so different from that of Norway, as were also the social conditions of Iceland, that the name *vin* was not employed there.

Tanner (1941: 35-95) accepts Söderberg's view with regard to the element *vin* in Vinland originally having meant meadow, pasture land. He points out that both the sagas describe grass in such a way that it seems clear that the Vinland voyagers were primarily concerned with pasture for their cattle; the salient point of the Vinland problem may, according to him, be found here. In his opinion there is no reason to believe that the word Vinland in its original form should have had anything to do with wine. The sagas' meaningless accounts dealing with grapes and vines show that their authors were not familiar with that plant.

A strange German by the name of Tyrkir is brought into Grœnlendinga Saga. His role is that of an expert on wine, he is to prove that grapes have been found. The members of the expedition pick grapes in spring. They load them into the ship's boat. They cut down vine trees as cargo for the ship.

Tanner rightly attaches great importance also to the fact that the earliest Icelandic sources make no mention of grapes and self-sown wheat. In his opinion it is obvious that the saga's mentions of grapes and vines represent a later loan from another part of the world. They may probably derive from Adam of Bremen, possibly influenced by the ancient legends about the Fortunate Isles, *Insulae Fortunatae*.

According to Halldór Laxness (1972: 11), the saga's mention of grapes and wild wheat derive from Adam of Bremen. In his opinion, the passage of Eirik's Saga dealing with these matters is a straight translation of Adam's Latin text.

Adam of Bremen's work was a classic, much used and quoted by scholars in many parts of Europe. With regard to Iceland we must bear in mind that the people there were in much closer contact with continental Europe at an early date than the remote situation of their country would let us suppose. A number of the Bishops of Iceland had studied on the Continent. Moreover, priests, pilgrims and other Icelanders journeyed to many different parts of Europe. One could make oneself understood in most countries by speaking Latin.

Many of these travellers brought European culture home with them. Foreign literature came to Iceland, religious tracts, learned works, legends, text books, and many of these were translated. At the beginning of the eleventh century a school was founded at Hólar, and it appears from the *Saga of Jón Qgmundarson* that Ovid's *Ars amatoria* was known in Iceland at that time. In the remote island far in the north, there seems to have been a thirst for knowledge.

Under these conditions it would be remarkable if the Icelanders had not been familiar also with Adam of Bremen's classic, or at least with the fourth book of this work, which deals with Iceland and with the bishops of that country.

It is quite clear that certain erudite constructions and imaginative embellishments found in the Icelandic sagas are based on Adam's history (*Kult. Leks.* V: col. 285). *Flateyjarbók*, which was written towards the end of the fourteenth century, quotes Adam's work. In view of Iceland's cultural contacts with Europe, it seems very likely that the Icelanders should have become acquainted with Adam's work at a comparatively early date, an opinion shared by Sigurður Nordal and other scholars.

There are also other aspects of this matter. We know that the author of *Historia Norvegiae* (*Monumenta Historica Norvegiæ* 1880, ed. Storm) was familiar with the work of Adam of Bremen, for he employed it as a source for his own book; according to Gustav Storm, it would seem to have been his model. *Historia Norvegiae* was probably written during the 1170s or somewhat later (*Kult. Leks.* VI: cols. 585-6), and it is the earliest history of Norway. It is of particular interest also because it represents a tradition which is quite independent of the Icelandic sagas. The author was probably Norwegian.

It is striking that the author, in spite of his detailed knowledge of Adam's work, has totally omitted the entire romantic story about a Vinland with vines, excellent wine and self-grown wheat. Gustav Storm (1888a: 8) is undoubtedly right when he states:

'Even though the author of "Historia Norvegiae", probably a Norwegian, must have been familiar not only with Adam but also with the local legends about Vinland, he must have considered this story too fantastic, and therefore he omitted it. He knew too well that Greenland was a northern, ice-filled polar island to believe that there could be a "Vinland" nearby.'

It appears clearly from *Historia Norvegiae* that the author of this work was familiar with sources about the North of which we have no knowledge today. He has, for instance, the earliest fairly detailed mention of the Eskimos of Greenland, and of their tools and implements. This account seems, on the whole, to be reliable. Instead of Adam's fanciful account of Vinland, the author of *Historia Norvegiae* writes that 'Greenland extends almost to the African islands'. The author is, in other words, aware of the fact that certain islands had been found not very far from Greenland. The phrase 'the African islands' was presumably used in order to adapt these islands to the cosmography current during the Middle Ages. Greenland was 'the last frontier of Europe', and as only three continents were known, it seems natural to assume that islands which lay beyond Europe, and which could not belong to Asia, must form part of a hitherto unknown, projecting African promontory.

The fact that the author of *Historia Norvegiae*, who was clearly well versed in geographical matters concerning the North, including Greenland, rejected Adam's embellished account of Vinland as a fable, is of significance.

The available material illustrating the language of Greenland is very modest. The most common place-names describe features of the landscape, some being compounded with personal names. This limited material does not include any *vin*-names, but their absence does not entitle us to any conclusion as to the use of this term.

The landscape of distant Greenland is different from that of Iceland in important respects, but this mountainous land with its deep fjords has much in common with Norway. Norse outfarms, unknown in Iceland, have been found there. Greenland has more natural meadows than Iceland, like those known as *vin* in Norway. In view of these natural conditions, combined with the highly conservative language of distant Greenland, it seems not at all unlikely that the word *vin* should have been preserved there, and that the Greenlanders should have used it to describe features of the landscape in about A.D. 1000.

One factor would seem to be of special importance in this connection. Eirik the Red, the Greenlander, came from Jæren on the south-west coast of Norway, a region where *vin*-names, in the sense of meadow, were comparatively numerous (Olsen 1928: 207). Taking into consideration the profound importance which the Norsemen of the Viking Age attached to the family and its traditions, it seems hardly too bold to assume that Eirik kept up many of the traditions of that part of Norway from which his family had come, and that Leif had learned much about these traditions from his father during his childhood. It seems reasonable to suppose that place-names compounded with *vin* meaning meadow, which were so common in the region from which his family came, must often have been mentioned when Eirik instructed his sons in the traditions of their family.

With regard to the isolation of the distant Greenland community, the following statement by Valter Jansson, the Swedish philologist, is of interest (1951: 107): 'We should also note that those parts of the north where *vin*-names are most common belong to the regions where foreign influences are weakest.'

In the above, we have discussed in some detail two essential problems in connection with Adam of Bremen's description of Vinland. One of these deals with elements pointing to the location of Vinland which, according to Adam, must border on a polar sea with intolerable ice and immense fog. But at the same time he emphasizes that grapes which produce the most excellent wine grew in this Vinland of his, which is, of course, utterly absurd.

The other problem concerns the name Vinland – according to Adam, this meant the Land of Grapes. His interpretation must be due to a false etymological derivation; moreover, Adam was not aware of the linguistic finesses in Old Norse, according to which Vinland with a short *i* means Land of Meadows, while the same word, but with a long *i*, means Land of Grapes. For the Norse emigrants, pasture for their cattle was the most important aspect when they considered settling in a new land.

Thus we have studied this question from two angles, and in my view there are many strong arguments in favour of the theory that the sagas' accounts dealing with grapes, wine and wild wheat must be unhistorical additions. The authors of the sagas are not likely to have falsified the text intentionally; they undoubtedly believed that the information given by a classic European source such as Adam of Bremen, must be correct. They must have enjoyed adding these romantic reports about grapes and wine to the sagas, as in this way the renown of their ancestors would be enhanced.

It should be remembered that the Sagas were not written merely as accounts of historic evidence but were also intended to entertain.

Fig. 30. Aerial photo of southeastern Baffin Island. Cape Dyer and the east coast on the right, Cumberland Sound on the left. Photo courtesy of The Department of Energy, Mines and Resources, Canada.

STEFANSSON'S
AND RESEN'S MAPS

MAPS

We have two remarkable maps, both dating
from around the year 1600. Apart from the
west coast of Norway, Iceland, etc., they also
show Greenland and the north-eastern parts of
North America, where the names *Helluland,
Markland* and *Vinland* appear. There is a striking
resemblance between the two maps.

One of them, the so-called *Skálholt-map*, is the
work of an Icelander, Sigurður Stefánsson. The
original of this map is lost, but the Royal
Library in Copenhagen has a copy from 1668,
drawn by Þórður Þorláksson, who was bishop in
Iceland. The copy is incorrectly dated 1570, but
the map cannot be earlier than from about
1590. The other map was drawn by a Danish
bishop and scholar, Hans Poulson Resen, and
dates from 1605.

Sigurður Stefánsson belonged to a prominent
Icelandic family. His father was a clergyman, his
grandfather was Bishop Gísli Jónsson. Stefánson
was born in about 1570, and died around 1595,
by drowning in a river in Iceland. We know that
he studied in Copenhagen in 1592-3, where he
was in the company of his erudite compatriot
Arngrímur Jónsson. After his Copenhagen
period he became principal of the school at
Skálholt (Thorarinsson 1945, *Íslenzkar æviskrár*
IV: 267-8).

Stefánsson was a man of many talents, and he
was held in high esteem in Iceland. His interests
included history, music, literature and painting.
He wrote several learned treatises, but these are
now lost.

Hans Poulson Resen (1561-1638) studied at
the University of Copenhagen. In 1591 he
was appointed professor of dialectics there, and
in 1615, he became Bishop of Zealand. We must
also note that he was on three occasions elected
President of the University, and that a reform of
the learned schools was largely a result of his

*Fig. 31. Part of H.R Resen's map from 1605. From
G.M. Gathorne-Hardy 1921. See fig. 33.*

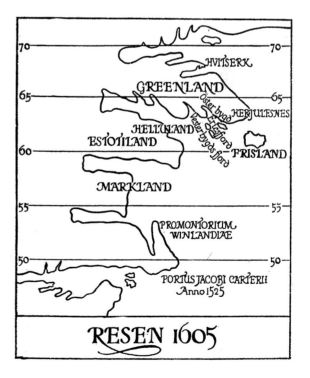

111

Characterum in hac mappa occurrentium, explicatio ipsius Auctoris.

A. Hi sunt ad quos Angli per venerunt, ab ariditate nomen habent, tanquam, vel solis vel frigoris adustione torridi et exsiccati.

B. His proxime est Vinlandia quam propter terrae fœcunditatem et utilium rerum uberem proventum, Bonam dixere. Hanc a meridie oceanum finire voluere nostri, sed ego ex recentiorum historiis colligo, aut fretu aut sinum hanc ab America distinguere.

C. Regionem Gigantum vocant quod ibi Gigantes cornuti sint quos Skrickfinna dixere.

D. Orientaliores sunt, quos klofinna ab unguibus appellarunt.

E. Jotunheimar idem est ac regio Gigantum monstrosorum, hic Regiam Geruthi et Gudmundi fuisse existimare licet.

F. Sinum hic ingentem intelligimus in Russiam excurrentem.

G. Regio petrosa, hujus in historia saepe fit mentio.

H. Haec quae sit insula nescio nisi ea forte quam Venetus ille invenit Frislandiamq; Germani vocant.

Autor hujus tabellae Geographicae perhibetur esse Sigurdus Stephanius Islandus vir eruditus, Scholæ Schalholtinæ quendam Rector dignissimus, qui etiam alia nonnulla ingenii et eruditionis specimina edidit videlicet Descriptionem Islandiae, quam apud Serenissimæ Regiæ Maj.tis Antiquarium Thormodu Torfæum vidisse me memini, nec non opusculum de Spletris, quod præterita æstate ab amico quodam in Patria mecum comunicatum, penes me asservatur. Delineationem autem hanc suam, ex antiquitatibus Islandiae maxima sui parte desumpsisse videtur. De Hellulandia Marclandia et Skrælingialandia videri poterit Arngrimus Jonas, qui ad Calcem opusculi de Gronlandia, Gronlandorum aliquot navigationes ad has terras annotavit, in terrarum etiam hyperborearum ex ultra Gronlandiam delineatione non Risaland et Jothunheima collocat, antiquitates quoq; Islandicas secutum esse Autorem, sat scio, sed an authenticæ illæ sint dubito. Cum priore Gronlandiæ mappa Dñi Gudbrandi sarum consentire hanc satis constat. Islandia hic justo majorem habet latitudinem, Promontorium etiam Huitsark, ingentis continentis potius quam isthmi, vel promontorii speciem præfert, ut cætera omittam, quæ ita curiositatis potius quam necessitatis ergo hanc mappam annotavi.

112

efforts. Resen published a number of textbooks and theological treatises. It is clear that he was particularly interested in the ancient history of Iceland. He was for instance in close contact with Arngrimur Jónsson, whose manuscript Resen read. He was the unchallenged leader of the Dano-Norwegian church, and was known as one of Denmark's most eminent men (cf. *Dansk Biographisk Lexicon* 1982, Vol 12: 144-6).

In Gustav Storm's view (1888a: 28ff.), Stefánsson's map was based on the descriptions contained in Eirik's Saga, while Resen's, according to Storm, was merely an 'improvement' of the earlier map. Storm considered that neither of these two maps can serve as evidence, both are according to him, derivative. Several other scholars hold a similar opinion, while a few, including Gathorne-Hardy (1921: 289ff), consider the maps to be reliable sources based on ancient traditions.

Both these maps were inserted into a Zeno type of map, probably Mercator's map of the world of 1596 or a variant of this, an addition which led to radical changes in the basic map with regard to Greenland and the north-east coast of North America.

Both maps have explanatory texts. The main text of Stefánsson's map is placed at the side and below the map; it is probably his own. Some regions on the map bear names referring to this explanatory text, but there are also other names. Stefánsson's explanations do not lead to a better understanding of his map and its origin; to some extent they are based on Norse mythology. But one aspect is extremely interesting: it is evident that Stefánsson did not himself construct this map, he did his utmost to explain a map which was not his own.

The Latin texts of Resen's map are far more numerous, and prepared with much greater care. Parts were written by Resen himself, parts by his assistants. In translation, the introductory text, which is in the nature of a title, runs:

'Indication of Greenland and the regions in the vicinity, towards the north and the west, according to an ancient map which was drawn in a rough fashion several hundred of years ago by Icelanders, who at that time were very familiar with this region, and according to nautical observations of our own day.'

It appears that Resen possessed considerable geographical knowledge; he refers to Zeno (1380), Johannes Scolvus (1476), Cabot (1497), Corte Reale (1501), Verazzano (1524), Estâvao Gomes (1525), Cartier (1534-43), Frobisher (1576-78), Davis (1585-87), the first Danish expedition to Greenland in 1605, as well as to other expeditions.

It is of particular interest in this connection that Resen, in spite of his learning and knowledge of contemporary geographical ideas, retained the representation given by a map which, with regard to Greenland and the north-eastern parts of North America, deviates radically from the maps of his own day.

Fig. 32. The Icelandic map, c. 1590, drawn by Sigurður Stefánsson. The original is lost; this copy, which dates from 1670, was drawn by Bishop Þorður Þórláksson. The headland inscribed Promontorium Winlandiae *apparently corresponds to northern Newfoundland. Photo courtesy of The Royal Library, Copenhagen.*

GREENLAND

The geographical elements of Stefánsson's and Resen's maps must be considered. In the regions east and south of Greenland both these maps retain the essential features of the basic map of Mercator type.

Greenland, however, displays entirely new features, which do not occur on other maps of the time. In the first place, Greenland is shown running south-east – north-west, while other maps have a south-west – north-east orientation. Further, the shape of Greenland is quite different from that shown on other maps. It is of particular interest to note that Stefánsson's and Resen's maps both show two fjords on the south-west coast of Greenland; on Resen's map these are called Ericsfjord and Vesterbygdsfjord. This correct position is in conflict with the idea held at the time, according to which the Norse settlements were believed to lie on the east coast of Greenland.

Gustav Storm (1888a: 31) maintains that the orientation and shape of Greenland are simply a result of this being a freehand map. But such a postulation is incompatible with the fact that the fjords by which the settlements lay are correctly marked only on these two maps. Moreover, Storm and others with him also assert that the map was drawn after its author had read Eirik's Saga, but the sagas do not contain any information which would induce a cartographer to give Greenland a shape and orientation different from those shown on the maps of the time. As far as the regions east of Greenland are concerned, both Stefánsson and Resen followed a map of a well-known type, but both deviated radically from the cartographic conceptions obtaining in their day when dealing with Greenland; this can hardly be explained unless they had a weighty reason for so doing, probably an ancient map.

This is borne out particularly by the fact that the fjords of the Eastern and the Western settlements are marked on the west coast on the maps drawn by Stefánsson and Resen. Right until the eighteenth century cartographers and historians were firmly convinced that these settlements lay either on the east coast or the south coast of Greenland.

A sketch map drawn by the erudite Icelandic Bishop Guðbrandur Þorláksson (Hermannsson 1926: 31 ff.) in 1606 shows two imaginary fjords on the south coast of Greenland, obviously intended to indicate the position of the Eastern and the Western settlements. Immediately south of the south coast this map has a land called Estotelandia, accompanied by the words *pars Americæ versus gronlandia*. The channel between Greenland and the imaginary Estotelandia is called Ginungagap. In his explanatory text Guðbrandur states that the west coast of Greenland was uninhabited, and that the Greenlanders had no knowledge of it. This is one of the striking examples of the confused geographical conception of the Norse Greenland and Vinland expansion obtaining at the time. It is of interest to note that Resen made a copy of Guðrandur's map, but that he took no account of it when preparing his own. On Jón Gudmundsson's map dating from about 1640 the settlements are shown on the east coast of Greenland; this situation was accepted by Thormod Torfæus, who reproduced the map (1706). A similar position is indicated on Þórður Þorláksson's map of 1668, as well as on certain Dutch maps, for instance those by Joris Carolus (1634) and Hendrick Doncker (1669). The idea that the Eastern Settlement lay on the east coast of Greenland was so firmly established that King Christian IV expressly instructed the leader of the expedition which set out to find the Eastern Settlement in Greenland in 1607, to search along the east coast.

It is of particular interest to note that a long Latin text on Resen's map, placed by the east coast, also describes the Eastern Settlement as lying on the east coast, in direct conflict with his actual map, which shows the fjords of the Eastern and Western settlements correctly on the south-west coast, marked with the names Ericsfjord and Vesterbygdsfjord.

We are here confronted with an author who drew

114

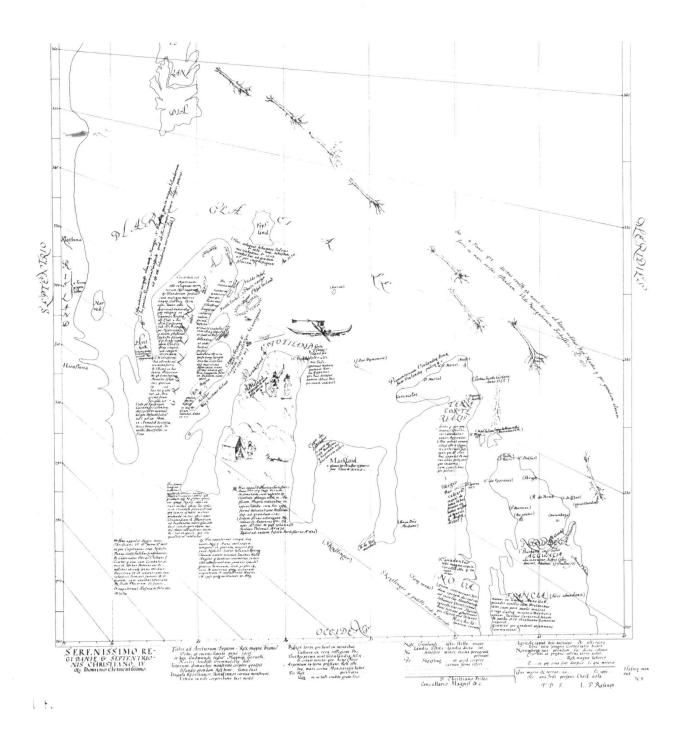

Fig. 33. The lower part of Bishop Hans Poulsen Resen's map of the North, 1605. Photo courtesy of Royal Library, Cpn.

115

and named the fjords of the Eastern and Western settlements of western Greenland correctly, but who nevertheless was apparently so firmly rooted in the ideas of his day that he, in a lengthy text, placed the Eastern Settlement on the east coast, in direct conflict with his own map. This shows that he cannot have constructed the Greenland map himself, but that he must have copied an existing map.

Stefánsson's map has no text to the effect that the Eastern Settlement lay on the east coast of Greenland. Thus this map has no element conflicting with the historically correct fact, according to which the fjords of the two settlements are shown on the west coast.

HELLULAND AND MARKLAND

Stefánsson's and Resen's maps contain important elements different from those of other contemporary maps also with regard to the regions north-west and west of Greenland. When we appraise these elements it is important that we keep in mind the fact that the Greenlanders probably sailed along these coasts for hundreds of years. This nautical activity started with the Vinland voyages, which went first to Disko Island off north-western Greenland, then across the narrow part of the Davis Strait to Baffin Island, and finally south along the coast of Labrador to the northern point of Newfoundland. In the centuries following these expeditions, this route was presumably sailed with a view to hunting, trapping and fetching timber from the coasts of Labrador and Newfoundland. The two peninsulas west of Greenland are shown somewhat differently on the two maps, although they are of the same type. It appears that they correspond to Baffin Island and Labrador. On Stefánsson's map the legend *Helleland* is written right across the northern peninsula, and *Markland* across the other, so that the two names cover all of this projecting region. Resen's map

calls the first of the two peninsulas *Estotiland* (a term borrowed from Mercator or Zeno), while the name *Helleland* – and this is remarkable – is applied to a restricted area up along the coast of Estotiland, i.e. Baffin Island. As on Stefánsson's map, the name *Markland* is written right across the other peninsula.

It is striking that both maps are nearly correct in important respects with regard to Baffin Island and Labrador. There are hardly any parallels to this in other maps of the period. Gathorne-Hardy (1921: 293) was aware of this, and he states:

'There is, moreover, as will be seen by a comparison with the map on p. 219, a striking resemblance to the actual form of Baffin Island and northern Labrador, the shape of the latter peninsula especially in Resen's map being remarkably accurate in points not traceable to any map of the period known to me. The indications of Ungava Bay and Cape Chidley in particular are features unrepresented by contemporary cartographers ...'

We must note, as we saw above, that Resen's texts show that he was aware of several of the arctic expeditions of his day, such as Frobisher's (1576-78) and Davis's (1585-87).

Maps showing Frobisher's discoveries, including Baffin Island, differ greatly from those by Stefánsson and Resen, however; as examples of this we would cite a map of the world published in 1578, and one illustrating the voyages he undertook in 1576-78, both possibly the work of James Bear. The same applies also to maps of Davis's discoveries included in Emery Molyneux' globe (1592), which was made with the help of Davis. Mercator's map of the world of 1569 – which may have been Resen's base map – and his map showing arctic regions dating from 1595 both also differ greatly from those by Stefánsson and Resen with regard to the northerly regions. On Resen's map, as we saw above, the large peninsula which corresponds to Baffin Island is called *Estotiland*. The name Helleland is associated with a limited area quite a way north along the east coast, by the narrow arm of the sea which obviously corresponds to the Davis Strait. This is strange. Why did the cartographer not assign this name to the entire land, as Stefánsson had done, and as he himself had done in the case of Markland? Why did he not at least place Helleland far south on the peninsula, for with such a position the Vinland voyagers would have cut the voyage north along the coast of Greenland short, and sailed straight across the Davis Strait to the southern point of Baffin Island, Cape Dyer.

Here I would refer to the above account of my expedition to Baffin Island (*p.* 41), where I found a landscape strikingly similar to that described as Helluland in Grœnlendinga Saga, near Cape Aston at 70° N – an immense land of plains, stretching from the ocean towards ranges of glaciered mountains (*p.* 42). I also showed that Disko Island off Greenland lies immediately opposite this land, and referred to sources which would seem to show that the voyage across the Davis Strait is likely to have started from this island. The fact that Resen's map, purportedly derived from a centuries-old Icelandic map, also shows a limited Helluland can hardly be due to concidence. Though Disko Island does not appear on Resen's map, Helluland is shown so far north along the Davis Strait that its latitude may well correspond to that of the islands. It is also worth noting that Resen's map shows Helleland north of a bay which looks not unlike Home Bay on the east coast of Baffin Island.

The assertion that the Skálholt map and Resen's map were constructed as a result of their authors having read the sagas does not seem to agree with the fact that the position and form of both Helluland and Markland are, on important points, so close to the actual geographical reality. It seems quite inconceivable that the scant information given by the sagas should have resulted in such close correspondence. Resen's meaningless text about Markland testifies to his meagre knowledge of the Vinland sagas. The text in question runs: *vel plana terra instar æquoris sine silvis et saxis &c* (a land as flat as the sea, without forests, cliffs, etc.), and yet *Markland* means Wood Land.

PROMONTORIUM WINLANDIÆ,

The most remarkable feature of these two maps is the long and narrow headland facing north, which is marked '*Promontorium Winlandiæ*. On Resen's map, this name is furnished with an addition – *bonæ forte Vinlandiæ pulchræ &c* (the promontory of Vinland the Good).

Stefánsson's map does not go further south than this headland, which borders on a deep bay in the west. Beyond this bay lies a region labelled *Skrælingeland*. Resen's map, on the other hand, continues a little further south, and includes much of the Gulf of St. Lawrence and Nova Scotia, where *Norumbega* occurs as an important name. As far as these southerly regions are concerned, Resen based his map on the cartographical science of his own day; he may have made use of Mercator's map of 1569 or of Michael Lok's of 1582.

This is in agreement with the plan on which his map was based; we saw above that he states quite clearly that he was making use of an ancient Icelandic map as well as of the experience gained during later ages.

As Skelton has shown (1965: 205), Resen also included other elements of Mercator's map in his own; thus there are twenty-three names derived from Mercator on the stretch from the Davis Strait southwards. These seem to have been placed very approximately along the coast, and some of them appear on Promontorium Winlandiæ and in other regions not found on Mercator's map.

Promontorium Winlandiæ bears a striking resemblance to northern Newfoundland, and its position indicates that it can hardly represent any other region. According to Stefánsson's map this long headland lies between 52° and 56° N, according to Resen's between 49° and 51° N. This means, in the former case, a position somewhat further north than that of Newfoundland, in the latter, a position which includes the greater part of northern Newfoundland as well as some other areas. L'Anse aux Meadows, farthest north on the coast, lies at 51°36'N.

But accuracy with regard to latitude was not to be expected. Resen makes it clear that he employed an Icelandic map several hundreds of years old – if this is correct, he must have inserted parts of such a map into a sixteenth-century map, a process which must presumably have been somewhat approximate.

The narrow, deep fjord running south immediately west of Promontorium Winlandiæ is an interesting feature of these two maps. Newfoundland was rediscovered by Cabot in 1497, but it was not until 1534 that Cartier's expedition made it clear that a strait, the Strait of Belle Isle, separated Newfoundland from the mainland. Here we must note that from the Labrador Sea in the north, this strait has the appearance of a fjord. Johannes Ruysch, the very able cartographer, who had clearly been north of the strait as early as in 1502, also took it to be a fjord. His map of the world, which dates from 1508, has a fjord roughly in the position of the Strait of Belle Isle. Thus the deep fjord immediately west of Promontoriurn Winlandiæ may refer to an ancient tradition.

To the best of my knowledge no other maps of this coast from the period in question include a region similar in form to Promontorium Winlandiæ and its immediate surroundings. Skelton (1965: 206) admits that it is difficult to find such parallels, but points to Michael Lok's map of the world of 1582, on which the Cortereal peninsula,

according to him, looks somewhat similar. However, this roundish peninsula, which extends towards the north-east, seems to have little in common with Promontorium Winlandiæ. In fact, on studying the earliest maps of Newfoundland, one is struck by the very misleading way in which Newfoundland is generally represented.

Coincidence can hardly be the reason why Stefánsson's and Resen's maps both show Vinland on a long peninsula extending northwards – which must represent Newfoundland – and the fact that the Norse settlement at L'Anse aux Meadows lies farthest north on the distinctly long and narrow peninsula which is Newfoundland, and that the deep fjord shown on both maps would seem to correspond to the Strait of Belle Isle.

We saw above that Gustav Storm and other authors consider Resen's map to be a copy of Stefánsson's, but no pertinent reason for this view is given. Several factors would seem to indicate that Gathorne-Hardy is right when he maintains that the two maps are based on a common source. But Resen's map is more painstakingly constructed, and it includes certain important features which do not occur on Stefánsson's map, such as the position of Helluland quite a way north on the east coast of Baffin Island. It seems unlikely, moreover, that a scholar of Resen's standing, who was in such close contact with his Icelandic colleagues, would not mention Stefánsson's name if he had really copied his map, the more so since Stefánsson was a well-known author, a contemporary of Resen's, and his map had been drawn only about fifteen years previously. On the contrary, one would be disposed to think that the credibility of Resen's map would have been enhanced if he had quoted Stefánsson, that eminent Icelander, as a source.

The assertion to the effect that Resen should have copied Stefánsson's map is also incompatible with the introductory text of Resen's map, which we cited above. There he states that he made use of an ancient map which had been roughly sketched by Icelanders some hundreds of years ago, and also on more recent nautical observations. He again refers to the Icelanders' ancient map in connection with Hvitserk, with the following text (in translation):

'It seems that Norwegian and Icelandic seafarers sailed here long ago, since the promontory Hvitserck is placed here *on the Icelanders' map*, and they could see it (Hvitserck) in the middle of the fairway, as appears from the Icelanders' narrations.'

One is left with the impression that Resen had the Icelandic map before him.

Most authors consider Resen's express statement to the effect that his map was based on an Icelandic map several hundreds of years old to be unreliable. To the best of my knowledge, however, no one has ever given any satisfactory reason to show why Resen should not have told the truth. Resen enjoyed a great reputation as one of the most eminent theologians and scholars in the North, and that is an important point. Add to this the many weighty arguments in favour of the great age of the map he was using, and the burden of proof must devolve on those who assert that Bishop Resen was lying.

THE HUNGARIAN MAP

On an earlier occasion I presented an unknown map of the same type as Stefánsson's. I became aware of this in Hungary. It belonged to Géza Szepessy, who had purchased it from J. Verebes in 1945.

The latter had found it among mixed-up papers at Estergom, after the Germans had evacuated after World War II. It is now in the National Library of Hungary in Budapest (*fig.* 34).

During my investigations in Hungary concerning this map, I conferred with the well-known historian György Györffy, who subsequently kindly sent me in manuscript form his very thorough report about the map, a report he had prepared together with a runologist, István Vésáry, and a librarian, István Bogdén. The report is too lengthy to be quoted verbatim here; its main points are the following:

The shape of the map, the names, and the projection employed show that it is most likely to derive from Stefánsson's map. Of the twenty-one names on Stefánsson's map, eighteen appear on the Hungarian one, some in a corrupted form.

The Latin texts are absurdly incorrect. The runes may date from the first half of the eighteenth century, or they may have been copied from publications. Some of them are incorrectly written, e.g. *Tengar* instead of *Tenger*, which means ocean. The runic text on the left side of the map 'is evidently in Anglo-Saxon with certain English words'. The translation of this reads: 'Orosius. Then along the northern world and the northern new world, there are/were/ York and Vinland.' This is an anachronistic use of King Alfred's Orosius, which has *Winedaland*, a name without any connection whatever with Vinland.

An analysis of the paper showed that this may date from the latter half of the eighteenth century; it is also possible that it is a later forgery. As there are so many elements of uncertainty, nothing definite can be said about the age of the ink. An examination under ultraviolet light showed that the entire map was drawn at one and the same time.

Györffy arrived at the following conclusion: 'We can establish that the map indicates such material of knowledge which were published in the 18th or 19th century.' His demonstration of the incorrect, in part meaningless, texts is undoubtedly correct. They testify not only to a lack of knowledge, but also to an almost childish eagerness to make the map appear mysterious.

There can be no doubt that the author of this

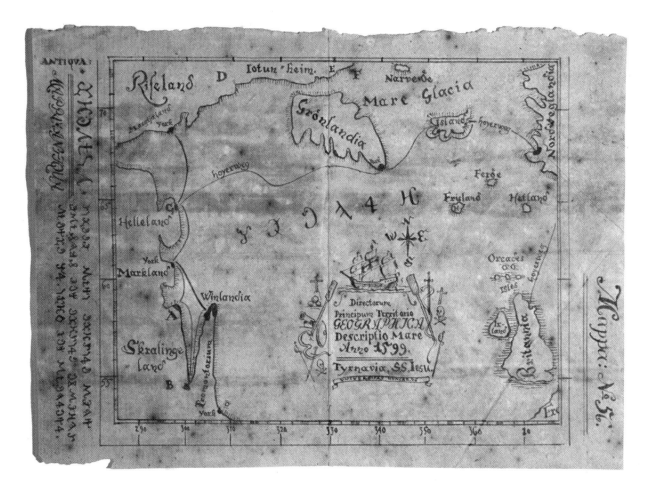

Fig. 34. Map found in Hungary, in the private collection of Géza Szepessy, former museum director. It has important features in common with Stefánsson's map; moreover, a route leading to Winlandiæ is shown in black. Dimensions: 29.8 cm x 21.5 cm.

map had as his model a map of the same type as Stefánsson's. But a great deal of uncertainty attaches to this question.

Györffy rightly dismisses Torfæus' map of 1715 as a model, and Lucas' map of 1898 is a copy of Torfæus'.

We saw above that the earliest known version of Stefánsson's map is in the Royal Library of Denmark. In 1768-69, two Hungarian astronomers had been invited by the King of Denmark to observe the passage of Venus in Vardø in northern Norway. At least one of them stayed in Copenhagen for some time on the way back, and he was elected member of the Danish Learned Society. He may have heard about Stefánsson's map from his Danish colleagues, and may have been given a copy of it.

In 1770, this astronomer, the Jesuit Pater Sajonovics, published his famous book on the Lappish language in Tyrnavia. If we again turn to the Hungarian map, we find that its title includes the name *Tyrnavia* as well as the signature symbolizing the Society of Jesus, 'S. S. Jesu'. But all these interesting elements form sufficient basis only for conjecture. It is hardly possible to show which map formed the model of the Hungarian one.

120

THE SO-CALLED 'VINLAND MAP'

In 1965 Yale University Press published a work by R.A. Skelton, T.E. Marston and G.D. Painter, entitled *The Vinland Map and the Tartar Relation*. An ostensibly very ancient map was presented here: on this Greenland was shown as an island, and west and south-west of this, there was another large island bearing a Latin text which, in translation, reads: 'Island of Vinland, discovered by Bjarni and Leif in company.' Above both Greenland and Vinland a longer text appears; in Skelton's translation, this reads:

'By God's will, after a long voyage from the island of Greenland to the south toward the most distant remaining parts of the western ocean, sailing southward amidst ice, the companions Bjarni and Leif Eiriksson discovered a new land, extremely fertile and even having vines, the which island they named Vinland. Eric (Henricus), legate of the Apostolic See and bishop of Greenland and the neighbouring regions, arrived in this truly vast and very rich land, in the name of Almighty God, in the last year of our most blessed father Pascal, remained a long time in both summer and winter, and later returned north-eastward toward Greenland then proceeded (home to Europe?) in most humble obedience to the will of his superior.'

This map led to an intense discussion as to its authenticity. However, the matter appears now to be quite clear: Yale University had the ink of the map subjected to a modern technical analysis, and after this the university announced (26.1.1974) that the ink contained an element which was not taken into use until the twentieth century. Thus this map must be a forgery.

Fig. 35. Mercator's map of 1569 showing the Arctic regions. From Jomard: Monuments de la géographie. *Mercator based his work partly on information about a polar expedition by an English monk and astronomer, who set out in 1360 from the Eastern Settlement in Greenland. Royal Library, Cpn.*

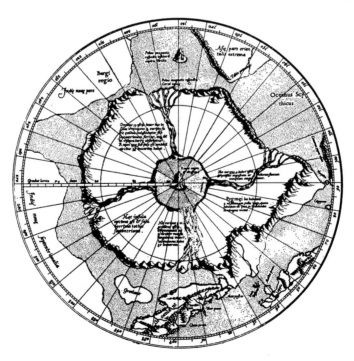

Where is Vinland? This problem has been debated by an untold number of authors for more than three hundred years; the earliest of these include Arngrimur Jónsson (1568-1648) and Thormod Torfæus (1636-1719). It is, with few exceptions, generally held in all this corpus of literature that the sagas' information about grapes is historical in character. As the northern limit of wild grapes lies roughly in the northern part of Massachusetts, it has been maintained that Vinland must lie south of this region. We saw above that several locations have been suggested: Massachusetts, Rhode Island, New York, Virginia and other, more southerly regions. But none of these suggestions has ever been proved.

As a result of studying the sources and other relevant matters, I arrived at a view opposed to that generally held – I came to the conclusion that Vinland must lie north of the regions where wild grapes grow. In *Land under the Pole Star* (1966) I gave my reasons for assuming that Vinland is likely to have lain in Newfoundland. A few other authors have also pointed to the island, for instance Torfæus (1705), Munn (1929), Tanner (1941), Mallery (1951) and Meldgaard (1961).

I further maintained that it should be possible to find traces of the Norse settlement in Vinland by investigating the coasts systematically, from the sea as well as from the air.

My theory was founded on the elements which indicate a northerly location of Vinland, the most important of which are discussed in the preceding chapters of the present book. Citing grounds in proof of my theory, I maintained, for instance, that the name Vinland probably means the land of meadows; that Stefánsson's and Resen's maps, which date from about 1590 and 1605 respectively, and include a peninsula marked Promontorium Winlandiæ, which corresponds to northern Newfoundland, are probably based on ancient Icelandic tradition; that Helluland and Markland are identical with parts of Baffin Island and Labrador, and that 'the Vinland

THE DISCOVERY
of
a Norse Settlement
in America

Fig. 36, p. 122: A National Parks guide waits with two re-enanactors to welcome visitors to the reconstructed Viking settlement near L' Anse aux Meadows, Newfoundland. Photo courtesy of Parks Canada.

Fig. 37. The Halten, the boat used for the expeditions, off the coast of Labrador. Great icebergs often drift southwards here, impelled by the current. Photo by Helge Ingstad.

voyagers could hardly avoid the coast of Newfoundland. And once they were here, these experienced men from the north would soon realize that this was a good country in which to settle', a country offering far better conditions than Greenland, and one suited to their northern culture. In *Land under the Pole Star* (1966: 157), I wrote the following about this matter:

'What must have made the strongest impression on the newcomers, was the pasture and the forest land...For the Norse Greenlanders, coming from an Arctic country, these forests must have represented great riches...Newfoundland was also rich in fish and game, and what is perhaps the world's largest concentration of cod is to be found here, while salmon run up the rivers – a larger variety than that of Greenland, as is noted in the saga. Along the coasts were whale and an abundance of seal, and some way north of the country the Greenland seal has one of its great breeding-grounds. In earlier times walrus came right into the Gulf of St. Lawrence, and polar bears were found farther south than today. Of the land animals the reindeer (caribou) must have been of the greatest importance; thousands of them migrated southward in winter and northward to the coast in the mild seasons. There were also furred animals and great quantities of birds... A good and fair land where Greenlanders and Icelanders would feel at home.'

In 1953, I set out on an expedition along the coast of western Greenland in my own boat, together with my wife, Anne Stine. We sailed to the ancient Norse settlements, and there we investigated a great number of ruins, farms, byres and other out-buildings, churches, convents and monasteries – reminiscences of a people who had disappeared so mysteriously. I gained a very good impression of what life must have been like in this harsh land with its wild mountains, and with great glaciers extending down to the sea, with inland ice stretching like an immense white mantle up to 3,000 metres thick towards the east and along the coast, with masses of drifting ice. Some touches of a brush, here and there in this barren country, lend colour to the landscape – sheltered spots with wind-blown, knurled birches, bright flowers, and the modest green fields by the ancient ruins.

The Greenlanders probably managed quite well here, for they had their roots in a northern culture, and they had grown up with the techniques which life in Greenland demanded, on land and at sea. But so much could happen in this exacting land, where men lived on the limits of human possibilities, where the struggle against the forces of nature was hard, often dangerous. Life was never secure. When the snow lay deep and the ground was covered by ice, the Greenland farmers faced many risks: their sheep could starve to death, their ships could be smashed by drift-ice, and their fishing and hunting efforts could prove to no avail.

These hardships should be taken into consideration in any appraisal of the Vinland voyages. It seems clear that people living in the Norse settlements of Greenland might be tempted to emigrate to more favourable lands, where life was easier. And when the Greenlanders were looking for new land, the standard by which they judged any country would be life in their own arctic home. They did not need to sail very far south along the coast of North America before they would find a land which was more favourable for settlement than Greenland, a land with richer pastures, game, marine animals and fish, a land which offered something new and extremely valuable – large forests. They meant materials for ship-building, and plenty of fuel for extracting iron from bogore.

In 1960 I investigated the coast of Newfoundland from the sea and the air, together with my daughter Benedicte, in the hope of finding traces of Leif Eiriksson's houses in Vinland. After

having searched for a long time without finding anything except relics deriving from Dorset Eskimos, Indians, whalers and fishermen, we came to the north coast of Newfoundland in the autumn. This was the coast in which I was most keenly interested, for the Vinland voyagers on their journey south along the coast of Labrador must have made straight for this shore, which extends eastwards towards the ocean.

As I approached the coast, a low, hilly land loomed ahead; not a single mountain was to be

Fig. 38. The fishing village of L'Anse aux Meadows.

seen. My thoughts turned to the account in Groenlendinga Saga, where the description of the first unknown land Bjarni came to occurs, the first of the lands he saw when he had lost his way at sea during his journey from Iceland to Greenland. This land, we read, was 'not mountainous, and was covered with forest, with low hills...'

One part of this land differed from the rest, a great plain with green meadows – this was L'Anse aux Meadows. We sailed in to a small fishing village, making our way between skerries and islets east of the green meadows.

About seventy people lived in this isolated, little village. There was no road here, nor did the coastal steamer call – and few elements of our modern age had reached this population of fishermen. We felt almost as though we had been transported back into the nineteenth century.

George Decker was the name of the man who took charge. He was a weather-beaten, friendly man, about sixty years old. I asked him about ruins in the vicinity, he said: 'Yes, follow me! We walked along a path leading westwards over a great plain, where some sheep and cows were grazing. Soon we came to a bay, Épaves Bay, where a small river ran out, Black Duck Brook, sparkling as it wound its way through the landscape, between heather, willows and grass. I caught a glimpse of a salmon leaping towards quite a small waterfall.

Not far from the head of the bay, an ancient marine terrace extended towards the river, about 4 m high. This was it. On the terrace one could see some vaguely elevated, very overgrown mounds; in some places they could hardly be discerned among the heather and the grass. There could be no doubt – these were the remains of very ancient house-sites.

I looked out over the plain towards the islands, and north over the ocean, where Belle Isle looked like a fairy-tale castle, towards the distant blue coast of Labrador, along which the Vinland voyagers of old had sailed south. It was almost a *déjà-vu*, so much was reminiscent of what I had seen in the Norse settlements of Greenland, and on the west coast of Norway – the houses built on ground higher than the surrounding land, with a view of the ocean, the green fields and meadows, the rippling brook in the open land-

Fig. 39. Reconstruction drawing of the houses which once stood at L'Anse aux Meadows. To the right, the charcoal kiln, with smoke rising from it. The smithy is close by, but is not visible as it was dug into the terrace down by the river. Håkon Christie.

scape, and perhaps also something else, less easily grasped. People from Greenland must have felt at home here.

But the answer was still hanging in the air, for Indians, Eskimos, whalers and fishermen had lived in these parts for centuries. Excavations were required.

During the years from 1961 to 1968, I led seven archaeological expeditions, in the course of which eight, possibly nine house-sites, as well as some other features, were excavated. Scholars from Canada, Iceland, Sweden, USA and Norway participated in the excavations. Anne Stine Ingstad was in charge of the archaeological work throughout. Her archaeological report, which is based on her comprehensive work *The Norse Discovery of America*, vol. I (1977), constitutes the next section of this book. For this reason, I shall only touch briefly on the archaeological aspects of L'Anse aux Meadows in the following chapter.

Fig. 40. George Decker, a fisherman from L'Anse aux Meadows. His ancestors were the first to settle here after the Norse men and women had left their houses about a thousand years ago.

Fig. 41. Black Duck Brook in flood. The depression in the background is house J, the smithy, prior to excavation.

L'ANSE AUX MEADOWS

L'Anse aux Meadows lies at the northern point of Newfoundland, at 51°36'N and 55°32'W, at approximately nine degrees south of the most centrally situated parts of the Eastern Settlement in Greenland, where Leif Eiriksson's home was. The north-eastern promontory, on whose north coast L'Anse aux Meadows lies, is gently undulating, and none of its knolly hillocks rise to a height greater than about 150 m. As we have seen, this landscape fits in well with Grœnlendinga Saga's description of the first unknown land which Bjarni sighted from the sea.

The Norse house-sites lie on an ancient marine terrace, about 4 m above sea-level, at the head of Épaves Bay. There is a large plain covered by grass and heather near the settlement. Black Duck Brook cuts through the terrace near house A; this picturesque little river rises from a lake a couple of kilometres further inland, runs down through a boggy valley, winding its way between grass and willows, until it slowly flows into the bay.

Épaves Bay is very shallow, extending a long way out to sea, and this is the reason why whalers and fishermen did not settle down by the river, preferring a site to the east of the plain, where there is no running water. For much of the day, their boats could not enter this shallow bay, and so the ancient sites were saved from destruction. Grœnlendinga Saga tells us that the inlet to Leif's Vinland was also so shallow that his ship went aground quite a long way from the shore at low tide, and that it could not be brought to the shore until high tide.

From the terrace one has a panorama view of the islands and skerries off L'Anse aux Meadows; the largest of them, farthest out to sea, is Great Sacred Isle. This is a landmark for sailors. – Beyond, one looks out over the Labrador Sea, where Belle Isle can be seen, sometimes hovering on the horizon, and over to the distant blue coast of Labrador in the north.

L'Anse aux Meadows has a highly pronounced

Fig. 42. This view of the reconstructed Viking settlement near L'Anse aux Meadows shows Épaves Bay behind. In this area, the Bay is quite shallow far out to sea. Photo courtesy of Parks Canada.

maritime climate, greatly influenced by the cold, sometimes ice-filled Labrador Current. This current flows southwards along the coast of Labrador, at a speed of up to 10 nautical miles an hour, towards the north coast of Newfoundland, where it branches out into two arms, one flowing along the east coast, the other along the west coast of this island. Nowhere else at so southerly a latitude can we find conditions as similar to those of the Arctic as those obtained in Newfoundland and the regions nearby.

The two nearest meteorological stations Belle Isle and St. Anthony have, according to Hare (1952), recorded mean temperatures of 50.4° F and 55.7° F respectively for the warmest month, August. The corresponding mean winter temperatures for the coldest months (January at Belle Isle, February at St. Anthony) are 14.9° F and 15.7° F (Henningsmoen 1977: 292 ff.).

Great masses of drift-ice from the Polar Basin and other arctic regions, as well as a great number of icebergs, come south on the Labrador Current. The coast by L'Anse aux Meadows is, as a rule, ice-free by the middle of June, but some years drift-ice makes for the shore until quite late in summer. One year we were only just able to make our way through the ice to L'Anse aux Meadows at the end of June.

Then there is the fog, which is so typical of the sea off the coasts of Newfoundland and Labrador. It is due to warm, humid air which rushes in over the cold ocean. In summer and autumn it can be troublesome, at times dangerous, for shipping in these waters; it may be as dense as a wall for days. This fog, combined with drift-ice and icebergs, can make navigation very difficult. This is in complete agreement with Adam of Bremen's description (c. 1075) of the ocean bordering on Vinland, which was written only about fifty to sixty years after Thorfinn Karlsefni, according to Grœnlendinga Saga, had undertaken his Vinland voyage. As we saw above, Adam writes: 'Beyond this island (Vinland), he said, no habitable land is found in this ocean, but all that is beyond is full of intolerable ice and immense mist.'

Another remarkable characteristic of the climate is constituted by the great variations from year to year. 1960 saw a wonderful summer, the sun was constantly shining and there was little wind, the temperature reached about 68° F at times. There were many flowers and berries that year. Other summers were cool, often with fog rolling in from the ocean. George Decker told me that the winter weather also varied considerably: in 1963 there was practically no snow before January or February, and it was quite mild, so that the cows grazed out in the open for much of that winter. But often the cold and the snow could come much earlier.

By the shore, the sea frequently freezes fairly early in December, and remains frozen all winter. The ice may extend so far out to sea that one can walk to the islands off L'Anse aux Meadows. The north coast of Newfoundland lies in a transitional zone between the subarctic forest and the tundra. The vegetative season is fairly short, lasting from 100 to 120 days. There were many kinds of flowers at L'Anse aux Meadows, colourful and sweet-smelling, and patches of blue iris glowed in the meadows. The bog behind the house-sites grew yellow with cloudberries, some slopes blushed with mountain-cranberries. There were blueberries, crowberries, red currants, black currants, gooseberries, raspberries, strawberries and squashberries.

All these berries, apart from squashberries, grow also in Norway, while blueberries, mountain-cranberries and crowberries are also found in Greenland.

The grass grows lush in the vicinity of the Norse house-sites, and the fishermen's cattle and sheep grazed here. There are other meadows, too, further along the shore, and on the nearest of these, the fishermen had built a barn. In fact, the grassland at L'Anse aux Meadows and the district around is more luxuriant than any to be found by the coast at this latitude. The natural precincts of the meadows are very clearly defined, this is highly reminiscent of Norway, where precisely such areas with clearly defined natural boundaries often have names compounded with *vin*, in the sense of meadow. As we saw above, the word *vin* in this sense is known to have been in use in Norway during the historical period. Moreover, we know that Norsemen who emigrated to Orkney and Shetland, where they settled, from about A.D. 800 onwards, used the term *vin* as part of place-names during the historical period, most often in the first syllable – as in Vinland (Olsen 1928: 190 ff.).

There is no forest at L'Anse aux Meadows today. As in the other parts of northern Newfoundland, the forest here was ruthlessly exploited by whalers and fishermen, but George Decker's grandfather had told him that there was considerable forest not far from L'Anse aux Meadows in his younger days. On the east coast of Pistolet Bay, about 10 kilometres from L'Anse aux Meadows, there is still a fairly large area of spruce forest, and the fishermen of the village used to fetch the building materials they required for their houses and their boats from here, transporting the timber by dog sleigh. Épaves Bay is a typical driftwood bay, as the name shows: it means *the bay where flotsam and jetsam are washed ashore*. This is where the fishermen of L'Anse aux Meadows used to fetch their fuel.

There are rich deposits of bogore in the outskirts of the bog behind the house-sites, and also in the boggy area by Black Duck Brook. In some places, one can find bluish-black lumps lying close together immediately below the sods. Thus a smith would have had no difficulties in obtaining a supply of the raw materials he required for producing iron according to the ancient Norse method.

Fig. 43. Icebergs, pack-ice, and drift-ice can all be serious problems for seafarers past and present. Photo by Xabi Otero.

The fauna of the entire northern promontory of Newfoundland is fairly sparse today, a circumstance which is largely due to hunting and to the fact that habitation at the isthmus connecting the promontory to the rest of Newfoundland makes it difficult for animals to reach the northern parts.

There is salmon in Black Duck Brook, we caught them with our bare hands. We would remind the reader of Grœnlendinga Saga's report about salmon at Leifsbúðir. Cod makes for the shore, but their number varies greatly from year to year. The fishermen do not go out on the high sea, but fish among the islands from their open, home-made boats.

Each year the Greenland seal (*Pagophilus groenlandicus*) migrates southwards, and one of their great breeding grounds lies off the coast of Labrador. The young are thrown on the ice in March, and the fishermen of L'Anse aux Meadows go over the ice in order to hunt seal-cubs that have drifted southwards. There is still whale along the coast of Newfoundland, and it is not uncommon that one of these animals is stranded in the shallows, where it then dies. An occasional polar bear may also come south on the ice; while

we were in Newfoundland, a polar bear was shot in the Strait of Belle Isle.

There were, as we have seen, about seventy people living at L'Anse aux Meadows, when I came there for the first time in 1960. There were four families: the Deckers, the Bartletts and the Colbourns, who had come from the east coast of Newfoundland, and the Andersons, who were descended from Torstein Anderson, a Norwegian who had lived at Makovik, Labrador, where he had worked for the Hudson Bay Company.

George Decker, who was born around 1900 or so, told me that his great-grandfather William had been the first to settle at L'Anse aux Meadows. He had come from Conception Bay, and it was said that he was of English descent. At that time there was no permanent settlement by these northern coasts, except at Noddy Bay a little way south of L'Anse aux Meadows, where a man by the name of Hedderson had settled with his family.

One of William Decker's two sons, William, stayed at L'Anse aux Meadows, and he was to become George's grandfather. George remembered him well; he had been a huge man, and it was to him he owed his great knowledge about the olden days. He had told George about the Beothuk Indians, some of whom he said still lived in the forests not far from L'Anse aux Meadows in his great-grandfather's day. These forests were thought to have been their last refuge after they had been hunted by the white man as though they had been wild beasts. At that time the caribou still migrated from the mountains down to the shore early in summer, with packs of wolves in their train – at L'Anse aux Meadows one could often hear wolves howling at night.

During his grandfather's lifetime, and until the days of George's own youth, a French three-mast schooner of about 300 tons used to anchor up in Noddy Bay. Then the French fishermen moved over to L'Anse aux Meadows, where they built five houses on the spot where the village lies today.

The people of L'Anse aux Meadows were on friendly terms with these French fishermen, whose schooner returned to France late in autumn. They looked after the houses and equipment of the Frenchmen while the latter were away.

George Decker also told me that there had always been someone at L'Anse aux Meadows who kept cows or sheep. The animals grazed out in the open for much of the winter, being taken in only when the storm grew too fierce, or the snow lay too deep.

L'Anse aux Meadows was still quite an isolated community when we came there; it was without a road, and the coastal steamer did not call. Life went on in the old-fashioned way, the people built their own boats and houses, they made their own tools and implements. They used muzzle loaders, and during the hunt they carried their powder horns slung across the chest. Their incomes were modest, their demands small. But they all seemed to be quite happy, this little fishing village on the northern point of Newfoundland had a peace of its own. I have rarely met more friendly, more hospitable people; we became close friends in the course of the years, and some of them were of great help during our excavations.

But after we had discovered and excavated the Norse settlement site, the peace which had reigned was shattered: a motor road was built, and every year a great number of tourists, most of them from Canada and the USA, came to the Norse site and the village. Later a National Park was established here, and this covered the settlement site and a large part of the surroundings. Much has changed up there in the north, and we can only hope that the authorities will always, in their work connected with the National Park and the increasing tourism, bear in mind that the old fishing village at L'Anse aux Meadows also rep-

132

resents an important, a fascinating part of the history of the coast, and that the interests of the fishing population will be safeguarded.

The name L'Anse aux Meadows is interesting. The English part of the name, Meadows, is here compounded with the French *L'Anse*, which means 'the bay'. The resulting name, *The Bay by the Meadows*, is most descriptive of the landscape here, and it corresponds closely to the name *Vinland* in the sense *The Land with the Meadows*. A descriptive name of this kind must have seemed natural to people who lived in close contact with nature, regardless of whether they lived a thousand years ago or later.

During the period around the year A.D. 1000, the time when Norsemen were living in the houses at L'Anse aux Meadows, the time of the Vinland voyages, conditions were different in several respects, and the land was more favourable.

First we must note that during the 'Norse period' at L'Anse aux Meadows, the sea-level was 1/2-1 m above today's (Henningsmoen 1977: 329). According to Henningsmoen's pollen investigations, the climate of L'Anse aux Meadows a thousand years ago did not differ much from that of the present. She states: 'The pollen curves in the present material give no more than weak indications of climatic changes.' Several recent authors have assumed that the climate of the North Atlantic–North American region was somewhat more favourable during the period when Iceland and Greenland were colonized. Henningsmoen (1977: 327) points out, however, 'that it is important to bear in mind that the published climate curves indicate a climate similar to today's a thousand years ago ...'

It is very interesting to note that Leif M. Paulssen's investigations (1977: 357 ff.), based on a point of departure entirely different from that of the pollen analyses, also suggest that the climate a thousand years ago can hardly have differed much from today's. His identifications, based on analyses of charcoal from Norse hearths at L'Anse aux Meadows, show that the trees and heather which grew in that region during the Norse period were of the same kinds as those growing in Newfoundland today. According to Henningsmoen's analyses, this applies to all of the vegetation, and it is out of the question that vines should have grown in Newfoundland during the Norse period. It seems that there must have been good pasture there also at that time; Kari Henningsmoen's statement to the effect that the testimony of the vegetation is certainly enough to justify the name Vinland meaning 'Meadowland' is based on her pollen analyses.

In the course of the ages, huge piles of driftwood must have accumulated along the shores of Épaves Bay, a typical driftwood bay. There the Norsemen who lived in the turf houses at L'Anse aux Meadows had a never-failing supply of fuel and building materials, practically on their doorstep. This was of particularly great importance to their iron production. Most of this driftwood came from the north, from the forests of Labrador.

The *Annals of Greenland* (AM 115 8°), compiled in 1625 by an Icelander, Björn Jónsson of Skarðsá, contain an interesting piece of information regarding driftwood from Markland, i.e. Labrador. In translation, an annotation to Eirik's Saga reads:

'From the inmost bay of Markland comes driftwood. The land is called Markland because of the dense forest which is there, and even on the shore of the fjords which are formed when the tide is high, but which are dry when the water has receded, as we shall speak of later.'

Brögger (1937: 46) describes this piece of information as being of the greatest interest, and he maintains that it would seem to indicate that Icelandic tradition, even as late as in Björn Jónsson's days, still included much more knowledge of the western lands, particularly Markland, than that which is contained in the literature.

Of vital importance to the lives of the Norsemen who lived at L'Anse aux Meadows were fishing, and hunting on land and at sea. When they came to Newfoundland about a thousand years ago, the stock of animals was practically virgin, there must have been a great amount of land and marine game of all kinds. The primitive hunting methods of the Eskimos and the Indians can hardly have led to any appreciable reduction. Accounts dating from the time shortly after Cabot's rediscovery of Newfoundland in 1497, moreover, contain information about a very rich fauna in that land. The animals mentioned include caribou, wolf, fox, bear, lynx, marten, all kinds of birds and fish, an abundance of seal and whale, and probably quite a number of walrus. The great herds of caribou, an animal of vital importance to the Beothuk Indians, receive particular attention.

There must have been a considerable stand of birds by the coast not so very long ago. George Decker told me that in his grandfather's days there used to be so many eiderducks brooding on the flat, grassy Green Island just off L'Anse aux Meadows, that one could hardly put down a foot without stepping on eggs. Eirik's Saga (VIII) contains a parallel to this, an account of Karlsefni's arrival at Straumsfjord, which is assumed to be a substitute for Leif's Vinland in Grœnlendinga Saga (see p. 87).

We must realize, however, that even in a land rich in game, the animals may disappear from much of the country for quite some time, as a result of wind, deep snow or the ground being covered by a sheet of ice. This may lead to famine, to catastrophe, for the people living there. According to Eirik's Saga, hunting and fishing failed during the first winter Karlsefni spent in the new land, so that his expedition experienced great difficulties. This may be one of the few authentic elements of that saga, and it would seem to correspond to conditions at L'Anse aux Meadows.

Even if the climate should have been somewhat milder a thousand years ago, there would still have been a great deal of drift-ice and a considerable number of icebergs in the Davis Strait and the Labrador Sea. The Davis Strait forms the outlet for ice from the Polar Basin, and we must also take into consideration the masses of ice from more southerly regions, such as the coasts of Greenland, Baffin Island and Labrador.

Because of these climatic conditions, the Vinland voyagers presumably started rather late in the year from Greenland, as we saw above, probably not until the end of July or, still more likely, the beginning of August. This corresponds with the sources' statement to the effect that the ship which sailed from Bergen to Greenland is also not likely to have left Norway before the beginning of August, because of the drift-ice (see pp. 104 ff.). As a result, the period when sailing was possible was limited, and it was of the greatest importance that one settled as quickly as possible, so that the preparations vital for a winter in the wilderness could be completed in time. Houses must be built and provisions for the winter must be secured by means of hunting and fishing.

During their stay at L'Anse aux Meadows, the Norse expeditions – which spent a year, and a couple of years there respectively – must surely have undertaken a considerable number of exploratory voyages along the coast, in order to get to know the land, and to be able to make use of its resources. Grœnlendinga Saga mentions, some such voyages, describing Thorvald's in particularly great detail. These accounts would seem to agree well with the direction of the north coast of Newfoundland, and with voyages starting out from L'Anse aux Meadows.

L'Anse aux Meadows today is not the same as it was a thousand years ago, the time when the Norsemen settled here. The land offered quite a different livelihood in those days. There was an almost virgin stock of animals on land and in the

Fig. 44. House F during excavation. Photo by Helge Ingstad.

sea; here the enormous herds of caribou are of prime importance. There was forest here, with timber for boat-building and for iron extraction–to the Norse Greenlanders, this must have seemed almost incredible. In this connection we must bear in mind that the Vinland voyagers assessed the conditions they found in the light of their own Norse culture. They had come to a favourable land fairly far south, but much was similar to the North there, and thus they felt at home. Their ancient techniques of hunting and catching whale, seal, caribou etc. fitted in well here. Once Leif Eiriksson had looked around, he must surely have thought: 'This is a good land.'

SECRETS FROM THE SOIL

The excavations were exciting from the moment we started digging, but often very difficult. The house-walls which were gradually uncovered consisted of turf which was, in part, so highly eroded that it had practically disappeared, and they were without stone settings which might have given some indication. A detailed study of the different layers of sand and earth was of vital importance, and Anne Stine soon gained much valuable experience. One of the largest houses, house F, lay completely covered under sand and earth, and it was found by mere chance: one evening, when the sun was low in the sky, we were just able to discern a slight irregularity in the

135

heather-covered ground, and started the excavation there.

True, conditions were not always so very pleasant – kneeling on the ground all day, come rain, wind or fog, and scraping away inch after inch of soil is not the most comfortable way of life. But these discomforts were soon forgotten. And when we really came across a find, and careful work with the brush revealed something of Norse character – when that happened, it was like a miracle. Suddenly we felt that we almost knew these Norse people who had lived here so long ago.

Already the first season brought to light finds that cheered our lives: a hearth with a stone setting, of the same type as a Norse hearth in Greenland. Another fascinating find was a small ember-pit, a close parallel to one excavated at Brattahlið in Greenland, the farm belonging to Eirik the Red. The people used to put the glowing embers into such a pit at night, and cover them with ashes, so that they could use them to kindle the next day's fire.

I was particularly interested in investigating more closely the strange long, white beaches in Markland (Labrador) of which Grœnlendinga Saga speaks, Leif Eiriksson's last port of call before he sailed south to Vinland. They must surely be the long beaches which extend for about 30 km north and south of Cape Porcupine in Labrador.

And so we sailed our ship, the Halten, to the north, and Poul Sørnes, our good skipper, was happy now that he was at sea again. We sailed along the coast of Labrador, while a brilliant sun shone over land and sea, where great bluish-white icebergs drifted south with the current.

After two days, we reached Cape Porcupine, a strange, long headland. The beach was a beautiful sight with its fine, white sand. It was about a hundred metres wide, and sloped very gently down towards the sea. The land looked flat, and the forest, with tall spruces, grew right down to the beach. Never shall I forget this view - the foaming waves washing over the white beach, while the green spruce forest formed the background. – This beach is visible from far out to sea, an important point.

The wilderness was unique in its beauty – shoals of cod chased shoals of capelin in towards the shore. Much fish had been washed ashore, and there it lay, a glittering silver ribbon in the sun. We were not alone, however, the black bear had also discovered the fish; on our first evening here we met four black bears ambling along the shore. They were gobbling capelin and enjoying life.

It was here, by these long, white beaches that Leif Eiriksson launched his ship's boat, rowed towards the land and looked around, according to Grœnlendinga Saga. But he soon realized that this land lacked an important factor for a possible later emigration – there was very little grass here, no pasture for their cattle. He rowed back to the ship, and sailed south.

136

At this point of Leif's voyage, the start of the last leg which was to bring the Norsemen to Vinland, Grœnlendinga Saga has the first information about times of sailing – two *dægr*. This is of special interest, for at this stage it was more essential than ever for the later Vinland voyagers to know roughly where Vinland lay. And the start of this last leg, the long, white beaches by the open sea, was a first-class landmark.

We sailed southwards along the coast of Labrador for two days, and then the north coast of Newfoundland appeared. We steered towards L'Anse aux Meadows, practically without having to alter our course.

After the first, promising excavations we continued work here for six more years. Slowly the ruins of a Norse Viking Age settlement came to light. Eight – possibly nine – turf houses of Norse type were uncovered. Some of them were surprisingly large, up to 24 m in length. This is in close agreement with Grœnlendinga Saga, which stresses the fact that Leif built 'large houses'.

Several years before these excavations I had, in *Land under the Pole Star*, written that finds of traces of iron extraction resulting from the smelting of bog-iron during the Viking Age must be one of the most reliable indications of Norse settlement in America. And I added, hypothetically, that it was quite possible that somewhere in North America, about a thousand years ago, a Norseman had stood at his stone anvil, working the red-hot iron with his sledge-hammer. A new sound in a new land.

Bearing this in mind, it is remarkable that we actually found a smithy at L'Anse aux Meadows, a small building dug down into the terrace, close by the river. Here there was an anvil, a large, earth-fast stone, and iron fragments lay strewn about on the earthen floor. There was slag here, there were lumps of bog-iron, the smith's raw material. This was the place where the smith had worked at his forge and anvil, while the sound of

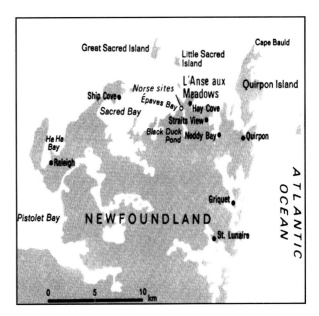

Map showing the northeastern part of Newfoundland with L'Anse aux Meadows, where the Norse house sites were discovered and excavated.

his sledge-hammer echoed over the small Norse community.

In the layer above the Norse stratum, we found two Dorset Eskimo arrowheads of quartzite, as well as a beautifully made soapstone lamp. These people must have lived in this area at about the same time as the Norsemen. A fair number of Indian artifacts also came to light.

These finds are in accordance with what Grœnlendinga Saga tells us about the Vinland voyagers who met natives – Skrælings – and first traded with them, and later fought them.

Other Norse finds include two of particular significance – a bronze ring-headed pin, and a soapstone spindle whorl. The latter indicates that the settlement included women, and this also agrees with the sagas.

A number of C^{14} analyses of Norse finds have yielded dates which indicate that the settlement dates from around the year A.D. 1000.

137

Marking the 1000th anniversary of Leif Eiriksson's arrival in Newfoundland, a fleet of replica Viking ships enters Épaves Bay near L'Anse aux Meadows. Photo by Paul Elliott.

Here I have merely mentioned some of the most fascinating features of the excavations, and especially such as appear to have a direct connection with the sagas. For the rest, I refer the reader to Anne Stine Ingstad's account of the excavations, which provides further evidence showing that the settlement at L'Anse aux Meadows was Norse.

In *The Norse Discovery of America*, Vol. 1 (A.S. Ingstad 1977), she has the following illustrative description of the settlement at L'Anse aux Meadows:

'The settlement at Épaves Bay, with all its houses, large and small, its smithy and its charcoal kiln, its boat-sheds and probably also its bath-house, whose closest parallels are to be found in the farm ruins of Iceland, Greenland and Scandinavia, provides a varied picture of many aspects of eleventh-century Norse life.'

*Holding a handmade chest on his shoulder, a
contemporary Viking explores St. John's harbour region.*

There are still some who firmly maintain that
there were grapes in Vinland. Although they
acknowledge that the settlement site at L'Anse
aux Meadows is Norse, they prefer to call it an
intermediate stop on the way to the land of
grapes and wine, the promised land, for as such,
it fits in with their theories.

I shall here confine myself to repeating that the
geographical descriptions and sailing times
given in Grœnlendinga Saga quite clearly indicate a coastal route leading directly to northern
Newfoundland and L'Anse aux Meadows, and
that Eirik's Saga must presumably be fiction.
Moreover, Adam of Bremen, the author of the
source on which the reports dealing with grapes
are based, himself contradicts his own statement
by emphasizing that the sea beyond Vinland is
full of intolerable ice and immense mist, a perfect description of the sea bordering on L'Anse
aux Meadows, a land where no grapes can grow.
Moreover, a point of particular importance
must be noted: the established date of the settlement at L'Anse aux Meadows, c. A.D. 1000 is
about the same as that of Leif Eiriksson's voyage,
according to Grœnlendinga Saga.

The Government of Canada has made a considerable area around L'Anse aux Meadows
into a National Park. A Viking museum has been
built there, and much has been done to establish
a fascinating tourist attraction. The Norse settlement site has been included in UNESCO's
'World Heritage List' as one of the most valuable
historical monuments in the world.

Fig. 1, p. 140. View of L'Anse aux Meadows and Black Duck Brook: Great Sacred Isle in the background.

On the 14th of June 1961 we cast anchor at the outlet of Épaves Bay, at a safe distance from a large, stranded iceberg. The bay is very shallow far out to sea, and the 'Halten' could not get any closer to shore, so we had to launch our small boat. But even this small craft could not put in to shore, so we waded across the last stretch. How this reminded me of Grœnlendinga Saga's vivid account, which had always struck me as being trustworthy!

'(The bay) was very shallow far out to sea at low tide, and their ship was grounded, and when they looked out from the ship, the sea was a long way away. But they were so eager to get ashore that they did not care to wait for the tide to rise under their ship, but hurried off to land where a river flowed out of a lake.'

We, too, went ashore where a river flowed out into the sea. This was a fair land, and L'Anse aux Meadows was bathed in sunshine.
Beyond the bay, a curving marine terrace rises gradually from the sea, up to about 4 metres above the highest water level. The lower part is fairly flat and covered in grass, which grows tall and lush in the course of the summer. In the east, the terrace passes into a heather and grass-covered headland jutting north out into the sea. Beyond, and north of this headland, lie two islands, Great and Small Sacred Isle. In the west, the land rises gradually, ending in a hilly ridge, no more than 20 to 40 metres high. It runs north/south, and drops sharply down to the sea below (*fig.* 1).
From 1961 to 1968 we conducted seven archaeological expeditions here, in which scholars from the following countries took part: Sweden, Iceland, Canada, U.S.A. and Norway. Eight complete house-sites were investigated as well as one fragmentary one. The excavations also included several lesser features.

THE EXCAVATION
of
a Norse Settlement
at L'Anse aux Meadows,
Newfoundland

By Anne Stine Ingstad

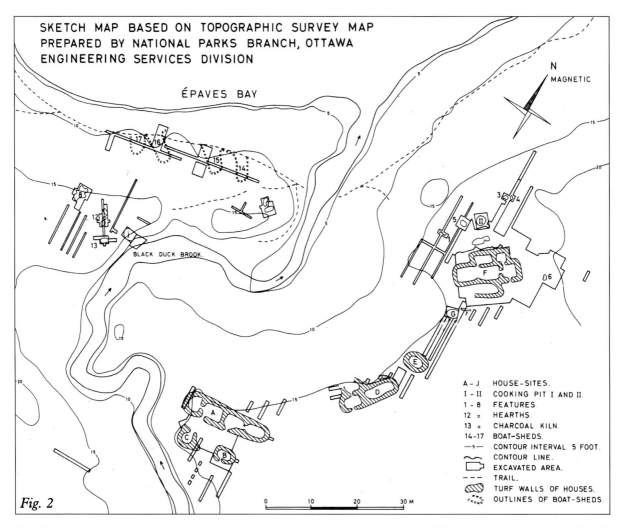

ÉPAVES BAY

N
MAGNETIC

BLACK DUCK BROOK

A - J	HOUSE-SITES.
I - II	COOKING PIT I AND II.
1 - 8	FEATURES.
12 =	HEARTHS.
13 =	CHARCOAL KILN.
14 - 17	BOAT-SHEDS.
—5—	CONTOUR INTERVAL 5 FOOT.
	CONTOUR LINE.
	EXCAVATED AREA.
- - -	TRAIL.
	TURF WALLS OF HOUSES.
	OUTLINES OF BOAT-SHEDS.

0   10   20   30 M

Fig. 2

The house-sites were numbered A to J in the order in which they were investigated (*fig. 2*).

Seven of the house-sites lie along the marine terrace east of the river, Black Duck Brook, together with the fragmentary site. The smithy was the only house on the west bank. It lies at the point where the river cuts its way through the terrace, which takes the form of a steep cliff here. The eastern part of the terrace is about 450 m long, and nowhere does its width exceed c. 40 m. Here, too, the land is covered with grass and heather. In the south, the meadow gradually merges into a bog with reddish-golden moss and a veritable carpet of cloudberry leaves. In the autumn, one could pick any amount of delicious cloudberries here.

A number of overgrown, irregular mounds could be discerned along the terrace. Some of them looked as though they might be faint traces of sill-beams, while others were so vague that it was impossible to say what they might represent. They were certainly traces of human life in the past, but excavations were essential if we were to discover what lay hidden under the turf; and what ethnic group these remains might represent. There were four possibilities: Eskimos, American Indians, Norsemen or fishermen and whalers from the time after Cabot's rediscovery in 1497.

It was obviously impossible to excavate everything concealed under the turf during one brief summer and autumn. We therefore decided on test excavations which were to be conducted in such a way that they would not be detrimental to any future excavations. Our aim during this first season was to find some evidence or other pointing to the ethnic affiliation of the settlement, if in fact it was a settlement. It was of crucial importance to us to find out whether the site was Norse; if it was, we were going to return the following summer and start work on more extensive excavations.

Our expectations were great. The very atmosphere of the place, its situation and landscape, seemed familiar to us, recalling both Greenland and Iceland. We really looked forward to starting work.

But there was a great deal to be done before we could begin the excavations. We had to find a place for our camp, and hire workmen to help us with the heavy, unskilled jobs. We raised our tent down by the river, at the spot where it winds below the steep, craggy bank. Here we found shelter from the sea wind, and there was a water supply to hand. A pleasant spot, where we were to camp for many a summer.

There were about seventy people living at L'Anse aux Meadows in those days. Life here was as isolated and hard as it had been ever since the first settler came some time during the eighteenth century. All those years had seen few changes. The coastal steamer had not started to call at the village, there was no road, no telephone, no electricity. Any mail had to be fetched once a fortnight at the nearest fishing village, which lay about three-quarters of an hour's way away. The home-made fishing tackle was old-fashioned, and they had very few of the facilities one normally associates with civilization. But I am convinced that the impression I gained was correct, these people were content with the little they had, they were happy together. They bestowed

their friendship on us, a friendship we value highly to this day. I know we will be close friends for the rest of our lives.

We hired some of the local fishermen to help us remove the surface turf. These men were to be my colleagues throughout all the years we spent at L'Anse aux Meadows, and they became really good at the job as time went on.

Once the most essential work of surveying and levelling had been done, we could at last start excavating. The first features to attract our attention were some parallel, overgrown banks, about 10 m long. They were clearest at the eastern end of the site, and here it looked as though they might be connected with one another, joined by a curving ridge. At the other, western end, the banks became less and less clear, and finally they faded out completely.

The turf was easily removed, as the soil below consisted largely of sand. I was very curious to find out what these banks actually consisted of. Imagine my disappointment when we saw that there was not a single stone in them! All there was, was soil in varying shades from black through brown to pale grey. At first I could not imagine where all these colours came from, until I realized that they represented the turves from which the banks had been built. Even the soil below the banks was without any stones which might have indicated where the walls had stood. Already at this early stage it was fairly certain that these banks represented walls, but I realized that it would not be easy to find them. As we dug, we found that we could trace the layer of black turf for about 10 metres; after this, it became paler and more eroded, only to disappear entirely in the end.

That first summer we cut only two trenches through this house-site, as the floor layer between the banks was unpromising. We found no structural traces, nor did we uncover any real cultural level. I could not understand the reason for this, so I abandoned this house-site for the

Fig. 3. House-site A, seen from the east. Photo by
Anne Stine Ingstad.
Fig. 4. Engraved stone slabs mark the locations of the
original buildings. Photo courtesy of Parks Canada.

time being. It was not excavated completely until
1968 – by that time I had the experience from
the other house-sites to go by. We called this site
House A (*fig. 3*).

Next we carried out a preliminary investigation
at a house-site which lies parallel to house A.
Here we could just make out all the four walls.
An exciting dig, as we were soon to realize.
Immediately under the greensward we found a
tough, black layer of soil, and below this, another layer, just as black, but less tough. After a
while, we found pieces of charcoal, and the soil
became richer and more fatty, almost like cheese.
We had found the cultural layer of this house.

At the western end of the site stones soon
appeared, and suddenly I found many pieces of
charcoal. An encouraging find, which turned
out to be a beautifully constructed hearth, lying
at an angle to the western end wall. I knew
hearths of this type from the literature - and I
ran back to the tent and fetched one of my
books. True enough, a hearth of this type had
been found at Brattahlið in Greenland, in Eirik

the Red's and Leif Eiriksson's farm, in the very
hall which is thought to have been Eirik's own!
I could not have wished for more.

I continued work in this house. Soon I found a
cooking pit, a little way east of the hearth (*fig.
5*), with a large lump of slag at the bottom.
There was no longer much doubt, since neither
the Eskimos nor the American Indians worked
iron, and it seemed unlikely that fishermen or
whalers should have spent their time extracting
iron. A continuous sooty patch ran across the
floor from the cooking pit. At the southern end
of this patch we found a small depression, beautifully lined with stone. This, too, was reminiscent of Greenland, it was an ember-pit, where
the Norsemen used to cover the glowing embers
at night, so that it would be easy to light the fire
next morning (*fig. 6*). There was a similar

ember-pit at Brattahliở, but this was not in Eirik's or Leif's houses, but in that part of the home-fields which archaeologists call The Fireplace Area.

Encouraged by these finds, we finished excavating this small house-site that first summer. The house measured 4.5 m x 3.2 m. The walls consisted entirely of turf, and they were thinner than those of house A.

We found out why when the river was in flood, and covered this entire part of the terrace: in the course of the years, the walls must have been eroded by the waters of the flooding river. We were soon to find out that the same had happened in the western part of house A.

This is the house designated B.

To the west of this house there was a peculiar, roundish depression surrounded by thick banks. An opening in the north faced house A. Small 'arms' of turf protruded from the wall in the east and the west. One of them ran towards the south wall of house B, the other ran at an angle towards the bank of the river. We were long puzzled by these 'arms'; at first I took them to be a natural phenomenon, but as we grew more familiar with the conditions here, we began to realize that they must be the remains of turf walls which once connected these three houses. The reason is obvious: they formed a dam stemming the water in spring, for Black Duck Brook floods the whole area each spring, when ice drifts down the river. The internal measurements of this small house site were 2.8 m x 4 m.

As soon as the greensward had been removed, a number of flat slates came to light. Below these lay a cultural layer, about 15 cm thick. The upper 5 – 8 cm of this layer clearly represented the turf roof of the house, being extremely tough. Now we knew that the slates had lain on top of the roof, probably in order to prevent the turf being blown off. We were to find that this was a

Fig. 5. The cooking pit of house-site B, with the long hearth in the background. Photo by Anne Stine Ingstad.

Fig. 6. The ember pit in house-site B. Photo by Anne Stine Ingstad.

common feature on the terrace; the same practice is not uncommon in modern Iceland.

Below this tough top-layer we found a looser stratum, greyish in colour. It was very similar to clay. It was highly discoloured by rust, and contained pieces of charcoal and slate fragments. The charcoal concentration was densest furthest inside the house, around a large stone. There was no hearth.

Fig. 7, 8. The buildings that were painstakingly excavated by Anne Stine Ingstad and her team were carefully recreated by a team of dedicated specialists. Photo courtesy of Parks Canada; André Cornellier photographer.

We found two lumps of slag, one fragmentary iron rivet, one fragment of iron, two slivers of bone (one of these was to prove to come from a domestic pig), and one piece of red jasper here. The jasper was analysed, and proved to be most closely akin to Icelandic jasper, and it seems most likely that it came from Iceland. These finds were most encouraging, for now we had two finds pointing in the right direction: as there has never been wild boar in Newfoundland, we have every reason to believe that this sliver of bone must have come from somewhere where pigs are kept.

Summer is late in coming to this northern part of Newfoundland, which faces the Labrador Sea. Huge icebergs drift on the ocean, carried by the Labrador Current. When we went ashore early in June, the snow had only just melted, and the vegetation was still dead, yellow. But the countryside was bathed in sunshine, and soon the grass turned green, and a blue carpet of wild iris covered the meadow. Bluish-green willows with catkins glittered along the river, and that first summer at L'Anse aux Meadows was one of sunshine on land and at sea.

Helge had long since planned a journey to the north, following the Vinland route. He intended to investigate the country up there in the north, to see if he could find any traces of Norse settlement there.

At the end of July we stopped digging for the time being, and went north to Labrador on the 'Halten', our ship. This was an extremely interesting journey, where we saw some unusually long sandy beaches near Porcupine Point. They corresponded to the saga's description of the place where Leif Eiriksson went ashore and looked around.

At the beginning of August I returned to L'Anse aux Meadows on my own, this time on board a Grenfell Mission plane. It was late summer by now, the grass was tall and lush, and the flowers defy description. Everything would have been perfect had it not been for a violent forest fire farther south, which covered L'Anse aux Meadows with clouds of smoke.

I continued my test excavations on the terrace by Épaves Bay, together with Job and Blake, my assistants. One of the greatest difficulties we encountered was that of detecting turf walls in the final stage of erosion: in that state, they look simply like small mounds of grey, sterile sand. Only a trained eye can see any faint greyish or brownish stripes, which would indicate that there was once a turf wall there. The walls of one and the same house-site could represent all the various stages of erosion.

TEST EXCAVATION OF HOUSE D

Roughly at the middle of the terrace we could see a few mounds and something resembling the remnants of a wall. My test area ran along this 'wall'. Below the surface turves I found a layer of soil rather browner than those in the houses previously investigated.

The test excavation did not result in any structural finds. All I could be sure of was that this was a house-site, for three of the walls could clearly be traced in the profile of the trial trench. I abandoned this dig for the time being, with every intention of resuming it the following summer. By now it was obvious that we had to have at least one more expedition, possibly more. I must say, I am grateful that I did not at that time realize that eight years were to pass before we were able to say that our excavations were finished.

HOUSE E

Early on I had noticed a roundish depression near the edge of the terrace, a little way south of my test excavation of House D. There were distinct turf walls, 1.5 m thick, around this depression. The corners were rounded, giving the impression of a round building. But this was

147

nevertheless a small, rectangular house, 3.75 m x 3.25 m.

Once the surface turf had been removed, a large, flat stone came to light. As it lay immediately below the greensward, it seems that it must have covered the smoke opening in the roof.

The layers below contained some smaller stones, apparently haphazardly scattered about. The main hearth lay in the south-eastern corner of the house. It had been partly dug out of the gravel under the turf of the wall, but the bottom lay only very slightly below the floor. In the northwest, the hearth was bounded by a large slate standing on edge. It was brim-full of charcoal, ashes and brittle-burned stone. There were no finds from this excavation.

HOUSE F

When I had finished my test excavation of house E, I felt sure that there were no more houses on the terrace. How wrong I was! I walked over the terrace one evening after a violent thunderstorm, in the hope of finding cloudberries on the bog beyond. A black cloud covered the horizon in the north, almost touching the sea. Suddenly the sun, about to set, appeared below the cloud. In this almost eerie light I suddenly caught sight of faint traces of banks, forming an angle or a corner of a house. Then the sun set, the vision had gone. Everything was as it had always been.

That night I lay awake in my sleeping-bag, turning thoughts and ideas over in my mind for a long time before I was eventually able to sleep. One thing was quite clear, the digging season was not over before I had carried out another test excavation. The others had not yet returned from Labrador, so I had time for the job.

Next morning I sent for my helpers again; my plan was to cut test trenches in an area roughly 10m² in size.

At the north-eastern end of one of the trenches I found a complete stone packing immediately below the grass, consisting of flat, cracked stones. In the profile we could see that these stones lay immediately below the surface turf, but when we dug deeper, it appeared that there was a black layer of soil below them. The uppermost part of this layer was tough, rather like those in the other houses which I had interpreted as representing the one-time turf roofs. Here, however, there were many large lumps of charcoal in this black layer, some of them might almost be called small logs. There could be no doubt this was a burned level. An exciting discovery what would it lead to?

Under the stone packing at the north-western corner of the trench we found a well constructed hearth. It consisted of two built-up chambers of slate. On the floor in front of the hearth there were some large, charred logs and, under them, a round depression in the floor, filled with charcoal. As the bottom of this depression was quite flat, it seems most likely that it was the impression of a wooden vessel which once stood here, and burned down.

There is a hearth of the same type in the so-called Fireplace Area in the homefield of Brattahlið in Greenland, the farm of Eirik the Red and Leif Eiriksson! Hearths of this type were in use in Greenland for a very short period; as far as we know, they belong to the first period of Norse settlement.

In the cultural layer of this part of the house we found an oval beach pebble. A round depression had been hewn out of the upper surface. I knew that this was an Icelandic lamp! I had seen a number of similar lamps in the National Museum in Reykjavik (*fig. 10*). They are known as *kola*. As soapstone is not found in Iceland, lamps were most often made from beach pebbles.

In one spot my test trench cut through a patch

where the soil had a consistency different from that in the rest of this part of the house. Pale grey and black stripes appeared, with shades of reddish tones *(fig. 11)*. After a little while I realized that we must have cut through a transverse wall. Five layers appeared quite distinctly. This was a partition wall between two rooms.

It was getting quite late in autumn. The bog was full of the most delicious cloudberries, and the village women and children were busy all day long gathering berries for winter, not only cloudberries, but also raspberries and blueberries. One day, when I was washing clothes in the brook, I discovered a small redcurrant bush, and on another occasion I found a blackcurrant bush. There could be no doubt that we had come to a goodly land.

I was busy digging together with my assistants, but I could not help wondering where the others might be. Many weeks had passed since I left them in Labrador, and I really felt that I had dug enough for one season. The test excavations had made it quite clear that I would have to return for a really thorough excavation of these house sites, together with archaeologists from other countries, primarily from Iceland. But we would also need specialists in other subjects, first and foremost a pollen analyst.

The sky was still grey, the air thick, from the forest fire that raged south of us. The nasty little black flies did their best to plague me. But even so, I was in high spirits, thanks to the promising results of the excavation.

Fig. 10. Stone lamp from house-site F, together with two lamps from Iceland. Photo by Anne Stine Ingstad.

Fig. 11. Section of turf wall in house-site F, showing the horizontal layers of turf. Photo by Anne Stine Ingstad.

Suddenly one day all the village children came running to the terrace, the *Halten* had been sighted, I could expect the others soon! Now I really had to get busy! The feast must be ready when they arrived. Job got hold of a first-class salmon, I rushed out to the bog to pick cloudberries. A meal fit for a king! I put fragrant balsam fir twigs down on the ground inside the tent, with joy I anticipated the reunion with all my men! I must admit that I had not had time to think about them for the last few hours, but now I looked forward to showing Helge what I had found. Then I suddenly heard voices outside the tent. There they were, bearded and grimy, but oh so happy and full of smiles. Now we were all together again for the last time before leaving L'Anse aux Meadows that season.

After we had eaten, we all went up to the terrace, where I showed them everything that had come to light while they were away. Helge was all smiles, for he, too, realized that this was a promising result.

Winter was approaching, and it was time to leave for more southerly parts. We intended to sail the *Halten* to Halifax in Nova Scotia where we were to leave her. From there we were to go to New York, and take the Stavangerfjord home. It is a good thing we did not know what was going to happen on the way south – the *Halten* just about managed to get us to Halifax harbour late one night, in the nick of time before the hurricane Esther broke loose. We had had contact with the hurricane for several days, with great breakers washing over the 'Halten. The coastal radio had instructed all boats to put into a port of refuge, but our receiver must have had trouble with all the water, for we heard no such instructions. We continued our voyage south, alone on the ocean, with a broken spanker gaff and a motor that was not working. With a half spread of canvas we arrived in Halifax late at night on the 22nd of September. We were the last who made the harbour, all the other boats,

large and small, were secured behind a web of rope to protect them against the storm. Forewarned is forearmed, so they say, but sometimes it is a blessing not to be forewarned!

That winter Helge and I went to Iceland, to ask Kristján Eldjárn, who was then Director of the Historical Museum in Reykjavík, to take part in the next expedition, the following summer. He liked the idea, and asked to be allowed to take along Gísli Gestsson, his assistant, who had excavated a number of turf houses and other monuments in Iceland. Professor Holger Arbmann at the University of Lund was so kind as to help us find a Swedish archaeologist participant, Rolf Petré.

No Norwegian archaeologist was able to take part that year, as they were all busily engaged in the mountains, in connection with the extensive watercourse regulations that were planned. But fortunately Kari Egede-Nissen, botanist and pollen analyst, was willing to come with us. I was particularly pleased about this, not only because of her scientific qualifications, but also because I would no longer be the only woman taking part. Female company was something I had longed for.

That year we flew to Halifax, and from there, we had been offered to go on in one of the Royal Canadian Navy's vessels, north as far as St. Anthony at the northern point of Newfoundland. From there we had to make our own way to L'Anse aux Meadows with all our equipment, as best we could.

As we made our way north, it started to rain, and the weather grew cold. Soon we were met by drifting ice, more and more closely packed the further north we came. Finally it almost formed a solidly packed layer, and the ship had to force her way through at very slow speed. We only just managed to reach the good harbour at St. Anthony.

Now we had to wait for a fortnight, for all the bays north of St. Anthony were completely blocked with ice. The days grew longer and longer, or so it seemed, for we were eager to get to L'Anse aux Meadows and start digging. One day we heard that the wind had turned more southerly, and that the drift-ice at Épaves Bay, the bay where the ruins lay, might have broken up or drifted away. We arranged for two fishermen to meet us with their boats at Pistolet Bay; we loaded our equipment on to a lorry and made our way there.

There was only just about room for our equipment, the fishermen and us on these small boats. We did not encounter any trouble during the first part of our journey north, but then we met the ice. Loathsome ice, with swells below and very few openings, and those there were, would suddenly close up. For hours we struggled on our way north, and it was bitterly cold. Nor did the sight of land help our state of mind. The land was covered with snow.

When L'Anse aux Meadows at last loomed ahead, we realized that the boats could not possibly make it to shore, since the ice lay packed right up to the coast. We had to unload our equipment on to the ice, and after hours of hard work we finally managed to get it all safely on land. The date was the 23rd of June, Midsummer Day!

The weather that summer was quite different from what the previous year had led us to expect. It rained when we arrived, there was ice and fog everywhere. It went on raining for days, for weeks, throughout most of the summer. Eventually the snow disappeared, but it was long before the snow-drift behind our tent melted. In the end the ice dissolved, too, and the huge icebergs that drift south from Baffin Island on the Labrador Current took over. In spite of all, we did get some kind of summer that year, too. Our team that year included Kristján Eldjárn and Gísli Gestsson from Iceland, as well as Rolf Petré from Sweden. The Icelanders started to excavate the south-western part of house A, cut-

ting several trenches here. Under the grass turf they found a thick cultural layer, up to 15 – 30 cm in depth. It consisted largely of earth, fine gravel and sand, with a stone here and there, but there seemed to be no kind of system, It turned out that the cultural layer was thickest where my test excavation the year before had stopped. It looked as though it filled some kind of depression here, which grew more shallow towards the edge. An iron rivet was found in one of the trenches, but even so, the Icelanders did not consider this site so promising that it was worth more of their time. And so the trenches were filled up, and the site remained untouched until 1967, when I decided to resume excavation here.

HOUSE J – THE SMITHY

It was quite some time since I had noticed a depression in the river-bank, west of Black Duck Brook. I knew that in Iceland smithies used to lie in this kind of position, on the riverbank and at a safe distance from the rest of the houses. This, I felt sure, was an interesting investigation for our Icelandic archaeologists, and I left this excavation to them.

Immediately under the greensward lay a beautiful little soapstone lamp, of Dorset Eskimo type. As it lay so high up above the floor, it was obvious that it had no connection with this small house. The Eskimos must have found a sheltered spot for their camp in the depression, most probably after the houses had collapsed.

The Icelanders cut trenches here, to the full extent of the cultural layer. The entire depression was excavated in this way. In the middle of the floor there was a large, smooth stone, granite (fig. 13).

There were marks from blows on it, and a piece had been broken off (this piece later turned up in the brook, below the 'smithy'). This stone must have served as an anvil. The floor around it was hard-trodden, and the cultural deposit included some small iron scales, interpreted by the excavators as forging scales. There were also lumps of bog-iron, some slag and some burned clay, which may have some connection with the slag.

There was also a great deal of charcoal in the cultural level. Right from the start we referred to this depression as the 'smithy', and there can hardly be any doubt that this really was the function of house J (fig. 14).

Fig. 12. Traditional Viking smithwork is demonstrated by a re-enactor using authentic tools and methods. Photo courtesy of Parks Canada.

Fig. 13. The earthfast stone anvil in house-site J. Photo by Anne Stine Ingstad.

THE CHARCOAL KILN

Once the excavation of the 'smithy' was finished, the Icelanders started to investigate the terrace behind house J. About 7 m south-west of the 'smithy', they found traces of human activity, including a shallow depression which was only barely visible before the excavation. They investigated this pit; the uppermost 15 cm of the cultural layer consisted of reddish-brown earth which contained some turf. Immediately below this level there was pure sand, a striking contrast to the layer above.

A circular deposit of charcoal came to light in the sand, with the greatest concentration of charcoal at the centre of the pit. In one spot, the sand was burned to a reddish-brown colour. About 20 cm above the bottom, the pit measured 1.80 m x 1.10 m. The lowest 5 cm of the cultural layer consisted of pure charcoal, and there was also a great deal of charcoal further up along the edge of the pit. This depression must obviously have been a charcoal kiln.

We thought a great deal about the possibility of iron extraction at L'Anse aux Meadows during the Viking Age. Surely, there must have been some activity of this kind here? In that case, there must also be an occurrence of bogore in the vicinity.

And so Helge took some of the men along, and they started to search for ore in the bog behind the settlement. They did not need to dig for long. Soon they were back with their hands full of bluish-black, rusty lumps of bog-ore. This must have been a veritable eldorado for the Norsemen. Not only was there any amount of ore just below the turf in the bog immediately behind their houses, but the forest was not far away either, and this was something they were not accustomed to from either Greenland or Iceland. Moreover, there was any amount of driftwood on the beach, and thus they could easily produce the charcoal they needed for iron extraction.

Fig. 14. House-site J – the smithy, after excavation. In the background, left, the kiln. Photo by Anne Stine Ingstad.

Now only one feature was missing: the smelting pit. Where was that? This was a question to which we returned year after year. We searched in the vicinity of the bog as well as everywhere else. Finally we came to the conclusion that it might well have been beside the 'smithy', at the top of the river-bank. There was a scar at the edge of the terrace there, from which a good deal of sand had slid out in the course of the years. This sand contained a fairly large amount of charcoal.

HOUSE D

Rolf Petré had started an excavation at the middle of the terrace, in line with my test excavation there the year before. It soon became clear that these two sites were connected, although a turf wall separated them. There could be no doubt that the excavated area here represented one house, two of whose rooms were now laid bare. They were aligned with each other, and shared an end wall.

153

There was a long hearth in the middle of the floor of Petré's excavation, a hearth without any stone surround. At one end there was a small ember pit made of slate, very similar to that we had earlier found in house B. Ember pits are a typically Norse feature, and these two pits would seem to indicate a cultural relationship between the two houses.

This room (room III) with its central hearth is of the type we know as a Norse hall. On either side of the hearth we found sterile patches, which may once have been covered with twigs, since we found many small twigs in the cultural deposit.

This house yielded a number of finds deriving from two different cultures:

1 *fragmentary iron rivet*, found at 4 cm above floor level.
1 *fragment of copper*, possibly a prong, found at floor level immediately beside the ember pit.
2 *fragments of iron rivets*, found at 1 cm and 8cm above floor level respectively.

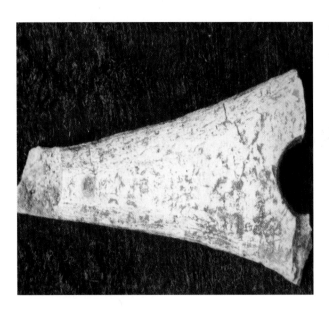

Fig. 15. Bone needle from house-site D. Photo by Anne Stine Ingstad.

A fragment of a bone needle (fig. 15), found at 2 cm above the bottom of the ember pit.
A quartz arrow-head of Dorset Eskimo type, found at 6 cm above floor level.

It is quite clear that Eskimos must have lived in this house at some time after it had been abandoned by the Norsemen.

During one of the following years we found yet another room which formed part of this house. It had been added to the north wall, which faced the sea. It lay at a slightly lower level than the rest of the house, and had been dug into the edge of the terrace. There was a thick cultural layer here. Three of the walls were quite clear after excavation, but the north wall, which may have been wooden, had disappeared completely. An iron rivet was found in this room.

Thus house D consisted of three rooms, one of which had been built on to the back wall of the house. This was the normal building practice in Iceland during the late Viking Age.

It was late summer by now, almost the end of July. The Icelanders had finished excavating the smithy, as well as the charcoal kiln and a large cooking pit a little way east of these. They had also uncovered a number of primitive hearths, obviously open-air hearths. There were no finds from these features, and thus we cannot know whether they were built by the Norsemen or by natives.

I had resumed the excavation of house F. The year before I had uncovered two rooms in this house, and now the excavation began to be really fascinating. As the work proceeded, we realized that house F must have been a large building, even though little was visible above the turf.

That summer I excavated another room in this house, of the same type as a Norse hall. There was a long hearth in the middle of the floor: a large, flat stone, a nicely built ember pit, and a cooking pit. On either side of the hearth the floor was raised, there must have been earthen benches here, where the people could sit or lie down. Another, quite small room formed an extension of the 'hall'. Moreover, the trenches showed that there were yet two more rooms, one on either side of the ones excavated. It was impossible to excavate also these two rooms that summer, for it was already growing colder, and autumn was not far off. By now the tent down by the river was a most uninviting shelter.

We were expecting an archaeologist from Ottawa any day, Bill Taylor. We had asked him to come and look at our excavations. He was an expert on the cultures of the Eskimos and the American Indians, and we wanted to hear his opinion on some stone implements which must derive from Indians and Eskimos.

One night the wind grew so strong that the tent-pole started to creak and groan, and early next morning the storm broke. On the east wind the rain gushed horizontally in from the ocean; it streamed in through the tent canvas, the floor turned into a pond. And outside, the river roared past, growing ever larger. Foaming, it rushed down to the ocean.

We woke up to a bright, sunny morning, with wisps of mist here and there. In its fury the river had flooded the whole plain, our tent was an island in the middle of it all. The ocean was in an uproar, white froth all but covered the skerries. Bill Taylor's tent had not only been blown down, it was lying in the water. One of

Fig. 17. House-site F, seen from north-east, during excavation. In the background the river bank with the depression of the smithy before excavation. Photo by Helge Ingstad.

the fishermen came dragging our big tin can, which we kept in the river to cool our butter. He had found it far out at sea, where it bobbed in the morning sun – still full of butter.

In the afternoon, an unfamiliar fishing boat came to Colbourne's jetty. Bill Taylor had come! We had forgotten all about him during the storm. Where were we to put him? His tent was completely useless, and the river rushed straight through ours...

Bill Taylor stayed for a while. Once everything was reasonably ship-shape again, he was able to see the excavations. His view tallied with ours. In his opinion, the house-sites could not derive from either American Indians or Eskimos, nor could they have been raised by whalers or fishermen.

As the autumn went on, the rain and fog made it so depressing to lie on the ground and dig, that we decided to make for home, for Norway. Another summer had passed, another autumn too, but it was obvious that there was more work to be done here, that we would have to excavate here for several years yet. We were pleased with the results of that year's work, for now we thought there was no doubt that the settlement

Fig. 19. The spindle whorl of house-site F (bottom) together with a spindle whorl from a Norse farm in Greenland (top). Photo by P. Maurtvedt.

Fig. 18. The excavated house-site F seen from the north-east. Photo by Helge Ingstad.

Grønland.

Grønland.

Amerika.

Amerika.

was Norse.

When I now look back on the years we spent at L'Anse aux Meadows, I find it hard to tell one summer from another. We went on excavating house F, the large house-site. We cut test trenches beyond it, and they confirmed my belief that a large house had once stood there. In 1965 we uncovered the fifth room and the sixth. They lay on either side of the great hall, which formed the centre of the house.

There was a cooking-pit in the floor of each of these newly excavated rooms. The room built on to the north wall of the hall was connected with the latter by a door opening. The southern room

156

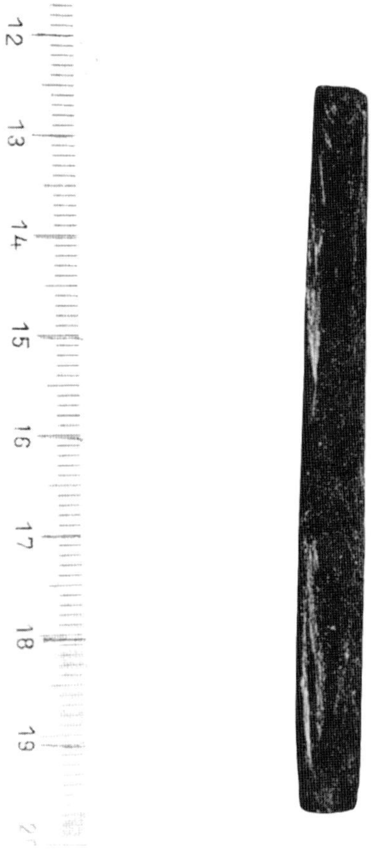

had no such opening either to the central room, or to any of the others *(fig. 18)*.

One of the most significant finds came from outside the southern room: a soapstone spindle whorl, of decidedly Norse type *(fig. 19)*. This find was a great joy! An American student found it; he had no idea of the importance of his find, and he must have thought that the rest of us had gone completely mad when we performed a veritable war dance. That year our team included an American anthropologist, Junius Bird from the American Museum of Natural History in New York. He understood the significance of the spindle whorl, and shared our delight. In the southern room we also found a beautiful little needle-hone of quartzite; this was also a Norse type *(fig. 20)*. The room also yielded iron rivets and slag.

In 1967 we were expecting important visitors, a Swede and a Norwegian. Professor Mårten Stenberger from the University of Uppsala and Professor Bjørn Hougen from the University of Oslo had been invited by the government of Newfoundland to see the excavations, and to express their opinion. We had had a beautiful summer, and we were looking forward to their visit.

One afternoon we heard a plane, and soon we saw a small aircraft circling above our heads. Of course the two professors wanted to see the whole site from the air, but soon they were to land, and to join us. I was looking forward to showing them the excavations, and to the chance of discussing them with nordic archaeologists who were familiar with the house types of the Viking Age.

By now we had acquired a small wooden shed, and for the first time we were able to dry our clothes!

That evening in the shed with our visitors from far away was a memorable occasion. As soon as we had eaten, we went to the excavation site. Going from house-site to house-site, we discussed all the possible interpretations, but their

Fig. 20. Needle-hone from house-site F. Photo by Helge Ingstad.

opinions apparently coincided completely with ours. Mårten Stenberger had excavated Viking Age houses in Iceland and he had also, together with the Danish archaeologist Nørlund, excavated Leif Eiriksson's farm in Greenland, Brattahlið, to which I have referred several times in the above. I wanted to show Stenberger and Hougen the oval depressions surrounded by very faint banks down by the shore. I had always thought of them as boat-sheds. I did not mention them at all, I wanted the two visitors to discover them on their own.

And true enough, no sooner had we got there than Stenberger said: 'So here are the boat-sheds!' I was very pleased that he interpreted them in the same way as we had done.

About 5 m from house F, there was a round depression in the edge of the terrace (*fig. 21*). This I wanted to investigate before stopping work for the season. Undoubtedly there had been a small house there, dug down into the terrace to a depth of 118 cm. The earth of the terrace had served as walls for this house, which measured no more than 2 m x 2.5 m. We were unable to find any traces of a wall in the north, the side facing the sea, and it seems most likely that there was a wooden wall with a door in this position.

Immediately under the grass lay a large, cracked slate, with two big, water-worn stones on top. The slate must have covered the smoke-opening in the roof, and the two stones weighed it down, so that it would not blow off. Under the slate there was a black cultural layer, 60 cm thick. It contained pieces of charcoal. The floor layer of the house was about 10 cm thick, hard-trodden, black, and full of charcoal which had been trodden down into it. A thick, flat flag-stone, fire-cracked, stood on edge by the west wall. In front of it, we found a compact layer of charcoal, which included very many fire-cracked stones and stone chippings.

It seemed very likely that this small house was a bath-house, not least because of the very large number of fire-cracked stones in the cultural layer. An iron rivet was found high up in this layer. It most probably belongs to a wooden door, which in the course of time had fallen into the house after the collapsed walls had partly filled it with sand. This house also yielded two fragments of iron.

The summer of 1968 was to be our last season at L'Anse aux Meadows. The meadows lay bathed in sunshine practically every day, and the weather was lovely and warm. This time our team included two Norwegian archaeologists, Sigrid Kaland and Arne Emil Christensen. Arne Emil, a Viking ship expert, knew all about ships

Fig. 21. House-site G during excavation. Photo by Helge Ingstad.

Fig. 22. Building and repairing ships was a vital part of Viking livelihoods. Photo courtesy of Parks Canada; Shane Kelly, photographer.

and boats. He was to investigate the faint traces of boat-sheds or boat-houses down by the shore. I resumed the excavation of house A, and reopened the trenches which the Icelanders had dug, but which they had filled before they left. This part of the settlement proved to be extremely interesting.

To my mind, the thick cultural layer which could be seen in the trenches could not be the result of an occasional stay here, it must represent the remains of a house.

I also had to start digging at my own test excavation again. The first year I thought that I had reached sterile gravel and sand, but now I saw that this was merely a layer deposited by the river in flood. I found a thick, cultural layer also below this sterile sand. House A had four rooms in a row, and one of the two in the middle was of Norse hall type, with a hearth in the middle of the floor, and raised, earthen benches on either side.

When this excavation was finished, the walls were clearly visible at the eastern end of the house; in the west, they were highly eroded, but sufficiently clear for us to be able to trace them. All the rooms were equipped with hearths; in the western part of the house they were in the form of longish depressions in the floor, without any stone setting. Both the two rooms in the eastern half of the house had a large cooking pit in the corner. The rooms were separated by thick turf walls with door openings.

The excavation of this house-site was almost finished, but we still had one trench to investigate. This ran east-west. Sigrid Kaland and I were kneeling side by side, scraping here (fig. 23). Suddenly she let out a yell: 'Anne Stine, I've found bronze.' My reaction was to say no, that was impossible. 'It must be that green stone I've been near a couple of times.' But Sigrid insisted, and when I looked at her find, I saw one end of a green bronze object, about 10 cm long. Carefully Sigrid started to brush it clean; one more turn of the brush, and there was the ring! There could be no doubt at all, this was a Norse ring-headed pin, and it lay at the edge of a cooking pit (fig. 24).

We practically exploded in our excitement. We called Helge and Arne Emil – they were digging the boat-sheds down by the shore. No reaction. We called and we shouted, and finally they real-

Fig. 23. Sigrid: Anne Stine, I have found bronze!

ized that something was up. They came up to our excavation, and when they saw the verdigrised ring-headed pin lying at the edge of the cooking pit, their joy was no less unrestrained than ours! It was incredible. We had dug in this very place during our first summer here, but not deep enough. Now, on the last day of our last season at L'Anse aux Meadows, in the last spot to be dug, we found this bronze pin! The best find of all was in truth the final clue!

We have the following finds from house A:

1   bronze ring-headed pin of Norse Celtic type
4   fragmentary iron rivets
13 fragments of iron
6   lumps of slag
1   arrow-head, Dorset Eskimo type, found in a turf layer in the western end wall
2   pieces of red jasper
1   flint chipping
1   piece of iron pyrite
1   fragment of bone (pig)

159

Fig. 24. The ring-headed pin, in situ. Photo by Helge Ingstad.

And thus we had finished at last, we had achieved our aim: a Norse settlement site had been found and excavated. There could surely be no doubt that the site by Épaves Bay was proof of Norse settlers in these far-distant parts around the year A.D. 1000.

Helge and I walked over the site for the last time, going from house-site to house-site along the terrace. There had been at least eight houses here, possibly nine. The smithy lies on its own, on the other river bank, which is just how the Norsemen used to position their smithies, so that they were at a safe distance from the dwelling houses, in case of fire. Moreover, water was close at hand here. Three of the houses were over 20 m long, and had several rooms each.

The houses lie along the terrace in groups of two or three, and these groups give the appearance of representing separate complexes. As they are indubitably Norse, there is no reason to discuss their cultural affinities in detail, but an investigation of their place within the culture of the Norsemen may be of interest.

It seems reasonable to assume that the first settlers by Épaves Bay would build their houses down by the river, so that water was easily accessible. We shall therefore begin with houses A, B and C, the most westerly houses on the terrace. House A, 24 m long, has four rooms, which all lie along the longitudinal axis of the house. The

160